Map by Morgan

HOSTILE ALLIES

MILTON VIORST

Hostile Allies

FDR AND CHARLES DE GAULLE

The Macmillan Company, New York

Collier-Macmillan Limited, London

To My Wife
JUDY

Second Printing 1965

The Macmillan Company, New York
Collier-Macmillan Canada, Ltd., Toronto, Ontario

Library of Congress catalog card number: 65-10382

Printed in the United States of America

DESIGNED BY RONALD FARBER

Foreword

THE WORK on *Hostile Allies* was begun in 1957, a year before de Gaulle's return to power. I had only scratched the surface of my research when the *coup d'état* of 1958 thrust de Gaulle once again into prominence. What began as a history necessarily became the study of a leader of enormous current importance. To many Americans, the de Gaulle of the Fifth Republic has seemed an enigma, an anachronism or simply a capricious old man. But as my research proceeded, it became evident that de Gaulle's character and aspirations have remained remarkably constant over the course of twenty years. I became convinced, in fact, that the de Gaulle of the late 1950's and early 1960's could only be understood in the framework of the events of the Second World War, when the man known to the world today was molded. *Hostile Allies* focuses on the incompatibility, both political and personal, of Franklin Roosevelt and Charles de Gaulle. This incompatibility, which revealed so much of these men and the countries they led, contains the roots of the American differences with France today.

In writing *Hostile Allies*, I could have had no finer editors than my wife, Judith, and my good friend, Stephen S. Rosenfeld, both of whom studied the text with dedication, insisting on the right word, the proper emphasis and the pursuit of each thought to its logical conclusion. Their wisdom and perception contributed much.

v

I would also like to thank Jean Baubé, Lawrence Mirel, Forrest Pogue, Herbert Stein-Schneider, Seth Tillman and Marcel Vigneras, who read all or parts of the manuscript and offered useful suggestions. Countless others have given me their help or encouragement during the long years that this book has been in preparation. Apologizing to those I have overlooked, I would like to cite particularly Forrest Pogue and Marcel Vigneras, excellent historians who were generous in offering direction when it was needed; Joseph Avery, who, with others of the National Archives' World War II Records Division, searched tirelessly for documents for me; Stetson Conn and his colleagues in the Office of the Chief of Military History, who cut much red tape and answered countless questions; Jean Baubé, who not only shared his special knowledge but made his wartime records available to me; Herman Kahn of the Roosevelt Library in Hyde Park, who responded to my queries in most scholarly fashion; Paul Péronnet, my old schoolmate, who dispatched the latest books to me from France; Monique Polgar and the French Information Service, who put a fine photographic collection at my disposal; Dorothy Sankey, who indefatigably handled the typing; Peter Ritner, my editor at Macmillan, who had faith in me and the book. I would like to acknowledge special appreciation to Judy and my two sons, Anthony and Nicholas, who were understanding during the long hours I remained locked in my study in front of the typewriter and the note cards.

MILTON VIORST

Washington
May, 1964

Contents

Weak Reed in the Crisis

May–June, 1940

Oₙ THE TWELFTH OF JUNE, 1940, when the disorganized remnants of the French Army were reeling dizzily before German armor, Winston Churchill dispatched to the President of the United States a message which contained this line:

Reynaud . . . is for fighting on, and he has a young General de Gaulle who believes much can be done.[1]*

On this promising note, Franklin Roosevelt was introduced to Charles de Gaulle. He took no notice. Roosevelt was much too preoccupied with the disaster in France to pay attention to an obscure young general, whatever de Gaulle believed could be done. Churchill has claimed that he already recognized Charles de Gaulle as *"l'homme du destin."*[2] But neither then nor at any time in the five remaining years of the war did Roosevelt perceive any special qualities in de Gaulle, any nobility that distinguished him from other mortals. Roosevelt's introduction to de Gaulle was not auspicious. If it was an omen, it accurately foretold a relationship of bitterness and discord.

For de Gaulle was not an ordinary mortal. As much as any man can, he had prepared himself for an exalted mission. Since boyhood

* Superior numbers refer to Sources and Notes (p. 257), to be used in conjunction with Comments on Sources and Notes (p. 249) and Bibliography (p. 251).

he had looked upon his existence with the utmost seriousness. He had designs upon greatness. It was not by accident that he was thrust into a grand endeavor. Only because he had subjected himself to the most rigorous preparation was he able to master it.

Charles de Gaulle was born in 1890 into a family with a distinguished military tradition, enriched by an impressive scholarly heritage. His father, Henri de Gaulle, was Professor of Philosophy, Mathematics and Literature at St. Stanislas, the foremost Jesuit College in Paris. At home, de Gaulle's environment was both intellectual and pious. He was deeply affected by both aspects of it. At school, he was a good student. He read avidly, especially in the history of France, and he was intensely interested in public affairs.[3]

De Gaulle belonged to a generation which thirsted to avenge the French defeat of 1870. *"Revanche"* was its watchword. Bergson, who taught that the discovery of truth required intuition as well as intellect, was its great teacher. Bergson brought a quality of mysticism to a young generation's search for wisdom. He influenced Proust and the Impressionists. Péguy, the poet, most powerfully exalted his ideas in his mystical paeans to French patriotism. It was a heady age for young men, and de Gaulle was profoundly moved by it. In the context of his military background, de Gaulle's upbringing and temperament virtually foreordained him to a career in the Army. There seemed no more natural vehicle for his self-expression.

At Saint-Cyr, de Gaulle made an excellent record. He possessed an instinctive capacity to command. His classmates already knew him as distant and cold, self-assured and haughty. They dubbed him "The Tall Asparagus," in recognition of his long, gangling frame. They also styled him *"le Connétable,"* title of the military commanders of the kings of France, but it was meant more as a gibe at his demeanor than as a tribute to his capacity. Graduated in 1912, de Gaulle ranked high enough to choose his unit. He selected the 33rd Infantry Regiment at Arras, commanded by Colonel Henri-Philippe Pétain.

De Gaulle was wounded for the first time in August, 1914, two weeks after the Great War began. He received his first citation in January, 1915. On March 2, 1916, at the foot of the fort of Douaumont, he was wounded for the third time and taken prisoner. His citation for bravery read:

Captain de Gaulle, company commander, known for his great intellectual and moral qualities, though his battalion suffered a dreadful bombardment, was decimated and enemy troops had surrounded his company, inspired his men to a furious assault and a savage hand-to-hand battle, the only resolution he judged compatible with his sense of military honor. Fallen in the engagement. Officer without equal in all respects.'

The citation was signed by his newly promoted commanding officer, General Pétain.

De Gaulle tried to escape five times from German prison camps, but his height invariably betrayed him. Incarcerated finally with other incorrigibles, he spent the last months of the war in relative comfort, reading and thinking. After the Armistice he returned briefly to warfare by joining the French volunteers who fought for Poland in its struggle against the Soviet Union. Amply decorated, he arrived back in France in the fall of 1920. It was then that he met Yvonne Vendroux, daughter of a wealthy biscuit manufacturer, whom he married the following spring. In the ensuing years, the de Gaulles had three children—Elisabeth, Philippe and Anne. De Gaulle's only son was named for the great hero of World War I, his former commander, Marshal Pétain.

In 1924, de Gaulle published his first book, *La Discorde chez l'ennemi*, a study of the social and political disintegration that led to Germany's downfall in 1918. His analysis of the German leadership crisis demonstrated a preoccupation with the problems of government which remained with him. The failure of the German state, he contended, grew from the insistence of military leaders on meddling in the domain of the civilian chiefs. De Gaulle strongly condemned the failure of the generals and admirals to observe the separation of powers. When field commanders usurp the functions of the policy-makers, he argued, governmental chaos follows. De Gaulle recognized the responsibility of military men to make their views known. But he denied them the prerogative of imposing these views upon the state.

Throughout the 1920's, de Gaulle advanced steadily, though not spectacularly, in army rank. Acknowledged to be an officer of great promise, he was frequently assigned to posts near the top of the military hierarchy. But as the years passed, he grew increasingly discontented with the French high command. He found France's military leaders, like French society generally, smug about the victory they had won in 1918. For three years he was aide-de-camp to Marshal Pétain, whose immense influence was directed toward creating for France a defensive system of fortifications and foot soldiers. De Gaulle, despite his junior status, challenged what he regarded as stagnant military thinking. In spirit as well as in military doctrine, he drew further and further away from his fellow officers. The generals, for their part, did not take well to a junior officer who chose for himself the role of Cassandra. On at least one occasion the War Ministry had to overrule the General Staff to award him a promotion he had earned. It was obvious that de Gaulle risked sacrificing a certain future in the highest ranks to sound an alarm about the future of the nation.

In 1932, de Gaulle published *Le Fil de l'épée*, which warned openly of the decay in the social and military establishment. But in it de Gaulle meticulously avoided any discussion of politics. Nothing in this book, nor in any other he wrote before the war, criticized the French Government. No chance phrase revealed whether he was republican or monarchist, rightist or leftist, clerical or anticlerical. In a book otherwise outspoken, de Gaulle so steadfastly refrained from discussing his political ideas that there is reason to wonder whether, at this stage of his life, he had any political philosophy at all. It was characteristic of him that his standard of measure was France, not the people or the Church or even the Army, but an almost abstract notion of France as a nation. When he attacked complacency or conventionality, it was on the grounds that they were a threat to the integrity of France. When he asserted that superior men must come to the defense of France, he wrote in terms of character and personality, not in terms of politics. De Gaulle clearly assigned himself the mission of preparing himself for a time of crisis. *Le Fil de l'épée* is an expression of his personal philosophy. It is a public acknowledgment of his belief in his own destiny. It is both a declaration of intention and a protestation of faith.

The man of character, he wrote,

is at a disadvantage in ordinary matters vis-à-vis his superiors. Confident of his judgment and conscious of his strength, he concedes nothing to the desire to please. The fact that he draws his decisiveness and his firmness from himself and not from any orders often separates him from passive obedience. He asks simply that he be given his assignment and left alone to do it, an unbearable requirement to many officers who, lacking a view of the whole, cultivate details and sustain themselves on formalities. They finally dread his audacity, which is not easy either on routine or on relaxation. "Vain, undisciplined," the mediocrities say of him . . . but as soon as times become difficult, when danger is pressing, when the nation suddenly needs initiative, a taste for risks, solidity, the perspective changes at once and he immediately receives his due. A kind of tidal wave propels the man of character to the front of the stage. His advice is accepted, his talent appreciated, his value relied upon. To him, naturally, goes the difficult task, the principal effort, the decisive mission.[4]

The year after *Le Fil de l'épée* was published, de Gaulle began a personal campaign for basic military reforms. He brought out *Vers l'armée de métier* in 1934 to plead for the formation of a relatively small, highly trained, mechanized army to act as a mobile striking force. This army, he argued, must be made up of professional soldiers, an elite capable of moving quickly in tanks and armored cars, possessing great fire power and supported by aircraft. It was not to replace the ponderous, unprotected masses of conscripts responsible, in concert with the Maginot Line, for the defense of France's frontiers. It was, instead, to act in advance of the defensive lines, to break up attacks and disrupt the attacker, to speed to the points of greatest danger and, most important, to give the men in the rear time to mobilize for defense in depth.

The conformists reacted vigorously. The Army Commission, of which Pétain was then head, characterized the proposal as "contrary to logic and history." General Maxime Weygand, then Chief of the General Staff, wrote: "Nothing of that nature needs to be created. It already exists." But it did not exist. Weygand either lied consciously or completely misunderstood his army. France would pay dearly for his complacence in the spring of 1940.

Parliament was equally hostile to de Gaulle's ideas. In a nation that had invented and remained dedicated to the principle of the *levée en masse*, the concept of a professional army was not popular. In addition, the Left feared the creation of a more powerful military elite. The Right would tolerate no censure of the elite that already existed. The result was a Parliament as dedicated as the Army to the *status quo*.

Among the parliamentarians, Paul Reynaud alone espoused the *armée de métier*. Fiery and outspoken, Reynaud was impressed by the young officer and, in 1935, made an impassioned plea on the floor of the Chamber for acceptance of his ideas. Reynaud sparked a searching debate, but he made no converts. He did, however, establish an association with de Gaulle that was to have great significance.

In the ensuing years, Reynaud, constantly inspired by de Gaulle, campaigned for a mechanized army. Their collaboration was well known and frowned upon by the General Staff. Their failure was a triumph for the General Staff from which the French Army has never quite recovered.

Germany, in contrast, gave de Gaulle's ideas a sympathetic welcome. General Guderian, the Wehrmacht's principal apostle of tank warfare, borrowed freely from them. De Gaulle's book sold much better in Germany than in France. In anguish, de Gaulle watched while a mechanized army grew up across the frontier. Had the French possessed a mobile striking force—and the determination to use it—they could have stopped Germany from seizing the Rhineland, absorbing Austria and devouring Czechoslovakia. The French had the largest army in the world sitting on their frontiers, but it was incapable of moving. France was dedicated to static defense. She lacked the means to bar the Nazi depredations.

But the leading generals somehow retained their confidence in the Army's prowess. In 1939, shortly before the war began, Pétain wrote that "our army is in a position to stop, with all certainty, any enemy who would like to penetrate our frontiers." The decimation of Poland by the Panzers did nothing to shake his conviction. At the very moment that German columns were moving into the Low Countries, he insisted that masses of tanks and tactical aircraft would not alter the outcome of the battle.

Colonel de Gaulle, commander of tanks for the Fifth Army in Alsace, continued nonetheless to sound the alarm. Through the fall and winter, the period of the "Phony War," he had pleaded whenever he could to whatever generals or politicians would listen. On January 26th, he submitted a long memorandum to eighty top French leaders, including Edouard Daladier, the Premier and War Minister. Though Daladier had no personal hostility toward de Gaulle, he was committed to the strategic convictions of his generals. Only Reynaud seemed to recognize the seriousness of the threat to France.

On March 21, 1940, Paul Reynaud, by a one-vote margin in Parliament, succeeded Daladier as head of the French Government. However late, the moment appeared to have arrived to undertake de Gaulle's reforms. But Reynaud's mandate, given the vicissitudes of French politics, was limited. Daladier remained Minister of War and, as such, implacably opposed to shaking up the General Staff and the military system he had helped to create. Reynaud, on taking his new post, at once summoned de Gaulle to Paris to discuss the conduct of the war. He proposed then to appoint de Gaulle as his personal military adviser, but Daladier, recognizing the challenge, succeeded in vetoing the idea. De Gaulle returned to the front to wait for Germany's crushing blow. But he did not despair, for he was now convinced that France would soon have need of him.

Those who aspire to command . . . those who are strong [he had written several years before] make themselves ready. Destined to make their mark, rather than submit to someone else's, they build in the secrecy of an inner life the structure of their attitudes, their belief, their will. That is why, in times of tragedy, when the winds blow down convention and habit, they alone remain standing and, consequently, they alone matter. Nothing is more important to the state than to keep these exceptional persons at their posts, for they will be its last resort.[5]

On May 12th, two days after the start of the offensive, German tanks cracked the French defensive line at Sedan and began pouring through the breach into northern France. The French Army retreated in disorder, the confidence of its commander, General Maurice Gamelin, irrevocably shaken. Early in the morning of May 15th, Reynaud woke Churchill out of bed to announce to him hysterically: "We have been defeated. We are beaten. We have lost the battle."[6] On Reynaud, who had tried harder than any Frenchman to rejuvenate the Army, was now thrust—as if in ironic jest—the burden of its decrepitude. But in the face of rout there was no time for recrimination. Reynaud had to act. Paradoxically, to save the nation, he chose to call on the very men who had brought it to the brink of disaster.

On May 18th, Reynaud issued an appeal to Marshal Pétain, *vainqueur de Verdun*, and General Weygand, deputy to the brilliant Foch, to lend themselves to the effort of deliverance. By enveloping the nation in the aura of an earlier victory, he hoped somehow to stiffen its capacity to resist. Pétain, at eighty-four, was the embodiment of French military glory. Weygand, at seventy-two, remained France's most esteemed general. Reynaud knew better than most that both were superannuated heroes who could add glitter but no substance to his troubled affairs. In France's moment of desperation, however, he felt he could avail himself of little else. Pétain, who had become ambassador in Madrid, and Weygand, who had taken command of the French forces in Syria, did not hesitate. Both headed at once for Paris.

Reynaud did have one other hope, though it was slim indeed. On the same day that he issued his plea to Pétain and Weygand, he called in the American Ambassador, William Bullitt, and informed him that France faced "absolute defeat . . . in less than two months" unless the United States somehow intervened. Reynaud told Bullitt that he intended to make a personal appeal to Roosevelt to obtain from Congress a declaration of war. Bullitt, though a committed Francophile, recognized that such an action would be absurd. Roosevelt may have understood the danger of a Nazi victory, but there was not the remotest chance that either the Congress or the people of the United States would agree to go to war to prevent it. Bullitt persuaded the French Premier to abandon his plan. Reynaud kept it in reserve, however, as if he could call on the United States as a last resort to come to France's rescue.[7]

Reynaud's petitions, to Roosevelt on the one hand and to Pétain and Weygand on the other, were clearly born of despondency. He wanted desperately to lead France to victory. A tiger in the parliamentary arena, he was thought to have no peer in his dedication to the ruthless prosecution of the war. But whether conscious of it or not, he was, behind a facade of determination, hedging his commitment to fight. The appeal he sought to make to Roosevelt was manifestly an empty gesture, politically because the President could not obtain a declaration of war, militarily because the United States in 1940 was powerless to alter the outcome of the battle. The offers to Pétain and Weygand cast even greater doubt upon his firmness. On the radio, Reynaud told the French people that "the victor of Verdun . . . is henceforth at my side. . . . He will remain there until victory." But the Marshal, a warrior in the public eye, had a private reputation for weakness and defeatism. It is inconceivable that Reynaud, as he later claimed, was unaware of Pétain's real character, for even the Germans knew of it and planned to make use of it.[8] As for Weygand, though famed for energy and aggressiveness, he indicated when he arrived from Syria that he had no stomach for a last-ditch fight. Had Reynaud been stronger, he would have surrounded himself with men of iron will, prepared to carry the war to the high seas and to the colonies. Then he, not de Gaulle, would have become the savior of France. He chose instead to look for help to Roosevelt on the outside and to Pétain and Weygand on the inside. He thus set the stage for capitulation.

Pétain, from the moment he joined the government as Vice-President and Minister of State, threw his weight behind an armistice. As the fortunes of the French Army deteriorated, he found more and more converts among the men who were supporters of Reynaud. Churchill, who had to contend with Pétain at his meetings with the French Cabinet, wrote that "the influence of his personality, his reputation, his serene acceptance of the march of adverse events, apart from the words he used, were almost overpowering to those under his spell."[9] By the end of May, the Marshal was openly and relentlessly pushing the doctrine that further resistance was useless.

Weygand was equally committed to surrender. When he assumed command on May 19th, he entertained no hope that he could stem the debacle. Another general, so pessimistic, would not have accepted the mission. Another premier, aware of this pessimism, would not have offered it. Thrust unprepared into an inferno, Weygand searched frantically for the means to extinguish the fire, without any belief that he could. The odds against him, to be sure, were insuperable. But if a second Miracle of the Marne was possible, Weygand, the shadow of a Joffre, was not the man to perform it. By the end of May, he was far more anxious to wind up a bad affair than to keep at the effort to make it a good one. Without the sanction of the Government he declared Paris an open city, thereby discarding his most valuable asset for retarding the German advance. Indulging himself more and more in recriminations against the British, he identified himself, in a fashion unbefitting his military duties, with the political decision in favor of capitulation. In the bosom of the Reynaud Cabinet, Weygand formed an unconcealed alliance with Pétain to hasten France's downfall.

Scarcely dissembled beneath the declamations of doom of both Pétain and Weygand lay the sentiment that the France they had been called upon to extricate from Nazi clutches was not worth saving at all. Neither man was a republican. Both were hostile to French liberal democracy. Their own patriotism they regarded as faultless. Neither was given to the least self-examination. Though they agreed that the collapse of the Third Republic reflected the infirmity of its ruling class, they completely rejected the notion that

they possessed any personal responsibility. On the contrary, rather
than blame themselves for France's failures, they made the Republic
itself their scapegoat. Both were blatant in their hostility to the very
government which commanded, or expected to command, their allegiance.

Marshal Pétain, bloated with two decades of adulation, had long
since persuaded himself that France could be saved only by obedience to him. As a general he had won the affection of the Left
through his concern for the well-being of his troops. But in the years
after the war he flirted more and more, usually in secret, with the
authoritarian doctrines of the Right. At one point in the debacle, he
told the English General Spears, Churchill's personal envoy to the
French Cabinet, that "we must pay now and pay dearly for the
anarchy we have indulged in for so long." Spears, a competent observer, noted "that his voice had sounded satisfied, almost as if he
accepted defeat joyfully."[10] Pétain burned with a passion to deliver
the French people personally from the corrupting influence of the
parliamentarians.

Weygand's antirepublicanism was not the product of personal
ambition though, at heart a royalist, he detested the Republic more
than did Pétain. To him, the Army was the incarnation of France,
parliamentary government nothing but a usurper. In arguing that
the Cabinet, as a gesture of solidarity with the French people, ought
to remain in Paris to be captured by the Germans, he was undoubtedly motivated, however subconsciously, by a desire to be rid
of the Republic then and there. Weygand decried Reynaud's contention that the nation, through its government, could fight on, as did
Norway and the Netherlands, after the Army was beaten in the
field. "The old order of things, a political regime made up of ma-
sonic, capitalist and international deals has brought us where we
stand," he cried. Weygand was persuaded that in defeat France had
the opportunity to banish its "worn-out personnel" and acquire a
sounder set of values.[11]

What Pétain and Weygand overlooked, in their dubious patriotic
yearnings, was the nature of the Nazi invader. Spears reports that on
May 31st, Churchill, in one of the most eloquent speeches of his life,
told the French Cabinet that "the peoples of France and Britain were
not born to slavery, nor can they endure it. . . . If Germany defeated
either ally or both, she would give no mercy. We should be reduced

to the status of slaves forever." Pétain and Weygand, Spears said, were both witnesses to his torrent of emotion but "it fell on . . . barren soil." For neither man acknowledged that the Germany of Hitler differed in any important aspect from the Germany of the Kaiser, of Bismarck or of Frederick the Great. For two millennia, Franks and Teutons had crossed the Rhine to make war on each other. Within the previous seventy years, each had brought home a victory. After every war, the vanquished recovered and, in a few decades, was ready to challenge its rival on the battlefield again. When Hitler said he was settling the fate of the Reich for a thousand years, they saw no reason to take him seriously. Weygand, in fact, fretted more that the Germans would leave him too few troops to prevent domestic disorder than that Nazism would despoil his country. At no point did either he or Pétain express any realization that they were flinging their people into the arms of a homicidal maniac.

On the contrary, Pétain and Weygand exalted defeatism to the level of virtue, while caviling at resistance as vice. Between them they reversed the normal criteria of fidelity and courage. "The country will never forgive you," Weygand screamed at Reynaud during one Cabinet meeting, "if, to remain faithful to England, you reject the possibility of peace."[12] "My own feelings," he wrote in his memoirs, "made preferable to me a struggle to the end, in which I should have been glad to perish with the last combatants. . . . But was that our duty? I should have been wanting in it if I had not done my utmost to put an end to a struggle which I regarded as more and more disastrous to France." Echoing this theme, Pétain proclaimed: "While ministers hesitate and think of their reputations, soldiers are being killed and the land of France is being ruined. . . . It is sheer pusillanimity to shirk the issue."[13]

Though no one doubted that the Battle of France was lost, Reynaud remained committed to fighting on. Was there some strategy that, in the final hour, could be devised to keep France in the war with a hope of ultimate victory? On May 29th, at the peak of the miraculous Dunkirk evacuation, Reynaud submitted written instructions to Weygand to take steps to turn the peninsula of Brittany into an armed fortress in which the Government and all available military forces could take refuge. The "Breton redoubt," in Reynaud's words, would become "a hand extended toward England and America." It could serve as a bridgehead for the concentration of a small but powerful army and as a fortified exit to the sea from which retreating armies, under air cover from England, could go on to the French colonies in Africa. Reynaud pointed out to Weygand that the French Navy, one of the strongest in the world, and the French Air Force, still largely intact, were available to support this strategy. He also announced his intention of sending two classes of recruits to North Africa to begin training, with arms presumably to be purchased in the United States. The Breton redoubt was to be the prelude to a long struggle for liberation.[14]

Many believe that the strategy of the Breton redoubt was inspired by de Gaulle, for Reynaud was no military thinker himself.[15] The two men had not met after their discussion on March 21st. But de Gaulle, persuaded that France was in for a beating, might have suggested it then. Or he might have transmitted it to Reynaud by letter or telephone during the final weeks of the Phony War. Almost certainly, he did not come into contact with Reynaud after May 10th. For once the Germans attacked, de Gaulle was swept up into the holocaust, working desperately, like other French commanders, to maintain his forces in effective fighting order.

On May 15th, amidst chaos, Colonel de Gaulle was promoted to command of the Fourth Armored Division. The post had been promised him several months before when Reynaud became Premier and Gamelin, in halfhearted reaction to the lessons of the Wehrmacht in Poland, agreed to regroup some of his tanks into an armored mass. But before the Fourth Division could be organized, the First, Second and Third Armored Divisions had already been annihilated. De Gaulle, with whatever remnants he could assemble under the Fourth Division banner, took on the mission of delaying the German advance so that a mass of French infantry might form a line behind him. During the last two weeks of May he fought successful holding actions, first around Laon, then, after moving northwest along the Somme, around Abbeville. In the Abbeville action, he temporarily checked the German spearhead, inflicted severe losses in men and equipment and barely missed driving the Nazis out of their beachhead on the southern bank of the river. But his cause was hopeless and, without reinforcements, his columns were forced to retire.

In the thick of the Abbeville fighting, de Gaulle was promoted to temporary brigadier general. At forty-nine, he was the youngest man in the French Army with general's rank. On June 2nd, an order of the day signed by Weygand contained this mention of him: "Admirable chief, audacious and energetic, attacked on the 30th and 31st of May an enemy bridgehead, penetrating 14 kilometers into his lines and capturing several hundred prisoners and considerable material." A few days later, Reynaud summoned him to Paris.

De Gaulle became a member of Reynaud's Cabinet on June 5th, when the Premier at last rid himself of Daladier and himself took over the War Ministry. The Cabinet shake-up was advertised as a purge of the appeasers. But by leaving Pétain in the vice-presidency, it fell far short of what was required to isolate the virus of defeat. "Better inside than out," Reynaud said when de Gaulle asked why the Marshal retained his office. But the Premier, once again, was hedging. Into the Cabinet came an uncompromising foe of capitulation. As Undersecretary of State for National Defense, de Gaulle was to be the Premier's personal military adviser. But the influence of a temporary brigadier general was insignificant next to that of the placid Marshal of France and the irascible generalissimo of the armies.

Churchill's man Spears set down his impression of de Gaulle after meeting him, for the first time, at one of Reynaud's Cabinet sessions.

A strange-looking man [he wrote], enormously tall. Sitting at the table he dominated everyone else by his height, as he had done when walking into the room. No chin, a long, drooping, elephantine nose over a closely-cut moustache, a shadow over a small mouth whose thick lips tended to protrude, as if in a pout before speaking, a high, receding forehead and pointed head surmounted by sparse black hair lying flat and neatly parted. His heavily hooded eyes were very shrewd. When about to speak he oscillated his head slightly, like a pendulum, while searching for words. . . . It was easy to imagine that head on a ruff, that secret face at Catherine de Medici's Council Chamber.[16]

Reynaud assigned to de Gaulle the mission of organizing the means for France to carry on the war against Germany from its overseas empire. De Gaulle was under no illusion about the chances of utilizing these means. He knew of the growing influence of Pétain and Weygand inside the Cabinet, even upon Reynaud himself. Ybarnégaray, a minister of state once considered implacable, illustrated the default of judgment generated by the disaster. "For me, a veteran," he told de Gaulle, "nothing matters but to obey my chiefs, Pétain and Weygand."[17] But if the Government did decide to continue the war, plans had to be made in France, in England and in Africa to make the most of the decision. Back and forth to London de Gaulle traveled to prepare with Churchill and his staff the next stage of the struggle. Despite the military and moral deterioration, de Gaulle functioned as if a miracle would occur.

In London, de Gaulle became convinced that if France fell the British not only meant to keep on fighting but that they might really win. He became converted there to the concept of global war. For French soldiers, the belief that a continental war could be won after the Continent was lost had always been apostasy, if not madness. It acknowledged defeat in Europe and abandonment of the homeland, a possibility they dared not contemplate. Pétain and Weygand, hardy practitioners of continental war, never entertained a thought that France, from outside the homeland, might fight a winning war. De Gaulle himself, in his writings on strategy during the 1920's and 1930's, nowhere suggests that either the French Empire or the French Navy might someday play a role in the national salvation. Like most Frenchmen, he regarded the Empire as a supplier of manpower and raw materials, the Navy as, at best, an auxiliary force. For the French, like the Germans but unlike the British, looked at war from the perspective of continentals. To France, Dunkirk was a fortress to defend; to Germany, it was a bastion to reduce. But to Britain, it was a gateway to the sea, through which troops could be evacuated to fight again at a time and place of their own choosing. Just as Hitler's failure to master maritime strategy ultimately cost him victory, the incapacity of Pétain and Weygand to elevate their thinking to a global level was to cause France to give up the fight before it was over. To them, it was self-evident that if a war was lost in France, France had lost a war. Churchill, however, looked back on Henry V and on Wellington, who came from the sea to win on the Continent. He recognized in the airplane and other modern instruments of war a capacity to penetrate the enemy's territory that earlier Englishmen never possessed. In defying the Marshal and the generalissimo, de Gaulle convinced himself that Churchill was right and that the British were not being cavalier. His mind was flexible enough to comprehend that France, too, could win if she persisted in the struggle.

In his *Memoirs*, de Gaulle acidly reported a conversation at Weygand's field headquarters on June 8th on the future conduct of the war. The Commander in chief, significantly, stated in his own memoirs that he had "no note worth recording of the interview." It vividly illuminates the differences in the strategic outlook of the two men. De Gaulle wrote:

"You see," the Commander-in-chief told me, "I wasn't wrong when I said several days ago that the Germans would attack on the Somme on June 6th. They are really attacking. Right now they're crossing the river. I can't stop them."

"So it is. They're crossing the Somme. And after that?"

"After? It's the Seine and the Marne."

"Yes. And after that?"

"After that? Why it's finished."

"What do you mean, finished? How about the world? And the Empire?" The General broke into a hopeless laugh.

"The Empire? Why, that's child's talk. As for the world, when I'm beaten here, England won't wait a week to negotiate with the Reich."[18]

De Gaulle, in his capacity of cabinet minister, urged Reynaud to dismiss Weygand at once. It was folly, he argued, that while the Premier wanted war, his commander in chief pleaded for surrender. Reynaud agreed, in principle, but did nothing. At one point, de Gaulle got Reynaud's permission to offer the post to Huntziger, commanding general of the Armies of the Center, but by the time he returned from Huntziger's headquarters, the Premier had again put the matter aside. The Premier recognized that at a moment when the nation was incredulous at its own downfall he would add to its bewilderment by choosing a third commander in chief within a few weeks. But, considering that Weygand pursued a policy directly contrary to the Government's, his was a weak excuse. Reynaud continued to tell himself that he would relieve his commander, but each time he seemed on the point of issuing the order his resolve vanished. If de Gaulle expected to keep France in the fight, he had to do so not in cooperation with a general determined to resist but over the objections of a man impatient to surrender.

When de Gaulle joined the Reynaud Cabinet, he unreservedly adopted the strategy of the Breton redoubt—if, indeed, he had not previously proposed it. He did not believe that a strategic trick could undo two decades of inadequate military preparation. But if France was to keep fighting, it made far better sense to try to delay the invaders in a rocky peninsular fortress, protected by sea and air, than in the open country in the South of France.

De Gaulle's antagonists to the execution of the Breton idea, however, were powerful. Weygand objected to both the premises of the Breton redoubt: last-ditch resistance and evacuation to the colonies. He argued that the Army lacked the strength to defend even the 100-mile entrance to the peninsula. Admiral Jean François Darlan, commander of the fleet, maintained that the ships needed to transport the men to the colonies were not available. General Noguès, military commander in North Africa, insisted that he would have no facilities for them once they arrived. Pétain, of course, was the most outspoken of all. He did not, like Weygand, plead that it was useless. On the contrary, he declared that it would expose the government to the "temptation" of continuing the war by abandoning the *patrie*. At best, the disorganization of the Army and the lateness of the hour made establishment of a Breton redoubt a task of huge magnitude. But the task itself was easier than mastering the opposition to it. In the face of the phalanx of foes, de Gaulle had small chance of gaining his objectives.

Nonetheless, on the morning of June 12th, de Gaulle appeared at Rennes, capital of Brittany, and after personally surveying the possibilities gave an order to the district army commander to begin at once the construction of concrete breastworks. That night he retuned to the Loire, where in a cluster of châteaux the Government had taken temporary refuge from the advancing Germans. De Gaulle beseeched Reynaud not to go on to Bordeaux, traditional seat of French governments in flight, but to Quimper in Brittany, which he regarded as "a step toward energetic decisions." But Reynaud was incapable of energetic decisions. Ostensibly, he compromised. He sent the Cabinet to Bordeaux and issued a written directive to Weygand to pursue the Breton strategy. But he remained silent about the Government's intentions on continuing the war from the Empire and he issued no orders to prepare for such a war. Weygand, out of a sense of discipline, gave a few perfunctory commands to his subordinates, but his heart was not in Brittany. Churchill, with Reynaud's determination so questionable, made no effort to coordinate a Breton strategy and committed no British forces to it. With the French Government already snug in Bordeaux, the Breton redoubt, despite de Gaulle, came to nothing.[19]

Paul Reynaud now fell back on his last resort, the United States of America. Since mid-May, when the Germans broke through at

Sedan, it was obvious that only the New World could save France. Salvation might come sooner if the resources were available to surmount the initial reverses. It would have to come later if they were not. But soon or late, America would need to come to the rescue, if indeed there was to be a rescue.

Churchill was explicit in declaring Britain's strategy. "We shall never surrender," the indomitable Prime Minister vowed to Parliament, "and even if, which I do not for a moment believe, this Island or a large part of it were subjugated and starving, then our Empire beyond the seas, armed and guarded by the British fleet, would carry on the struggle until, in God's good time, the New World, with all its power and might, steps forth to the rescue and the liberation of the Old."

Reynaud told Roosevelt his dreams with even braver words, none of which proved to be true, but which conveyed the same unmistakable idea. "We will fight before Paris," he said. "We will fight behind Paris. We will lock ourselves up in one of our provinces and if we are driven out we will go to North Africa, and, if need be, to our American possessions." But if France was to fight on, he tolled, the United States must stake her with guns, with planes and, perhaps, with men.

From the beginning of the crisis in Europe, Roosevelt was convinced that an Allied victory was essential to the security of the United States. But he resented being dragged into the war. Though far from being an American isolationist, he shared much of the loathing common to Americans—a loathing that dated back to Washington and Jefferson—for European politics. He had little faith in the capacity of the French to look after their own affairs. At least until Munich, Roosevelt was determined to let the European democracies find their own way out of the dilemma he felt they had created. In no measure did he share the European view that the crisis, at least in the larger sense, was partly of America's making. After Munich, Roosevelt became alarmed. From Paris, Ambassador Bullitt—then one of his great favorites— bombarded him with gloomy predictions and panicky advice. But Roosevelt remained cautious. It was bad politics to challenge the isolationist sentiment that dominated the country. On September 8th, a week after the blitzkrieg on Poland, the President had told the press that "there is no thought in any shape, manner or form of putting the nation, either in its defenses or in its internal economy, on a war basis."[20] Roosevelt would not yet acknowledge, however well he understood it, that the United States was unsafe without Britishers and Frenchmen manning the front lines.

After the rout began, Roosevelt, a step at a time, shifted his position. In response to a plea from Churchill on May 15th, he authorized emergency shipments of war matériel, but he refused to deliver planes unless the French sent an aircraft carrier to Canada to get them. When he heard the news of Dunkirk, he ordered the Army to relinquish all the equipment it could spare, but it was June 13th—too late to have an impact on the Battle of France—before the first shipment left the country. As late as June 1st, Roosevelt rejected Bullitt's request for destroyers—the same he designated "over-age" and turned over to Britain several months later—but, sheepishly, he advised his Ambassador that "several American republics have destroyers which they might be willing to sell and could sell under their laws."[21] Daladier, then War Minister, shamed Bullitt with the lament "that civilization in the world should fall because a great nation with a great President could simply talk." The Ambassador could not challenge the assertion. He knew his country was offering only words. "At the moment," he wired to the Secretary of State, "words are not enough. Indeed, unaccompanied by acts they are rather sickening."[22]

Roosevelt made his most dramatic commitment the day Mussolini declared war on France. "On this tenth day of June, 1940," he proclaimed, "the hand that held the dagger has struck it into the back of its neighbor." Even his closest associates were astonished to hear such strong language. The State Department, timid in the face of the holocaust, was mortified. In the same speech, Roosevelt outlined his new policy for dealing with the Axis menace. "We will pursue two obvious and simultaneous courses," he said. "We will extend to the opponents of force the material resources of this Nation and, at the same time, we will harness and speed up the use of those resources in order that we ourselves in the Americas may have equipment and training equal to the task of any emergency and every defense." But the intentions he proclaimed were more for the long run than for the short. Reynaud's survival depended on immediate deeds. Otherwise, France would be lost.

On the day of the now famous "stab-in-the-back" speech, Reynaud dispatched a fresh appeal to the White House. "It is my duty," he said, "to ask you for a new gesture of solidarity, even greater than before. At the same time that you tell the men and women of America about our plight, I implore you to declare publicly that the United States extends to the Allies moral and material support of every kind, except the sending of an expeditionary corps. I implore you to do this before it is too late." In excluding the "expeditionary corps," Reynaud was applying the lesson Bullitt had taught him, but his sense of restraint, as the pressure mounted, was clearly ebbing.

In equally melancholy though less flamboyant terms, Churchill wrote a similar plea to Roosevelt:

It seems to me that there must be many elements in France who will wish to continue the struggle either in France or in the French colonies or in both. This, therefore, is the moment for you to strengthen Reynaud the utmost you can, and try to tip the balance in favor of the best and longest possible French resistance.

But at the very moment that Churchill counseled Roosevelt to "tip the balance," the President of the United States was without his regular representative to the French Government. Reynaud and his Cabinet were in Touraine. William Bullitt was in Paris, indulging his romantic nature, confident that he alone could save the city from the Germanic brutes and the Parisian rabble. Instead of remaining at his post, Bullitt decided to join the tradition of American ambassadors who—during the Revolution, the Commune and the First War— assumed guardianship of the French capital. "My deepest personal reason for staying in Paris," he wrote to Roosevelt, "is that whatever I have as character, good or bad, is based on the fact that since the age of four I have never run away from anything, however painful and dangerous. . . . The fact that I am here is a strong element in preventing a fatal panic. . . . It will mean something always to the French and to the Foreign Service to remember that we do not leave though others do." Thus Bullitt, when he might have been at Reynaud's side, sat gloomily in his Embassy office, to bear witness to the Wehrmacht's triumph.

Roosevelt possesses at least some of the responsibility for Bullitt's action. The Ambassador notified him of his intention in May and, unwisely, Roosevelt gave his approval. He seems not to have foreseen that Bullitt, in a touch-and-go situation, might have been extremely useful. As Ambassador since 1936, Bullitt had built up an intimacy with France's leading politicians that offered ready access to the sources of power. However noble his motives, Bullitt failed in his duty by not realizing that he owed his first allegiance to Washington, not to Paris. In retrospect, it seems reasonably certain that his presence would have made no difference. The march of events, by the time the Government began its flight, appears to have been leading inexorably to a preordained climax. But the matter, in those middle days of June, was still not settled. Churchill, though he may have been thinking wishfully, believed the contest between surrender and fighting on was sufficiently close for some small factor to tip the balance. Bullitt might have been that factor. The Ambassador to Poland, Anthony Drexel Biddle, who went from Warsaw to France after the German occupation, served in Bullitt's place as Roosevelt's emissary. Though a skilled diplomat, he was unknown to the French. Through no fault of his, he sat in the anterooms of power while Frenchmen, without America's presence, debated France's future.

Roosevelt, meanwhile, continued to increase his commitment. On June 13th he wrote to Reynaud:

This government is doing everything in its power to make available to the Allied Governments the material they so urgently require and our efforts to do still more are being redoubled. . . . I am, personally, particularly impressed by your declaration that France will continue to fight on in behalf of democracy, even if it means slow withdrawal, even to North Africa and the Atlantic.

When Churchill learned the contents of this note, he immediately wired Reynaud an ebullient interpretation of its meaning.

The promise of redoubled material aid [he wrote] is coupled with definite advice and exhortation to France to continue the struggle even under the grievous conditions which you mentioned. If France on this message of President Roosevelt's continues in the field and in the war, we feel that the United States is committed beyond recall to take the only remaining step, namely, becoming a belligerent in form as she has already constituted herself in fact. The Constitution of the United States makes it impossible, as you foresaw, for the President to declare war himself but, if you act on his reply now received, we sincerely believe that this must inevitably follow.

In his *Memoirs*, Churchill admits that he exaggerated the President's meaning. "Perhaps," he wrote, "these points were stressed unduly; but it was necessary to make the most of everything we had or could get." When the President found out the next day about the Churchill interpretation, he wired his Ambassador in London, Joseph P. Kennedy, to inform the Prime Minister that his message in no way committed the United States to military participation in the war.[23]

But even on the farfetched assumption that Roosevelt agreed to military participation, would Reynaud have been able to keep France in the war? Weygand, for one, was unyielding in his demand for an armistice, no matter what the United States decided. At that late date, he declared, America's entry could have no effect on the outcome of the battle. And to him the battle in progress was all that mattered. It would take two or three years, he argued, before American factories could produce enough tanks and aircraft to reconquer the country. By that time, he predicted, any French government that established itself abroad would long since have lost its authority over the nation. Better, he suggested, to save what was possible by dealing with the enemy. "For my part,' he announced, "I was determined . . . not to quit the soil of France, though I were put into irons." To Weygand, any decision from Washington could be no more than symbolic, and symbolic gestures, he reckoned, do not win battles.[24]

Reynaud, nonetheless, decided to abandon all restraint. A month before, he had recognized that it would be embarrassing to ask Roosevelt for a declaration of war. In mid-June, he no longer felt bound by the requirements of diplomatic good taste. He had nothing to lose by taking a gamble. On the night of June 13th, Reynaud went before a microphone to tell the world that "the French Army has been the *avant-garde* of the democracies. . . . France has the right to turn toward the other democracies and say to them: 'I have rights on you.'" This doctrine, which made sense to Frenchmen in their moment of disaster, found little sympathy on the other side of the Atlantic.

Early the next morning, the French Premier dispatched his ultimate plea to the President of the United States.

From this moment onward [he declared], France cannot continue to fight unless American intervention arrives to reverse the situation, making an Allied victory certain. The only chance to save the French nation . . . is today to throw in the scales the weight of American strength. It is also the only chance to keep Hitler, after having destroyed France, then England, from attacking America. . . . I know that a declaration of war does not depend on you alone. But I say to you again, at this grave hour in our history, as in yours, that if you cannot give to France in the coming hours the certainty that the United States will enter the war in a short time, the destiny of the world will change. You will then see France go down like a drowning man and disappear, after having thrown a last look toward the land of liberty where she sought salvation.

While the Cabinet waited at Bordeaux for Roosevelt's reply, de Gaulle set out for London. Like Reynaud, he was grasping at straws. Officially, his mission was to arrange with the Royal Navy to assist in the transportation of Frenchmen to North Africa. But he understood clearly that unless some dramatic turn of events occurred, no Frenchmen would be going to North Africa. De Gaulle went to London in quest of a miracle, whatever it might be. By the time he arrived, Reynaud had already received the answer from Washington. The miracle was not to come from America.

In these hours which are so heart-rending for the French people and yourself [the President wrote], I send you the assurances of my utmost sympathy and I can further assure you that so long as the French people continue in defense of their liberty which constitutes the cause of popular institutions throughout the world, so long will they rest assured that matériel and supplies will be sent to them from the United States in ever-increasing quantities and kinds.

But, to make sure there was no mistake about the limitations in his phrases, Roosevelt added a clinching paragraph, as if to emphasize the finality of the rejection:

I know that you will understand that these statements carry with them no implication of military commitments. Only the Congress can make such commitments.

Thus the New World declared that it was not quite ready to come to the rescue of the Old.

In London, meanwhile, de Gaulle continued his desperate search for a way to reverse the torrent that, each moment, brought surrender closer. Churchill was ready to give him every assistance. On June 15th, the British Foreign Minister, Anthony Eden, had ordered the shaping of some sort of imaginative announcement of unspecified character. His permanent secretary, Sir Robert Vansittart, in conjunction with Charles Corbin, the French Ambassador, and Jean Monnet, head of the French economic mission, seized upon an astounding idea they believed might make the difference. Between them, they drafted a declaration that would unite France and England into a single country, a country forged in crisis but designed to endure after the war was won. When de Gaulle saw the declaration he adopted it at once, though he was not deceived about the magnitude of the practical problems it presented. Churchill reacted in similar fashion. Neither could have believed that a simple declaration, hastily drawn up, would easily erase a millennium of national independence for both countries. But this was not a moment for caution. At lunch on the sixteenth, de Gaulle persuaded the Prime Minister that, whatever the practical reservations, it was the last chance to keep France in the war. Churchill agreed to bring the matter before the British Cabinet for approval that afternoon.

At three-thirty, de Gaulle telephoned Reynaud at Bordeaux to hold fast, pending a magnificent pronouncement. Reynaud replied that he could delay his scheduled Cabinet meeting until five o'clock, when he expected to have to tender his resignation. After that, he said, it would be too late. De Gaulle stationed himself outside the room where Churchill was meeting with his Cabinet. At four-thirty, the British Government emerged, the Prime Minister in the lead, beaming his consent. De Gaulle immediately telephoned the exciting news to Reynaud. The Premier was transfigured with joy. Deep depression turned to high optimism. While de Gaulle at one end of the line dictated, Reynaud at the other took down with a pencil the terms of the proposed Declaration of Union:

At this most fateful moment in the history of the modern world, the Governments of the United Kingdom and the French Republic make this declaration of indissoluble union and unyielding resolution in their common defence of justice and freedom against subjection to a system which reduces mankind to a life of robots and slaves.

Paper in hand, with the assertion that he would "die defending these proposals," Reynaud then marched into the room where the French Cabinet waited for him.

His reading of this startling document left both his friends and his adversaries stupefied. One minister immediately said it would make France into a British dominion. Weygand rejected it as having nothing to do with the problem at hand. Another minister grumbled about a sellout. No voice was raised in its defense. The French Cabinet, in deep spiritual and intellectual disarray from the weeks of unbearable pressure, was completely incapable of considering the proposal in a reasonable manner. The Declaration of Union, the last hope, was rejected without even the dignity of a discussion or a vote.[25]

That night Reynaud resigned. He was replaced by Marshal Pétain, who immediately took steps to establish contact with the enemy.

De Gaulle left England in the early evening, before he learned that the declaration had been rejected or that Reynaud had fallen. But he was not optimistic. In his *Memoirs*, he says he told Churchill that he might return. The Prime Minister, he wrote, agreed that the aircraft which brought him to Bordeaux would wait there for his decision. Churchill gives a somewhat different version. He was informed of de Gaulle's intentions and gave his approval to them, he says, only when Spears phoned from France that night. Whichever details are accurate, there is no disagreement about the essentials. When de Gaulle landed in Bordeaux, he received notice that Pétain had taken over the Government and proposed to surrender. He resolved at once to go back to England to resist the capitulation.

De Gaulle's choice, however, was not made on the spur of the moment. An American reporter who interviewed him several months later quoted him as saying: "It was not a matter of minutes, not a matter of quick decision. The debacle was a long time in coming. I saw it arriving."[26] Many years after the war, de Gaulle told a crowd at Huppy, a tiny town outside Abbeville where, in 1940, his division had inflicted a beating on the Germans: "The effort expended at Huppy was not lost. It was here that the idea came to me to hold on, no matter what the cost. It is here that I measured the resolution of our British allies. I took an oath that if I ever returned to Huppy, it would not be after a defeat but after the victory . . ."[27] But whenever de Gaulle made his immediate decision to carry on the fight, in a larger sense he had chosen the direction long before. In 1932 he had written in *Le Fil de l'épée*:

In the face of crisis, the man of character turns to himself. His instinctive response is to impose his stamp on events, to submit them to his control, to make them his responsibility. Far from seeking shelter within the hierarchy, from hiding in the rule books, from covering himself with reports, he chooses to stand straight, assume a fighting stance and look ahead. Not that he willingly disregards orders or rejects advice, but he has a passion to impose his will, a jealousy to reach his own decisions. Not that he is unaware of risks or disdainful of consequences, but he assesses them carefully and accepts them honestly. Even better, he embraces action with the pride of the master, for if he commits himself to it, it becomes part of him; joyful of the success he earns even when he reaps no reward, bearing the full weight of his failures, but not without some bitter satisfaction. In short, a fighter who finds his ardor and his sustenance within himself. . . . The man of character gives nobility to action; without him it is the dreary task of the slave, thanks to him it is the divine game of the hero.[28]

On that night in Bordeaux—his last in France for four years—de Gaulle chose to play the "divine game of the hero."

From the airport where he landed, de Gaulle hastened into the city to see Spears. Between them, they made plans for their departure in the morning. No longer a minister, de Gaulle was fearful that Weygand might try to arrest him, so he spent the night in hiding. He awoke early and, to attract no attention to himself, went to his office and made appointments for the remainder of the day. Then, accompanied by his personal aide, Lieutenant Geoffroy de Courcel, he joined Spears at his hotel. De Gaulle's luggage was put into the car as if it belonged to the Englishman. Then de Gaulle and de Courcel drove to the airport, ostensibly to see Spears off. Spears describes the tension the men felt while de Gaulle's luggage was being loaded and lashed. At last, the Englishman climbed aboard. To the surprise of the French chauffeur, de Gaulle and Courcel promptly followed him into the plane. Quickly the craft taxied away, found an opening in the crowded runway and took off.[29]

"De Gaulle carried with him in this small aeroplane," wrote Churchill, "the honor of France."[30]

He also carried with him, if not animosity, disappointment in the realization that the United States, in France's moment of crisis, had proved a weak reed on which to lean.

The Spurning of the Rebel

June–October, 1940

WRITHING BENEATH THE DISHONOR of his country's capitulation, de Gaulle chose to reject the decision of the Government at Bordeaux. France, he determined, must fight on. Its fleet, one of the most powerful in the world, remained ready to do battle. The Empire, rich in resources and in men, displayed a combative disposition. De Gaulle meant to capitalize on the *élan* of the segments of the nation that had not been bested by the enemy. He saw that the virus of defeat was spreading. He hurried to head off a plague.

Several hours after he arrived back in London, de Gaulle, in a last plea to Bordeaux to reverse its course, proposed to dispatch to Africa all matériel en route from the United States, as well as the French ships docked in British harbors. His answer was a curt order to return to France at once. De Gaulle then chose to take the initiative. He directed the freighter *Pasteur* to change her destination from a French to a British port, so that her cargo of guns and ammunition could be used by Britain's Home Guard, rather than by the enemy. In contrast, Admiral Darlan instructed the aircraft carrier *Béarn*, carrying a hundred American planes, to sail to Martinique, where her cargo was to gather rust throughout the war. These conflicting commands symbolized de Gaulle's determination to wage war beside the British, Bordeaux's to abandon the British to their fate.[1]

That evening, de Gaulle conveyed to Churchill his decision to found a French resistance movement. His resources consisted of

26

100,000 francs (about $2000) given him by Reynaud from a secret fund and some small renown as warrior, tactician and former minister. His authority was nonexistent. Churchill recognized that the odds against him were enormous. But, hopeful himself that a segment of France would fight on, he gave de Gaulle the opportunity to try. On the word of Churchill, de Gaulle secured the transmitters of the B.B.C. to broadcast an appeal to France.

On the night of June 18th, de Gaulle made his famous *Appel aux Français* over the B.B.C. It was the first step in a long and arduous journey. To his stricken people, he proclaimed:

Has the last word been said? Must hope disappear? Is the defeat permanent. No!

For France is not alone. She is not alone. She is not alone. She has a vast Empire behind her. She can unite with the British Empire, which controls the seas and continues the fight. She can, like England, make unlimited use of the immense industry of the United States.

This war is not limited to the unhappy territory of our country. This war is not resolved by the Battle of France. This war is a world war. All the mistakes, all the delays, all the suffering do not change the fact that there is in the universe all the necessary means to crush our enemies one day. Overcome today by a mechanized force, we can win in the future by a superior mechanized force. Herein lies the destiny of the world.

I, General de Gaulle, now in London, invite French officers and soldiers who are on or can reach British territory, with or without their arms—I invite engineers and specialized workers of the armament industries who are on or who can reach British territory, to put themselves in contact with me.

Whatever happens, the flame of French resistance must not and will not go out.[2]

But even this, the most memorable of his addresses, was not fully a summons to mutiny. Its message was military, not political. The next day, in fact, de Gaulle wired to Noguès, commander in chief of the North African theater of operations: "Am in London in unofficial and direct contact with the British government. Remain at your disposal, either to fight under your orders or for whatever action appears useful to you." But for reasons that are not clear, de Gaulle made up his mind before he received an answer. He chose to be a rebel.

On the night of June 19th, de Gaulle appeared before a microphone of the B.B.C., and declared:

At this hour, all Frenchmen understand that the ordinary forms of power have disappeared.

In face of the confusion in French souls, in face of the liquidation of a government fallen into enemy servitude, in face of the impossibility of our institutions remaining in operation, I, General de Gaulle, French soldier and leader, *I am conscious of speaking in the name of France.**

Thus de Gaulle demonstrated his supreme audacity in taking on himself the burdens and responsibilities of France. In *Le Fil de l'épée*, he had quoted approvingly this critical assessment of an English admiral: "He has all of Nelson's qualities but one; he doesn't know how to disobey."[3] De Gaulle, on June 19th, demonstrated, for better or for worse, that disobedience was within his capacity.

De Gaulle has written that from the beginning his objective was clear. "For the effort to be worth making," he said in his *Memoirs*, "I had to succeed in putting back in the war not only Frenchmen but France." De Gaulle's goal was to eradicate the defeat and reestablish the French state. It was also to restore the French nation to its full dignity and grandeur.[4]

In 1932 de Gaulle had written:

Leaders of men—whether statesmen, prophets or soldiers—who have gotten the best out of others have always identified themselves with great ideas and drawn from them great vitality. Followed in their lifetimes because they convey the impression of greatness rather than self-interest, their fame is measured less by the usefulness than by the sweep of their endeavors. Though reason sometimes condemns them, emotion clothes them in glory.[5]

In assuming the identity of France, de Gaulle realized the great idea of the earlier contemplation. He lacked the power, to be sure, commensurate with the high mission he had taken upon himself. But to him, his poverty of means enlarged the sweep of his endeavor and provided him greater opportunity for glory.

De Gaulle, as leader of the Free French movement, would never have existed, however, without Churchill. The Prime Minister unhesitatingly adopted de Gaulle's premise that, morally at least, the Pétain regime did not represent France. He gave de Gaulle his most potent weapon, the microphone of the B.B.C. "His Majesty's Government," it was proclaimed, "now declares that they can no longer

---

* Author's italics.

regard the Bordeaux Government as a government of an independent country." Churchill, from the start, felt deep contempt for the men who betrayed the commitment of the French state, not only to Britain but, in his view, to France itself. In sharp contrast, he deeply admired what he called de Gaulle's "unconquerable heart."[6]

On June 22nd, in the railroad car in which the Germans surrendered in 1918, the representatives from Bordeaux accepted the Nazi armistice *diktat*. It gave the Germans direct control of three-fifths of the territory of France, including Paris and the entire coastline from Spain to Belgium. Most of the clauses were considered standard for armistice arrangements. But one paragraph excited particular attention. Article 8 provided that "The French war fleet, excepting that part which is left at the disposition of the French government for the safeguarding of its interests in its colonial empire, will be assembled in ports to be determined and must be demobilized and disarmed *under the control of Germany or of Italy*."* Both the Germans and the French insisted this was a guarantee that the fleet would not become part of the Nazi war machine. But to the British, Axis control of disarmament and demobilization meant only one thing: that Hitler planned to seize the ships.

The day after the armistice was signed, it was announced in London that the British Government had "taken note" of de Gaulle's proposal to form a French National Committee and would "recognize such provisional French National Committee and will deal with them in all matters concerning the prosecution of the war, so long as that committee continues to represent all French elements resolved to fight the common enemy."[7]

Still, Churchill, anticipating the appearance of a more prestigious figure than de Gaulle, was not prepared to give himself completely to the Free French cause. His first commitment did not preclude shifting his allegiance to some other French leader, say Darlan or Noguès, who had means more substantial than de Gaulle's "few kindred spirits" to contribute to Britain's defense. On June 25th, the Prime Minister told the House of Commons that "we shall certainly aid, to the best of our ability and resources, *any* movement or action by Frenchmen outside the power of the enemy to work for the defeat of Nazi barbarism and for the freedom and restoration of France." He still hoped that from within the French nation, despite

* Author's italics.

its spiritual and physical desolation, some major figure would emerge who would refuse to submit to the invader.

Churchill at first looked expectantly toward Reynaud and to his Minister of the Interior, Georges Mandel, who had been a relentless foe of surrender. For a while, in fact, he believed de Gaulle might be the first echelon of a flight of the Reynaud faction in the old cabinet to set up in England a rival government to Pétain's. But the days passed and no one came. Meanwhile, his emissaries made unsuccessful overtures to Lebrun, President of the Republic, Jeanneney, President of the Senate, and Herriot, President of the Assembly, each of whom had an illustrious past and had sided with Reynaud in opposition to surrender. In the capitals of the French colonies, British consuls felt out the governors-general and the military chiefs in the continuing search for a dissident. But everywhere the British were rebuffed.[8]

On June 25th, Churchill awoke to find that the French cruiser *Massilia* had arrived in Casablanca carrying a group of parliamentarians unreconciled to the armistice. Among them was Mandel, who, he learned, was preparing to issue a proclamation establishing a dissident government over the Empire, with himself as head. Churchill immediately dispatched Lord Gort, former commander of the British Expeditionary Force in France, and Duff Cooper, the Minister of Information, to make contact with Mandel. But by the time they reached Morocco, the proclamation had been intercepted by Noguès, who ordered Mandel arrested and put back aboard the ship. Gort and Duff Cooper were barred from any communication with the former Minister. The two Englishmen had no choice but to depart the next day. Churchill then ordered the Admiralty to try to rescue the *Massilia's* passengers, but the ship lay beneath the guns of Casablanca harbor and it was decided that the effort was not feasible.[9]

Not all British authorities shared Churchill's enthusiasm for a French resistance movement. Though the Prime Minister had ordered that help be extended to de Gaulle to recruit personnel, the military services were generally indifferent to the Free French. The intense pressure generated by the Battle of Britain left them little energy to spare for the cause of France. At one point, Churchill had to remind his General Staff that "it is the settled policy of his Majesty's government to make good strong French contingents for land, sea and air service, to encourage these men to volunteer to fight on with us, to look after them well, to indulge their sentiments about the French flag, etc., and to have them as representatives of a France which is continuing the war. . . . Mere questions of administrative inconvenience must not be allowed to stand in the way of this policy of the State."[10] But the services, on the one hand, sought to enlist skilled Frenchmen for their own purposes. On the other, the feeling existed that the French could not be trusted and ought now to keep to their own side of the Channel. In some instances, Britons behaved appallingly toward some Frenchmen in the British Isles. In the tremendous confusion of the days following the armistice, neither Britons nor Frenchmen understood clearly to whom patriotic French citizens owed their loyalty.

De Gaulle had become the pivotal point of this confusion of loyalties. In his own mind, he had made the leap to a higher conception of fidelity to France. He was himself unburdened by doubts. When Weygand, now Minister of Defense in the Pétain Cabinet, directed him to return home, he wrote: "I must tell you very simply that I desire for France and for you, General, that you recognize and are able to escape disaster, reach Overseas France and pursue the war." Weygand never read this advice, for much later de Gaulle's letter arrived back to him unopened, with a notice carefully typed in the corner: "If retired Colonel de Gaulle wishes to enter into communication with General Weygand, he must do so through regular channels." In mid-July, de Gaulle was notified, by way of the French chargé in London, that he had been court-martialed for disobedience and inciting insurrection. "I will appreciate," he advised the chargé, "if you will inform those who directed you to transmit it to me that their communication is not of the slightest interest to me."[11] When in August the Pétain Government condemned him to death, de Gaulle barely bothered to take note. But however sincere was his disdain for the condemnation heaped upon him, few Frenchmen possessed the self-assurance to share his boldness. Of Pétain, de Gaulle said: "To obtain and to accept such an act of servitude, we did not need you, *Monsieur le Maréchal*. We did not need the *vainqueur de Verdun*. Anybody would have sufficed."[12] But to the overwhelming majority of Frenchmen, it was easier to call de Gaulle a traitor than to question the criteria of duty prescribed by a Marshal of France.

The readiness of Darlan and the Navy to follow Pétain's lead was never in doubt. The Admiral was deeply dedicated to the Navy's Anglophobic heritage. Still, it is difficult to understand why this man, who had given his life to developing a first-class fighting fleet, should have foresworn the natural climax of his endeavors. Darlan was willing to dock his navy before it had ever been tested in battle. As early as June 17th, he sent messages to his admirals and to the captains of his ships justifying the request for an armistice. In the succeeding days, he used the full weight of his position and prestige to suppress any tendencies toward dissidence.[13]

Churchill was convinced that it was Darlan's passion for power that determined his decision to surrender. Pétain had offered him the Ministry of the Marine, his first cabinet post. With the Marshal nearing eighty-five, there was the promise of more power to come. As Churchill wrote scornfully in his *Memoirs:*

Admiral Darlan had but to sail in any one of his ships to any port outside France to become the master of all French interests beyond German control. . . . Acting thus, Darlan would have carried with him outside the German reach the fourth Navy in the world, whose officers and men were personally devoted to him. Acting thus, Darlan would have become the chief of the French Resistance with a mighty weapon in his hand. British and American dockyards and arsenals would have been at his disposal for the maintenance of his fleet. The French gold reserve in the United States would have assured him, once recognized, of ample resources. The whole French Empire would have rallied to him. Nothing could have prevented him from being the Liberator of France. The fame and power which he so ardently desired were in his grasp. Instead, he went forward through two years of worrying and ignominious office to a violent death, a dishonored grave, and a name long to be execrated by the French Navy and the nation he had hitherto served so well.[14]

But though the Navy's loyalty was a foregone conclusion, the Pétain Government was not nearly as certain about the Empire. Bordeaux was, in fact, apprehensive about its ability to impose defeat on the colonies. The morale of their inhabitants, absent from the debacle, was high. Not only were they confident of their own ability but, unconquered, they were fearful of having to submit to the conqueror. From such distant places as Damascus, Tunis, Dakar and Douala flashed messages of determination to dissociate the Empire from the armistice. De Gaulle's telegrams from London, proposing the immediate establishment of a Council of Overseas France, acted as a stimulant. "Can send you all the American air and land weapons already loaded and en route . . . " he wrote on June 25th.[15] But some Frenchman more eminent than he would have had to make the request, and none did.

The key to major colonial resistance was General Auguste Paul Noguès, commander of the 400,000-man North African Army. A British official in Morocco had described him as "a tiger straining at the leash" during the Battle of France. When Noguès heard Pétain's announcement of the surrender, he became so upset that, contrary to military discipline, he fired off an angry protest to the Government. Despite Weygand's reproach, he accused Bordeaux of panic and of blindness to North Africa's fighting potential, apparently having forgotten that several weeks before he had himself discouraged carrying the war across the Mediterranean. Weygand was so disconcerted that he at once dispatched his personal aide, General Koeltz, to bring Noguès back into line. The effort was unnecessary. Noguès had already written to Weygand that "in case you determine that to maintain order you must apply the Armistice to North Africa, it is with shame that I shall execute it and will ask you then to relieve me immediately of my command." The color of Noguès' face at the moment of execution is not on record. Neither is any formal request to be relieved of command. On the contrary, after assurances that the Germans would not occupy North Africa, Noguès agreed to stay at his post, where he remained contentedly for several more years. "So as not to cut France in two during its misery," he explained on June 26th to the Governor-General of Syria, "with death in my soul I had to resolve not to continue the fight."[16]

How can the almost universal collapse of bellicose spirits be explained? Churchill probably was right about Darlan's venality, but even he conceded that most Frenchmen who surrendered did not do so out of self-interest. Most were as patriotic as de Gaulle, though they interpreted patriotism differently. Churchill himself quite persuasively explained in a speech to the House of Commons the mentality that doomed resistance:

The Almighty in all His infinite wisdom did not see fit to create Frenchmen in the image of Englishmen. In a State like France, which has experienced so many convulsions—Monarchy, Convention, Directory, Consulate, Empire, Monarchy, Empire and finally Republic—there has grown up a principle founded on the *droit administratif* which undoubtedly governs the action of many French officers and officials in times of revolution and change. It is a highly legalistic habit of mind and it arises from a subconscious sense of national self-preservation against the dangers of sheer anarchy. For instance, any officer who obeys the command of his lawful superior is absolutely immune from subsequent punishment. Much therefore turns in the minds of French officers upon whether there is a direct, unbroken chain of lawful command and this is held by many Frenchmen to be more important than moral, national or international considerations.[17]

A Frenchman who spent the early years of the war close to Weygand called this the "functionary mind." It has dominated the French Army, he wrote, since the days of General Boulanger, a would-be revolutionary of the 1880's. "A functionary serves the state," he explained. "He never meddles in politics."[18]

Admiral Georges Robert, Governor of the French Antilles, similarly justified the decision he and his fellow colonial authorities took. He confirms the diagnosis that duty was easier to determine than morality. He also repeats Noguès' protestation that a nation undivided, in a time of crisis, is in itself the consummate objective. In his memoirs, he said:

If the consideration that we had for these men [Pétain and those around him], recognizing their glorious past, and if the sense of discipline with which we constantly lived were not enough to keep us in the strictest obedience behind the government, then his [Pétain's] appeal for unity could not fail to correspond to our own conceptions of the necessities of the hour.[19]

In the face of this inflexible outlook, almost universally held, de Gaulle's task appeared insuperable. At the time of the armistice, there were 20,000 or 30,000 French troops in England. Most were from the Alpine Division that had fought in Norway and been delayed in returning home. Several thousand were Dunkirk evacuees. Several thousand more were among wounded who had been transported directly to British hospitals from Belgium. In addition, an estimated 10,000 French sailors manned naval vessels still tied up in British ports. The manpower was thus on hand to make up a sizable French contingent. But among these men, the name "de Gaulle" was practically unknown. There had been some talk of his *appel*, but it had provoked little enthusiasm. Many of the officers were suspicious of this temporary brigadier general who took so much authority upon himself. A week after de Gaulle's campaign began, a rally he held at Olympia Hall in London attracted only a few hundred volunteers.

In France, de Gaulle's impact was even slighter. Pétain's authority, as well as his prestige, was uncontested. The Marshal was personally irritated by the behavior of a man he once considered a protegé, but his government did not take de Gaulle's rebellion seriously. The *appel*, lost in the din of the crumbling state, had only a handful of listeners and created no perceptible stir. "A handful of mercenaries huddled around a microphone," was the brand Pétain's propagandists sought to put on the Free French. Even Paul Reynaud abandoned de Gaulle and gave his loyalty to the Marshal's government.[20]

Jean Monnet, probably the most influential of the voluntary French exiles, pleaded with de Gaulle to abandon his efforts at forming a dissident movement. Monnet pledged never to relax his labors in behalf of France's liberation but he refused to give his services to the Free French. Three years later Monnet entered de Gaulle's camp, but on June 23rd, 1940, he wrote to the rebel general:

I consider that it would be a great mistake to try to establish in England an organization which would appear in France as an authority created abroad under the protection of England. I share completely your desire to keep France from giving up the fight. . . . But it is not from London that the effort of resurrection can, at this moment, begin. It would look to Frenchmen, in this form, like a movement protected by England, inspired by its interests and, because of that, condemned to a failure that will make later efforts to get back on our feet more difficult.[21]

De Gaulle rejected this contention. On June 26th, he submitted a memorandum to the British Government announcing that his aim was to unite all elements of resistance on British territory and to serve as liaison for any dissident activity in the Empire or in Metropolitan France. He asked Britain to recognize his committee as the intermediary in dealings between Frenchmen and British war agencies. He also asked for an advance of credit on France's account, presumably reimbursable after the war, to pay the soldiers and civilians who joined him.

The Churchill Government was not quite ready to grant de Gaulle all he wanted. The Prime Minister had not given up the hope that the colonies would remain in the war. He had offered publicly to make whatever financial arrangements were necessary after they were cut off from France. But as the days passed and his hopes diminished, de Gaulle emerged more strongly as the only Frenchman on whom he could count. On June 28th, Churchill issued a communiqué which stated: "His Majesty's Government recognize General de Gaulle as leader of all free Frenchmen, wherever they may be, who rally to him in support of the Allied cause."[22]

De Gaulle, meanwhile, had undertaken a personal tour of the French units still stationed in Britain and found a decent, if not overwhelming, response. Several battalions and many technicians rallied from the Alpine Division. Other soldiers, individually and in groups, enlisted in considerable numbers. A few small ships with their entire crews and about two dozen pilots joined up. Near the end of the month, boatloads of escapees from France began to appear. The movement was picking up momentum.

But on July 4th, the news reached Britain that the Royal Navy had sunk a large part of the French war fleet moored in the harbor of Mers el-Kébir, just outside Oran. At the same time, the British seized all French ships docked in home ports and instituted a blockade of a French squadron moored in the harbor at Alexandria. The disclosure broke with stunning force among Frenchmen, engendering renewed bitterness toward "Perfidious Albion." Britain justified Mers el-Kébir as an act of self-defense against an adversary of terrible potential. The Pétain Government retaliated by breaking diplomatic relations with London and hurling bombs at Gibraltar, though significantly it did not seize the pretext to declare war. De Gaulle, obviously injured, did not hesitate. He asserted that the incident, however unfortunate and ill-advised, had in no way changed his objective. "We did not choose dissidence out of love of the English," wrote one of his collaborators, "but to avenge and erase our defeat."[23]

Mers el-Kébir arrested the growth of the Free French movement but did not, as many feared at the time, wreck it. On Bastille Day, July 14th, a Free French column paraded down Whitehall behind the Cross of Lorraine, the symbol of Joan of Arc that de Gaulle had chosen for Free France. By the end of the month, de Gaulle could count a force of 7,000 men armed with the equipment and sailing the ships left behind by their repatriated comrades. It was a microscopic host for a country that three months before had two million men standing guard on its frontiers. But over the B.B.C., the dissident leader could now boast: "Frenchmen. Take note. You still have a combat army."[24]

Whatever the assets of the Free French movement, physical or moral, they failed to impress the Government of the United States. France's disgraceful performance on the battlefield had left Roosevelt, no less than the rest of the world, with a feeling of disgust. But he continued to respect the power of France's fleet and the strategic location of her colonies, which far exceeded any admiration he possessed for a handful of French insurgents. With only the Royal Navy standing between the Panzers and the American coast, Roosevelt was aware of the danger in losing the French fleet, especially its mighty capital ships, to the enemy. France's control over Martinique, a short distance from the Panama Canal, posed an additional threat to American security. While Churchill gave an increasing commitment to the anti-Nazism of the Free French, Roosevelt chose to do business where France's power lay, in the hands of the Pétain Government. For all he cared, de Gaulle did not exist.

In the beginning of July, Pétain transferred the seat of his government from Bordeaux to the resort city of Vichy in the mountains of central France. Here he abolished the Republic and in its place created an authoritarian state with himself as head. He called his program "The National Revolution" and offered Frenchmen "Work, Family, Country" instead of "Liberty, Equality, Fraternity." In Vichy's splendid hotels he installed the bureaucracy that he expected to direct the rejuvenation of the French nation. It was to Vichy, not to London, that Roosevelt's emissaries went to find the sovereignty of France.

Secretary of State Cordell Hull recalled in his memoirs that:

The President and I had no hesitation in continuing diplomatic relations with the Pétain government, while waiting to see what its ultimate policy would be. . . . The Pétain government was a legal government. . . . Our only excuse for breaking off diplomatic ties with Vichy could have been the fact that the Pétain cabinet was leaving the democratic traditions of France for a dictatorial form of government which smacked of fascism. But at that time we still maintained relations with such completely fascist governments as those of Germany, Italy and Spain.[25]

Neither Roosevelt nor Hull cared that the Vichy Government had been created on the sufferance of Hitler. Had France chosen to resist in June, 1940, the Nazis would have been forced to reduce the fleet and the colonies before they could go on to further conquests. Hitler bestowed on Pétain the administration of two-fifths of the country in return for the neutralization of France's remaining capacity to wage war. It was a good bargain for Hitler. He saw no need to expend further energy on the French. His objective was to dispose of Britain and Russia, the remaining obstacles to his European hegemony. Confident his war aims would soon be achieved, he could return to France any time he chose to claim the booty he had left behind. Only when Britain refused to be broken did the state at Vichy take on a life of its own. While Germany had enemies, Vichy could remain reasonably independent, for the Axis was as concerned as the Allies about the fate of the fleet and the colonies. Vichy's ability to maintain these assets guaranteed its existence and provided some bargaining power to achieve its objectives. It won for Pétain the solicitude of the American Government.

Pétain's aim, as head of the armistice regime, was to serve as a buffer between the victorious Nazis and the French people. His action would not have made sense had he admitted that the Nazi New Order would, when it could, swallow France. He took for granted that Germany would withdraw its troops after hostilities were over and leave France independent, just as the victor had freed the vanquished after the two previous wars. Many Frenchmen believed otherwise. Pierre Laval, a former premier and an admirer of Nazism, led the clique at Vichy that worked assiduously to commit France to Germany's side. In Laval's view, since Hitler would win the war France should seek his gratitude and his mercy by actively collaborating with him. Pétain, though no less convinced of a German victory, insisted on maintaining a "prudent balance" between Allies and Axis. He preferred to play a double game, using the colonies and the fleet not only to threaten but also to extract concessions from both sides. Pétain understood that skillful use of his assets could serve to mitigate the harshness of the occupation in a hundred ways. But if he committed himself to one side or the other, he would lose his independence and leave the Nazis free to administer his country as a conquered province.

The United States played into Pétain's hands. Roosevelt's policy was to woo the Vichy Government with sympathy and, whenever the British consented, a shipload of civilian supplies. This was precisely the policy that Pétain wanted. The American presence in Vichy, a source of anxiety to Berlin, helped him withstand Nazi pressure. In this perversion of the lovers' triangle, Vichy was the object of the attention of both Roosevelt and Hitler. But in the rivalry, the Nazi's capacity to intensify the rigors of his occupation gave him an overwhelming advantage. What the United States offered Vichy was insignificant compared to the pain the Nazis could inflict. The United States could help Vichy to remain out of the Nazi grip. But it could help only a little. The principal resolve had to come from Pétain himself.

For the United States to have broken with Vichy would have required a conviction that Pétain, under any circumstances, would not surrender the colonies or the fleet. Such a conviction would have permitted Roosevelt to set an inspiring example of moral concern for all those people under the Nazi heel. But a policy of ignoring Vichy would have required audacity. It would have been a gamble, despite the vows made in Vichy, as well as in Berlin, that the fleet and the colonies were inviolate. De Gaulle himself drew attention to the risks of such audacity when he declared after Mers el-Kébir that "there is not the slightest doubt that, through principle and through need, the enemy would one day have used [those ships], either against England or against our own Empire."[26] Roosevelt never for a moment contemplated such audacity. As long as Vichy had powerful ships and strategic territories, he followed the safest, most conservative course. Roosevelt regarded it as his responsibility, to the nation and to the Alliance, to help Pétain resist the pressure of the conqueror.

Roosevelt took no pride in his Vichy policy. The Pétain regime irritated him. When, after Mers el-Kébir, the French Ambassador ran to the White House for sympathy, the President dismissed him harshly. Another time, he told the Ambassador that "the less either of them said about the relations between the two countries, the better for both." But Roosevelt remained steadfastly silent on the reasons for his course, on the grounds that a public admission of scorn for Vichy would reduce the effectiveness of United States diplomacy. Whatever his private feelings, Roosevelt stood faithfully by his courtship of France's apostles of capitulation.[27]

Hull, by contrast, often boasted of the Vichy policy, claiming it was justified because "we could encourage the French people by convincing them we are still with them."[28] But encourage them to do what? The Vichy policy encouraged them, if anything, to accept surrender. Evidence strongly suggests that the speed of American recognition of the Pétain regime stifled resistance both in the colonies and at home. The United States, for reasons of its own security, had to be concerned about the colonies and the fleet. It did not have to be nearly so solicitous about the regime that controlled them. The United States inflated the moral standing of the Pétain Government. This aspect of the Vichy policy was a burden upon the struggle for victory.

Churchill, naturally, recognized the advantages to himself of Roosevelt's course. The United States performed the thankless tasks of everyday diplomacy—the tedious notes, the cajolery, the threats, the extravagant compliments and false deference toward the men who had degraded France. While Roosevelt submitted to opprobrium for consorting with knaves, Churchill could assume a bulldog stance toward Vichy and exalt the virtues of de Gaulle. By letting the President of the United States do his diplomatic dirty work, Churchill reaped the satisfactions of defying Vichy without suffering the consequences.

Despite Roosevelt's unswerving allegiance to America's Vichy doctrine, Churchill was not above playing a double game with Britain's. He proclaimed a rigorous blockade of the French coast, but he saw to it that enough merchantmen slipped through to avoid provoking Vichy's retaliation. Though in mid-July he vetoed a proposal that the United States send relief to France, a few days later he urged on his Foreign Secretary the use of "both food and other inducements" to promote a "collusive conspiracy in the Vichy government." Without notifying the United States, Britain several months later began secret negotiations with Vichy to permit the entry of foodstuffs into France. "It was our first duty," Churchill explained, "to give loyal support to General de Gaulle in his valiant constancy." But, he added roguishly, "our consistent policy was to make the Vichy Government and its members feel that, so far as we were concerned, it was never too late to mend."

One essential difference between Churchill's policy and Roosevelt's was that the British, in dealing with Vichy, made no effort to conceal their contempt. The United States, by treating the Pétain Government with honor and dignity, enhanced its status in France and throughout the nonfascist world.[29]

De Gaulle grew increasingly bewildered by American policy as the Free French movement grew stronger. Throughout the summer, capable if not prominent Frenchmen rallied to him in sufficient numbers for him to establish a working committee to handle the administration of the movement. The committee maintained close relations not only with the British but also with the governments-in-exile in London. De Gaulle established the embryo of a General Staff to organize Free French forces along standard military lines and to direct intelligence operations which aimed at restoring contact with the Continent. In the principal capitals abroad, de Gaulle found able men to act as his representatives for diplomatic assignment, recruitment and the dissemination of propaganda. Free France was still skeletal, but the skeleton was becoming that of a government.

In France, meanwhile, the feeling of shock was fading. As they regained their equilibrium, Frenchmen slowly became aware of the group of compatriots who had rejected surrender. By constantly denouncing de Gaulle, Vichy's propagandists, as well as Germany's, gilded a hitherto unknown figure. When the Pétain Government on August 3rd condemned de Gaulle to death, it conceded, in the eyes of most Frenchmen, that de Gaulle had become a formidable opponent. At the same time, de Gaulle's regular broadcasts over the B.B.C. started to be a normal feature of life under the occupation. More and more listeners heard his messages. As the months passed and Germany failed to destroy Great Britain, the notion spread that the war was perhaps not over after all. Hesitantly, Frenchmen started to wonder if they had been deceived by Pétain and his men. De Gaulle gave them grounds for believing that France might yet play a part in the war.

The British Government granted formal recognition to Free France and to de Gaulle, its chief, on August 7, 1940. In a signed agreement and an exchange of letters, Churchill now acknowledged that Free France alone represented the spirit of French resistance. Significantly, he dated the accord so that it was recorded as having come into force on July 1, 1940. Churchill agreed to arm whatever forces de Gaulle could assemble under his command, to give the Free French priority over the Royal Navy in manning ships seized from the French fleet and to advance as much money as de Gaulle needed to operate the movement, repayable from French funds at some subsequent date.

The agreement conceded less to Free France than de Gaulle wanted, for it did not recognize the movement as possessing sovereignty. It acknowledged de Gaulle as supreme commander of his force but limited his authority by putting him under "the general direction of the British high command." It guaranteed to Britain the privilege of examining Free French accounts to ascertain that its money was well spent. Though it assured de Gaulle that his force "will never be required to take up arms against France," there was a conflicting interpretation of what the provision meant. De Gaulle would have interpreted it to mean that Free French forces might fight against Frenchmen but never against the national interests of France. He would, of course, have left it to himself to decide what constituted French national interests. Churchill, however, insisted that "France" be understood to mean a France free of German domination. "For instance," he wrote to de Gaulle, "a declaration of war by the government of Vichy against the United Kingdom would not constitute a declaration of war by France." The nuance, which Churchill made de Gaulle accept in writing, signified that Britain would have final say over the disposition of Free French troops. De Gaulle, reluctantly, accepted Churchill's condition with the "hope that events will one day enable the British Government to consider these questions with less reserve." He did, however, succeed in committing Churchill to the "full restoration of the independence and greatness of France." Though de Gaulle lacked the freedom from foreign restraint he needed if he was to act in the name of France, Churchill's promise at least harmonized Britain's war aims with his own. The pact of August 7th, de Gaulle knew, was a first step. But it was a step that established Free France as the guardian of French integrity and as a virtually autonomous member of an alliance.[30]

As de Gaulle labored in London to knit together his organization, the personal life he led was quiet and, for the most part, secluded. Days were spent at his headquarters, first in St. Stephen's House on the Thames Embankment, then in the more spacious Carlton Gardens, which ultimately became famous as the capital building of Free France. In the beginning, de Gaulle occupied a modest room in the Connaught Hotel. On weekends, he went to the country, where he rented a house for his wife and children, who had arrived in England on one of the last boats from Brittany. Later, when his son, Philippe, went to sea with the Free French Navy and his daughter Elisabeth was enrolled in boarding school, Mme. de Gaulle and their younger daughter, Anne, moved back into the city. The deGaulles took a small house, where they did little entertaining. Rarely, in fact, did they appear in public. In his *Memoirs*, de Gaulle, who is little given to gratitude, cited the "kindly reserve" and "sympathetic discretion" that his London neighbors and the English generally showed for his private life. Jealous of his privacy, de Gaulle hardly ever allowed his role as a public figure to interfere with his role as husband and father.[31]

The style de Gaulle adopted as Free French leader was in distinct contrast to the unpretentious quality of his private life. De Gaulle, the chief, was always aggressive, rarely flexible and often pugnacious in the assertion of Free French interests and what he conceived to be the rights of France. Even in the bleakest moments, he rejected meekness as a means to his ends. "He had to be rude to the British," Churchill wrote, "to prove in French eyes that he was not a British puppet." The Prime Minister made no secret of his displeasure at de Gaulle's "proud and haughty demeanor toward 'perfidious Albion' although an exile dependent upon the British and dwelling in our midst."[32] However great his dependence, de Gaulle believed his objectives required this defiant attitude. He once told Churchill, in response to a plea for less rigidity: "It is possible for you because you are seated on a solid state, a unified nation, a united empire, great armies. But me, what do I have? Nonetheless, I am in possession, and you know it, of the interests and the destiny of France. They are too heavy and I am too poor to be able to yield."[33] Thus de Gaulle, quite consciously, adopted the harshness that few were able to understand and courted the dislike that many were quick to accord him.

Spears, now his chief liaison with the British Government, described de Gaulle as "like a medieval monk." Spears' wife, the novelist Mary Borden, wrote that during a dinner party held for him, "his face never showed the slightest change of expression as he talked. No flicker of interest lifted his hooded eyelids." Yet, she said, evenings in his company "were sometimes uncomfortable but always interesting. De Gaulle could be eloquent, he could make himself very agreeable if he felt so inclined. But he was often biting, scathing in his criticisms of England and the English, just as much or more so of France. His long lips would curl as if he were drinking gall and wormwood when he talked of France."[34]

De Gaulle, unquestionably, was consumed by an intense passion. Without imperturbable conviction, he would not have been prepared to challenge not only those who opposed him but also those whom he most needed as friends. De Gaulle could not afford the luxury of second thoughts. He had set a distant goal and made up his mind that he would not be diverted. His single-mindedness allowed his spirit no tranquillity. Even his trusted companions could not reach the heights where his senses dwelled. Except for his family, de Gaulle remained a stranger to all.

Dewavrin, the celebrated "Colonel Passy" of de Gaulle's intelligence service, said of his first meeting with his new chief:

The welcome was glacial and all I saw of the general was his gray, piercing look, his tenacious will more apparent in his speech than in his movements, perhaps also a bit haughty or scornful. . . . One must not be surprised to learn that many officers, somewhat lost in the confusion that followed the armistice, walked out completely chilled by their first and often their only encounter with General de Gaulle.[35]

Larminat, one of the first and most loyal of the high military officers to join Free France, said that de Gaulle showed toward his followers "something of the style one has for an old domestic whom one sometimes treats rudely but like a member of the family."[36]

Passy tells the story of how one night de Gaulle invited him to dinner. To his surprise, he found the General "relaxed, exquisitely polite, urbane and friendly, rid of the dry and frequently brutal coldness that characterized his attitude in the office at Carlton Gardens." As the evening wore on, Passy says, he began to warm to de Gaulle and finally felt himself equal to asking his chief to say an occasional kind word to his officers and men, most of whom felt lonely and insecure, cut off from their families and their country. De Gaulle immediately drew himself up and replied harshly, "I have no lessons to receive from a young squirt like you." But the next morning as he entered Carlton Gardens, Passy reports, he saw de Gaulle climbing the stairs ahead of him. As he reached a landing, the General turned to a guard standing at attention, "shook the hand of the terrorised lad and said to him in a tone that would have discouraged any feeling of intimacy: 'How are you? Do you have any news from your family?' Then he turned and continued up the stairs, leaving the sentinel behind him, stupefied and mumbling an inaudible answer. . . ."[37]

Passy, who worked as closely with de Gaulle as almost any man during the years in London, was convinced that timidity was at the root of the General's incivility. As he analyzed it, de Gaulle was among those souls "who hide their emotion and their discomfort under a brutal and cutting exterior." Passy, however, was at best only partly right. De Gaulle was far too calculating to be dismissed as timid. His was a mind that was constantly at work. Every action was designed to contribute to an objective. His very presence, whether at a Cabinet meeting or a dinner party, was reckoned for the impact it would make. De Gaulle never permitted himself the luxury of inattention. He had a deadly instinct for making the right move, but it was always preceded by the most rigorous calculation. Many passages in *Le Fil de l'épée* attest to his having settled years before on the qualities of personality he would require and the consequences to which he must resign himself to perform the great mission he envisioned for the future.

The passion to act alone [he wrote] must inevitably be accompanied by some roughness in method. The man of character incorporates in his person the severity necessary for the effort. His subordinates feel it and sometimes they complain. . . . But once action begins, criticism vanishes. Aspirations and hopes turn toward him as iron toward a magnet. In time of crisis, it is he whom they follow, who takes the burden upon his own shoulders, though it would break them. At the same time, the confidence of little men exalts the man of character. He recognizes an obligation from the trust they put in him. His determination grows apace but so does his benevolence, for he is a born protector. If the effort succeeds, he distributes the rewards generously. In the case of a reverse, he lets the blame fall only on himself. He is repaid in esteem what he offers in security[38]. . . .

The power to command requires mystery, for no one reveres the familiar. . . . In the designs, the style, the exercise of the mind, an element must remain which others cannot grasp, which moves them and leaves them breathless. Certainly one must not lock oneself up in an ivory tower, ignore his subordinates and remain inaccessible to them. On the contrary, a hold over men's minds requires watching them, making each believe he has been noticed. But, on the condition that he must also adopt the habit of giving nothing away, determined to keep within himself some secret of a surprise that can at any moment alter the course of events. The latent faith of the masses will do the rest[39]. . . .

For those who want to perform a mission which drives most men away, incessant self-discipline and constant risk test the personality to the most hidden fibers. Those who subject themselves to it face a perpetual inner struggle, the sharpness of which depends on the individual, but which remains a torment for the soul. . . . Keeping himself apart from others, the leader deprives himself of the sweetness of freedom, of familiarity, of friendship. He takes a vow of solitude which is, according to Faguet*, "the wretchedness of superior men." Satisfaction, tranquillity, simple

---

* Emile Faguet (1847–1916), a literary critic, member of the French Academy, known for an ingenious mind and a wit that was often excessively subtle.

pleasures, those things which are conventionally called happiness are excluded from his realm. One must make a choice, and the choice is cruel. From it emerges some vague quality of melancholy which lodges in whatever is majestic, whether men or things. Before an old and noble monument, someone once said to Bonaparte, "It is sad." "Yes," he answered, "just like greatness."[40]

De Gaulle, discontented with his slow progress, reached out in the direction of greatness in midsummer, 1940, after it became clear that Vichy had established its authority over the colonies of North Africa. De Gaulle looked a step beyond, to the French territories south of the Sahara. Too distant and too primitive to be tightly held by Metropolitan France, they depended at least as much upon the neighboring British colonies as upon each other to remain economically viable. De Gaulle's information indicated that they were ripe to break away from Vichy. But he recognized that if he sought to win them one at a time, Vichy would march in with superior force and bring his efforts to an end. He had to win all the central African colonies with a single blow of the sword. At the beginning of August, de Gaulle sent a team of conspirators into the British colonies that bordered on French territory. Its principal members were Pleven, Hettier de Boislambert, Leclerc and Larminat, all of them now famous in Free French annals. Their target date for winning the allegiance of the great mid-African segment of the French Empire was the last week of the month. Their campaign has since become known as "The Glorious Days" in the history of the Gaullist movement.

On August 26th, Governor Félix Eboué of Chad, in response to the persuasion of Pleven, proclaimed the adherence of his colony to Free France.

That same night, Leclerc and Boislambert arrived by canoe at Douala on the coast of Cameroun. They made contact with a group of waiting sympathizers and by morning had control of the town. The next day, escorted by two companies of native troops, they set out by train for the inland capital of Yaoundé, where their authority was recognized as soon as they arrived.

On the twenty-eighth, Larminat crossed the Congo River from Léopoldville in the Belgian Congo to Brazzaville, capital of French Equatorial Africa. The garrison there had already risen and driven out Vichy's governor-general. Larminat had only to assume power from the garrison commander. He then flew to Bangui, capital of Ubangi, where a coup had installed a shaky Gaullist regime. His appearance ended opposition and stabilized the new arrangement.

On the twenty-ninth, the Governor of Gabon in Libreville renounced his allegiance to Vichy and declared in favor of Free France.

All of central Africa was now in de Gaulle's hands, without a drop of blood having been shed.

Vichy, though taken completely by surprise, reacted with unanticipated vigor. The counterattack began in Gabon. The naval commander at Libreville reaffirmed his loyalty to Pétain, trained his guns on the city and persuaded the Governor to reverse his decision. A short time later, a plane landed from Dakar, disembarking a group of faithful Vichyite officials, who took over the administration, carrying the important rebels away. Next, a general arrived, escorted by several heavy bombers, to take command of the military forces. A squadron of ships left Toulon, slipped unnoticed through the Strait of Gibraltar and began steaming full speed toward the south. It was clear that Vichy intended a major effort to get its colonies back. But at that moment a more significant showdown was impending several thousand miles northwest. The affair was not to be settled in the center of Africa but at Dakar, the fortress city on the West African coast.[41]

De Gaulle, anxious to win an important imperial center, proposed to Churchill in late July that they undertake a joint venture to seize Dakar. Churchill's imagination was ignited at the prospect. Impatient for action, he was too weak to provoke the Germans but, avid for a victory, he was willing to challenge the Vichy French. The operation was strategically justified, because Dakar looked out over the British lifeline around the Cape. Reports—later proved false—indicated that large numbers of Germans were present, possibly to build a submarine base. Churchill recognized that Dakar was defended by powerful guns, important naval units and a sizable garrison. He was willing to gamble that Vichy would not retaliate against an attack by declaring war. More significantly, he thought it possible, despite de Gaulle's warnings to the contrary, that Dakar would rally bloodlessly to the Allied cause.

When de Gaulle's troops learned of their mission, they were exultant. They had joined Free France to fight. This was their first opportunity. But in their elation, they gave way to indiscretion. Many of them spoke openly of their destination. In cafés around London, they drank toasts "*à Dakar*." These were the days, early in the war, when security procedures were still primitive. It would have been relatively simple for agents in their midst to transmit the nature of their operation to Vichy.[42]

De Gaulle, who was personally to accompany the attacking force, had originally proposed a prudent flanking operation to take the fortress from the rear. But because the Royal Navy was pressed for time, Churchill decided to confront Dakar head on. Like the Americans two years later, he was persuaded that the defenders would recognize that it was in France's interest not to fire on their friends. De Gaulle accepted the plan with misgivings, anticipating that Free French presence in the expeditionary force might rally the garrison. The attacking flotilla, which carried 2,000 Free French soldiers, appeared off Dakar on September 23rd. The welcome it received demonstrated that Vichy did not draw distinctions between enemies. Dakar resisted with all its strength.

Because of a serious blunder, the Royal Navy had failed to stop the squadron of powerful French cruisers that had left Toulon with a contingent of troops heading for Gabon. By chance, they were at Dakar when the British fleet arrived. Thus the attackers found the defense even stronger than they had anticipated. The attempt to rally the city peacefully failed completely. De Gaulle's emissaries were fired on and wounded as they entered the harbor carrying a white flag. In the heavy though sporadic fighting that followed, three British ships were seriously damaged, while the British sunk three French submarines, burned out two destroyers and scored important hits on the battleship *Richelieu*. No troops were landed, although several Free French soldiers were killed in a futile effort to put a patrol ashore. The reinforcements Vichy had sent had so stiffened the garrison that only a costly, all-out assault could have reduced the fort. On orders from London, and with the sanction of de Gaulle, the fight was abandoned after the third day.

De Gaulle suffered a serious defeat at Dakar. The momentum the Free French appeared to be generating in Africa was brought to an end. The hope that Dakar would be a step to Morocco, then to all of North Africa, was shattered. De Gaulle himself admitted as the fleet withdrew that he was never so depressed, never so unsure of the future of his movement.

To make matters worse, the Free French were blamed for disclosing the secret of Dakar and for bringing the Vichy squadron into the battle. It was never proved. The justice of the charge seems doubtful, since the initial destination of the ships was Libreville in central Africa. But it left the Free French with a reputation for being "leaky" that long remained with them.

More important, the defiance of the Dakar garrison was cited as proof that de Gaulle not only failed to attract Frenchmen but actually repelled them. De Gaulle was never to forgive Dakar's governor-general, Pierre Boisson, whom he came to associate with all that was corrupt in Vichy. Because of Boisson, Free France was badly hurt. Despite the British share, the fiasco was to have its most serious repercussions on the Gaullist movement.[43]

Churchill, however, stood by de Gaulle, as if adversity had made him more worthy. A week before Dakar, he had been ready to replace him, on the grounds that de Gaulle had failed to rally enough prominent Frenchmen. He found a candidate in General Georges Catroux, a full general with an authoritative presence, a fine reputation and an agreeable disposition. Catroux, however, rejected Churchill's overtures and, though he surpassed de Gaulle by several grades, put himself under de Gaulle's orders with the explanation that the Free French leader had lifted himself above considerations of military rank. When Churchill learned of what had happened at Dakar, he chose not to persist. The reports that reached him indicated de Gaulle's demeanor had been superb. Though he gave the House of Commons almost no details about the Dakar defeat, Churchill announced that de Gaulle's conduct and bearing "had made my confidence in him greater than ever."[44]

Despite the setback at Dakar, the enterprise had not been all in vain. The three cruisers that had done so much to thwart the operation were excluded from the reconquest of central Africa, which had been their original mission. Unprepared to challenge the Royal Navy, they remained in shelter in Dakar. The Free French troops who had failed in their first objective successfully achieved a second by consolidating de Gaulle's possession of the central African territory and by winning back, in a bloody battle with Vichy troops, the seacoast colony of Gabon. Though he was unable to extend his domain, de Gaulle, as a by-product of Dakar, solidified his base of operations and his capacity for independent action.

The month of September brought other significant advancement to Free French fortunes. On the second, it was learned that the islands of French Oceania in the Pacific had declared their allegiance. A week later, the tiny colonies of French India rallied. On the fourteenth, the Atlantic islands of Saint-Pierre and Miquelon were shaken by a Gaullist coup, which Vichy suppressed, but which left no doubts about popular sympathies. A few days later, France's possessions in the New Hebrides swung to de Gaulle, followed on the twentieth by the important island of New Caledonia. The hegemony in the Pacific offered little in terms of men and resources but had great potential significance as military and naval bases, in view of the growing antagonism between the United States and Japan.

The Free French were now a factor in the war, however modest. De Gaulle had contingents in England and the Middle East under British command and an autonomous force in Africa. He named Leclerc the commander of the African division, then assigned him the electrifying mission of marching north across the desert to threaten the flank of the Axis forces on the Mediterranean shore and, ultimately, to link up with Britain's desert army. In all, by late fall, de Gaulle had an estimated 30,000 men under arms, prepared to kill Germans and Italians in the name of France.[45]

Pétain, however, provided what ultimately became the best endorsement for Free France. On October 24th, in the tiny village of Montoire in the occupied zone, he met Hitler in a railroad car and, without making specific commitments, agreed to recommend a policy of collaboration to his people. A few days later, the Marshal went before a microphone to announce that "it is with honor and in order to maintain French unity—ten centuries of unity within the framework of constructive activity of the new European order— that I embark today on a course of collaboration."[46] The words, as Hitler angrily learned later, meant nothing. Churchill, though apprehensive, suspected as much, since Pétain had a few days before sent a secret emissary to him to propose a *modus vivendi*. But whatever Pétain intended, the Montoire meeting set a tone of submission for Vichy that was bound to have an impact on all self-respecting Frenchmen.

When he learned of Montoire, Roosevelt feared the worst, dispatched a harsh note to the Marshal, and prepared to seize Martinique. But in the end, Montoire persuaded him that he must try harder to woo the Vichy Government. It was at this point, when

Roosevelt conspicuously rewarded pusillanimity with indulgence, that his Vichy policy became most vulnerable. A chorus of abuse followed the decision, most of it from Roosevelt's ardent liberal supporters. But the President, who either failed to understand or rejected the popular loathing for Pétain, considered the criticism "factious, ignorant or unwarranted." The State Department went a step further and blamed the propaganda organs of the Free French, the British Government and the Communist Party, rather than any native American feeling, for the censure. Roosevelt's response to Montoire was to seek some American so eminent to represent him in Vichy that Pétain would have to take notice of his generosity and, in gratitude, stand firm against German pressure.

To de Gaulle, Pétain's meeting at Montoire, even if it was only to shake the Führer's hand, demonstrated unquestionable depravity. On October 27th, he was in Brazzaville, capital of Free French Africa. It was there that he issued the manifesto which was to guide his conduct and set the standard for his movement throughout the remainder of the war. The Brazzaville Manifesto represents de Gaulle's claim of legitimacy and his plea for acceptance to Frenchmen and the world:

There exists no longer a truly French government [he declared]. In point of fact, the body that sits at Vichy and that pretends to bear that name is unconstitutional and in subjection to the invader. In its state of servitude, this body can only be and is in fact an instrument used by the enemies of France against the honor and interest of the country. It is necessary therefore for a new power to assume the burden of directing the French war effort. Events impose this sacred duty upon me. I shall not fail to discharge it.

I will exercise my powers in the name of France and only to defend it. I solemnly undertake to render an account of my acts to the representatives of the French people as soon as they may be freely chosen.[47]

Thus de Gaulle submitted his claim, at the very moment that Roosevelt turned most fervidly to Pétain.

THREE

Courtship of the Dishonorable

November, 1940–December, 1941

Montoire had much more impact than Brazzaville on Roosevelt. The United States Government had nothing to say about de Gaulle's manifesto, if indeed it had even heard of it. But it reacted quickly to the proposal conceived at Montoire, a Franco-German entente. Roosevelt decided that it was necessary now to show more attention to Vichy, to intensify his effort to keep the Pétain Government out of the clutches of the Axis.

In mid-November, 1940, Roosevelt asked Admiral William D. Leahy, former Chief of Naval Operations, to become his ambassador. "We are confronting an increasingly serious situation in France," he wrote to the Admiral. "There is even the possibility that France may actually engage in war against Great Britain and, in particular, that the French fleet may be utilized under the control of Germany. We need in France at this time an American who can gain the confidence of Marshal Pétain, who at the present moment is the one powerful element of the French Government who is standing firm against selling out to Germany." Leahy's assignment, Roosevelt said in his letter of instructions, was "to cultivate as close relations with Marshal Pétain as possible."[1]

Churchill, at the same time, was coming to an opposite judgment about Pétain and his men. "We have never received the slightest good treatment or even courtesy from Vichy," he wrote to a cabinet minister, "and the Free French movement remains our dominant policy. . . . I am sure de Gaulle is much the best Frenchman now in the arena and I want him taken care of as much as possible." He sent the same instructions to the Foreign Office, with the comment that "General de Gaulle and the Free French movement . . . are the only people who have done anything for us and to whom we have made very solemn engagements."[2]

It was not that Churchill planned to abandon his efforts to swing the men of Vichy over to his side. On the contrary, on December 31st, a few days before Leahy reached his new post, Churchill sent a personal message to Pétain through the Canadian legation saying that "if at any time in the near future the French Government decide to cross to North Africa or resume the war there against Italy and Germany, we should be willing to send a strong and well-equipped Expeditionary Force of up to six divisions to aid the defence of Morocco, Algiers and Tunis. These divisions would sail as fast as ships and landing facilities were available." Pétain's refusal even to answer confirmed Churchill's sense of outrage toward the Vichy regime. "It passes my comprehension," he said, "why no French leaders secede to Africa, when they would have an empire, command of the seas and all the frozen French gold in the United States. . . . Surely the opportunity is the most splendid ever offered to daring men."[8] Churchill deplored a policy that bestowed rewards on those he regarded as the antithesis of daring men.

Throughout 1940, Churchill had been content with the divergence of British and American policies toward France. By accident or design, the policies complemented each other usefully. But by the beginning of the new year, Churchill was tired of pampering Pétain.

It would be a mistake [he told the Cabinet] to suppose that a solution of our difficulties with Vichy will be reached by a policy of conciliation and forgiveness. The Vichy Government is under heavy pressure from Germany, and there is nothing that they would like better than to feel a nice, soft, cosy, forgiving England on their side. This would enable them to win minor favours from Germany at our expense, and hang on as long as possible to see how the war goes. We, on the contrary, should not hesitate, when our interests require it, to confront them with difficult and rough situations, and make them feel that *we* have teeth as well as Hitler. It must be remembered that these men have committed acts of baseness on a scale which have earned them the lasting contempt of the world. . . . Certainly we should have contacts with them. But in order to promote such favourable tendencies we must make sure the Vichy folk are kept well ground between the upper and nether millstones of Germany and Britain. In this way they are most likely to be brought into a more serviceable mood during the short run which remains to them.[4]

Though the differences between the President and the Prime Minister over Vichy focused on tactics, it was obviously growing into a more profound conflict. Churchill and Roosevelt, it was apparent, had brought totally divergent premises to their dealings with France. Only after Montoire did disagreement swell into serious discord. As each man reacted to military requirements, it was often difficult to see consistency in either of their positions. But underlying their actions a thread ran through the thinking of both that revealed, more and more clearly as time passed, that they disagreed on the nature of France and, consequently, on the role of France in the war and the liberation.

Churchill looked across the English Channel and saw a people who, through triumph and defeat, had for a millennium been a worthy adversary or a noble friend. He shared with de Gaulle the conviction that France's resort to wretched men was a temporary aberration. At the same time as he fought to win the war, Churchill felt the need to unshackle the French nation from its thralldom to Vichy. When he pledged to restore France's greatness he was not being merely generous. Churchill recognized the importance of a free and independent France to the future of England. Aware that France was a land of many contradictions, his objective was to encourage its best tendencies. Churchill was solicitous of France's self-esteem. He was conscious that Britain and France would have to live together in Europe long after the Pétains and the Hitlers were gone.

Roosevelt had no comparable feeling of responsibility or concern. He did not share Churchill's faith in the inherent vitality of the French nation. His perspective, both forward and backward, was far more limited than that of Churchill—the European, historian and statesman. Roosevelt, irritated by French politics, without deep understanding of French history, with no experience in European diplomacy, took a condescending view of France and its prospects as a nation. "In more pessimistic moments I have of necessity come to believe [the worst] . . . about France and the French future," he had written some years before, "yet I always say to myself that in previous parties France has always snapped out of it. This optimism, I must frankly confess, has little foundation." Another time, the President said, "France faces a revolution when the Germans have been driven out." Characteristically, he predicted that it would result in a reform of the political system along American lines. William Hassett, one of his closest aides, summed up Roosevelt's remarks in his diary: "Probably federal form of government will be established, with limitation on number of political parties. There have been some eighteen factions acting as political parties in France, with sometimes three different governments a week. No stability in such a system. He thought the revolution, which he considers inevitable, would result in fixed tenure of office for Premier so that these swift and short terms of office would be done away with. Thought three political parties should be limit in France or in this country. . . ."⁵ Thus Roosevelt seemed to believe that France would never again be a first-class nation without, as a prior condition, becoming more American.

The President was unwilling to invest his military or diplomatic resources in what he regarded as the uncertain future of France. He looked upon such a move as an unwarranted risk of good capital. To him, France was simply one more factor to manipulate—much as he might manipulate Congressional factions to pass legislation—in the drive to achieve victory over the Axis.

Roosevelt was thus free of Churchill's instinctive aversion to Pétain. He possessed for the old Marshal the mixed feeling of veneration and sympathy that a hardy man in the prime of life might have for yesterday's war hero. Pétain, he felt, was good enough for France. No American, after all, had observed the collapse of the Reynaud Government closely enough to tell him of Pétain's role. The mercurial Bullitt had returned with high praise for the Marshal. The State Department retained the popular notion of Pétain as the rugged savior of Verdun, a man devoid of political ambition. Leahy, in his first report to the President, said that Pétain "gave me a definite impression of vigor and strength of character, and of personal appreciation of the friendly attitude of America." Those assessments reaffirmed Roosevelt's conviction that the Marshal was a sound figure on which to base American policy. The times, he believed, did not demand a Foch or a Clemenceau.⁶

In February, Roosevelt dispatched to Pétain a personal letter that Churchill, had he seen it, would have torn to shreds. "I wish to send you in the moments of great difficulty which you are confronting," Roosevelt wrote, "a message of sympathy and understanding. . . .

I earnestly hope that the outcome [of current developments] may be favorable to the continuation of *the free and independent France for which you have fought with such steadfast courage and determination*."* There was barely a word among those sentences with which Churchill would have concurred. Even Roosevelt could not have believed that whatever "steadfast courage and determination" Pétain demonstrated was in behalf of a "free and independent France." Churchill had rejected presenting the Marshal with a "nice, soft, cosy, forgiving England." But Roosevelt, it appeared, was quite prepared to console the old man with a "nice, soft, cosy, forgiving" America.[7]

Pétain also learned to his delight that the United States, and particularly its Ambassador, sympathized with his fierce hatred of de Gaulle. Leahy assiduously refused to deal with anyone who came to his office to speak for the Gaullist cause. He faithfully reported back to Washington such of Pétain's invectives as "a poisonous viper that I warmed at my own bosom," and "a traitor to his country." He noted, approvingly, Pétain's complaint that Gaullists in Syria gave the Germans a pretext for intervention. Pétain once said of de Gaulle, Leahy recorded, "He claims to be a patriot. Why doesn't he come back to France and suffer with the rest of us?" On a day when Pétain's fulminations against de Gaulle were particularly biting, Leahy chortled: "The old gentleman, whom I hold in the highest regard as a patriot completely devoted to the welfare of his people, has of late been hitting on all cylinders." Once Leahy granted he had received many letters which conveyed "a sense that the de Gaulle movement is much stronger in France than is indicated by officials of the Marshal's government." His words suggest the limitations he imposed on himself in procuring information and betray his uncritical assessment of it. More characteristically, he transmitted to the State Department opinions like this: "I have no doubt whatsoever that the Marshal feels personally very strongly about de Gaulle and that his elimination would go far in swinging the old soldier more toward the British camp." His advice had a strong impact on the thinking of Roosevelt and the Department of State.[8]

But despite Roosevelt's conviction that Leahy's presence would exercise a strong corrective influence on Pétain, Vichy's drift toward the Germans was not abated by the Admiral's arrival. In February,

* Author's italics.

six weeks after Leahy reached Vichy, the Marshal named Admiral Jean François Darlan as the head of government, foreign minister and his own heir apparent. Darlan had some time before committed himself to a pro-German policy, though, unlike Laval, he did not favor unreservedly embracing the Nazi cause. His politics, in practice more complex than Laval's, reduced themselves to simple opportunism. Darlan believed that France had to come out of the war on the side of the winner, and in early 1941 he had ample reason to believe that the winner would be Germany.

"It would have been better," Churchill told the Foreign Office, "to have had Laval, from our point of view, than Darlan, who is a dangerous, bitter, ambitious man, without the odium that attaches to Laval."[9]

Roosevelt and Leahy thought differently. They regarded Darlan as manageable and Vichy as, at worst, unpredictable. They were convinced that by offering Pétain kindness, as relief from German pressure, the United States could exercise an appreciable influence over Vichy's politics.

"Marshal Pétain," Leahy wrote in an early letter to Roosevelt, "stated that his only hope for the coming months is that the good offices of the United States will succeed in easing blockade restrictions on the import of essential foodstuffs to France, and in assistance by the American Red Cross."[10]

Shortly afterward, he laid out more explicitly the rules of play in Vichy's game of blackmail. There are two schools of thought in the Pétain Government, he said. One favors complete collaboration with Germany. The other favors strict neutrality. The proponents of neutrality have nothing concrete to show for their stand, while the collaborationists promise tangible results. Leahy understood that Pétain's France was hungry because Germany was seizing its food supplies. In the British view, the more the Allies sent to France, the more the Germans would take away. Nonetheless, Leahy subscribed to Pétain's argument. "Anything that we may do to provide food for the hungry people of unoccupied France," he wrote, "should help much in keeping the Marshal's vertebrae in a vertical position when he is under pressure from the invader to 'cooperate.' "[11]

Hull was furious when Churchill rejected American requests to loosen the Royal Navy's blockade of France. He summoned the British Ambassador, Lord Halifax, and sternly warned him that "unless the British allowed a little flexibility in this matter . . . we could not be responsible for keeping the French fleet out of German hands." Churchill showed how flexible he was by reversing his position when Darlan threatened to fire on British warships that interfered with French merchantmen. He proposed that Roosevelt devise a "working agreement" between his government and Vichy. "We do not want to push things to extremes," he wrote. But, as he learned, neither did Pétain. Before the policy was tested, Darlan withdrew the threat and Churchill promptly resumed his firm stand.[12]

"Parliament and the public," the Prime Minister wrote to the President in politician-to-politician intimacy, "will ask me why, when we are ourselves suffering a grievous blockade and British rations are reduced week by week, the French and Germans should have these advantages, thus prolonging the war." Churchill pointed out that he could not justify denying equivalent rights to the Belgians, Dutch and Norwegians, who were more loyal allies and who suffered greater hardships than the Vichy French. "I am therefore instructing the Admiralty to tighten up the blockade of unoccupied France as far as our naval resources and opportunities allow," he asserted, "and I hope that you will not think that this is unwise or unreasonable."[13]

Roosevelt certainly did think it was unwise and unreasonable. Hull wasted little time in complaining to Halifax that "British official sources" had inspired a press campaign depicting the United States as "sentimentally humanitarian." Then he delivered a stern lecture that he concluded thus:

We have been struggling almost daily since the French Government left Paris to uphold that element in the French Government which opposes Hitlerism and Hitler. It is very tedious and delicate work, especially when so many leading Britishers seem to have no comprehension of its nature and importance to them.[14]

If there was any shortage of comprehension, however, it was the Secretary of State who was the most seriously delinquent. He blamed the British for "numerous disagreeable incidents . . . occurring to keep Great Britain and France alienated and which deny the slightest hope or encouragement to Marshal Pétain in his most crucial trial." Britain and France, he said, "could work out many existing questions to their mutual advantage if they would only meet and proceed in a spirit of mutual concession and cooperation."[15]

What he failed utterly to comprehend was that Britain had no desire to offer hope or encouragement to Marshal Pétain, much less concessions and cooperation. Hull was completely unaware that Britain waged war, in part, to bring down Pétain. He could not understand that establishing a relationship between London and Vichy was not like implementing his own inoffensive Good Neighbor Policy in South America. The solid, practical considerations that normally govern the ties between states, whatever Hull thought, simply did not apply to Churchill's Britain and Pétain's France.

Hull was particularly indignant at Britain's indifference to the North African facet of his Vichy policy, which was his own inspiration. Since the lands from Tunis to Dakar had, for obvious geographic reasons, greater potential for resistance than Metropolitan France, the State Department had decided to put special effort into encouraging a spirit of autonomy there. This strategy focused on one man who had been fainthearted in battle but who had become intransigent in defeat. Maxime Weygand now ruled the African colonies in Pétain's name. Hull, in his innocence, could discover no reason for Britain's lack of enthusiasm toward a policy built around him.

Under the Marshal, Weygand had become a loyal servant of the Government, deeply committed to its "work of restoration."[16] But, far more vigorously than any other member of the Pétain entourage, he stood for rigid observance of the armistice terms, for conceding the Germans nothing beyond what they were explicitly authorized. Weygand, so anxious for the Republic to capitulate to the Germans had, ironically, become Vichy's symbol of obduracy. Pétain, for whom Darlan's opportunism struck just the right note, wanted none of Weygand's extremism, any more than he wanted, at the opposite pole, Laval's. So, in the fall of 1940, he exiled the General to Algiers. There Weygand was not as likely to irritate the Germans, but as a loyal Pétainist he could be counted on to crush the seeds of dissidence that had sprouted from de Gaulle's successes in central Africa. Weygand's mission, for which he was given virtually unlimited civil and military powers, was to keep North Africa independent—of the Axis, of the Allies and of the Gaullists.

Churchill tested Weygand's anti-Axis reputation on several occasions by offering, as he had to Pétain, to dispatch an army to support an insurrectionary movement. He even persuaded de Gaulle to support the idea with a letter to Weygand, which proved unwise since the Free French leader could not resist the opportunity to be insolent. De Gaulle's most trusted collaborator, Catroux, was more gracious, however. He sent a personal emissary to propose a major British-French pincer drive against the Italians, starting from Egypt in the east and Tunisia in the west, to free Africa of Axis military power. The rejection of these overtures confirmed Churchill's opinion that Weygand had "not one scrap of nobility or courage" and that he ought to be put on "short commons."[17]

The information that Hull received led him to a contrary conclusion. His chief agent in North Africa, outgoing, hardworking Robert Murphy, extolled Weygand's virtues and championed his cause. Murphy was impressed that Weygand, who had once predicted that England's neck would be "wrung like a chicken," now said, "Obviously I hope for a British victory." Murphy, who took no offense from Weygand's background and politics and who shared his devotion to the Catholic religion, soon established a close friendship with the General. Impressed by the efforts to rebuild the army in North Africa, he told Hull that "General Weygand and his associates are laying the foundation for substantial military action against Germany and Italy." Murphy specifically recommended that the United States ship gasoline to Weygand to keep the North African economy from disintegrating. Hull accepted Murphy's evaluation of the General and backed Murphy's proposals for supporting him.[18]

The British, far from sharing the State Department's esteem, were not at all certain Weygand would use his strength against the Axis rather than the Allies. They were willing to relax their blockade of North Africa, however, if they had some tangible *quid pro quo* to show for it. The American Government, they complained, was too anxious to grant benefits without assurances of some return. When Weygand then offered to let a dozen "vice-consuls" supervise the distribution of cargo, the State Department, recognizing their intelligence potential, was satisfied that he had met Britain's stipulation. Churchill's Government decided that a dozen vice-consuls were less useful than the British ships interned in North African ports. But they submitted to the pressure from Washington and gave their approval to the agreement Murphy and Weygand had negotiated. Even then, however, they raised obstacles to the actual shipments. They simply did not trust Weygand. The following year, his North

African army showed there had been good reason for their apprehension.[19]

Neither did the British look on Weygand's repression of the Free French with the same equanimity as the United States. The former generalissimo detested de Gaulle. The Free French broadcasts from England, recently supplemented by transmissions from Gaullist Africa, constantly reminded him of his failures. De Gaulle's propaganda, Weygand admitted, "increased the anxiety in men's minds." In his memoirs, he wrote that he did not object to de Gaulle's vow to carry on the fight. In itself, that would have been tolerable, he said. But de Gaulle's denunciations of Vichy, "against which no reproach could then be levelled," his disdain "for the suffering of commanders who had carried on the struggle to the end to the best of their powers" and his "besmirching martyred France in the eyes of the world," Weygand regarded as inexcusable. They were, it was clear, a reproach to him personally. De Gaulle focused a bright light on Weygand's own weakness.[20] Weygand wanted to destroy de Gaulle and, though the United States assented, Britain did not.

Weygand pursued Gaullism in the colonies relentlessly. By vigorous police action, both open and secret, he succeeded in crushing active support for the Free French movement in the Army, the administration and the civilian population. His methods were not necessarily harsh. Sometimes he exiled troublemakers, sometimes he merely warned them. When necessary, he sent them to prison. But as long as he was in charge, Gaullism did not thrive.[21]

The reconquest of de Gaulle's colonies in central Africa had more complex implications, however. Vichy, as part of its double game, profited from its belligerence toward the Allies by extracting concessions from the Axis. Germany had rewarded the stubborn defense of Dakar by authorizing reinforcement of the African army. The Gaullist threat had become such an effective argument for strengthening North Africa that Darlan was reported to have quipped: "If de Gaulle did not exist, we would have to invent him." Weygand tempted the Germans with the prospect of a march on the Free French colonies. The Nazis were, at the least, interested in an airfield at Fort Lamy, which the British used as a relay point in flying to Suez. Weygand has since claimed that the plans to regain the lost colonies were a deception to permit Vichy to justify a buildup of its forces. Personally, he said, he rejected a "fratricidal struggle." Nonetheless, while restoration remained Vichy's official policy, the Free French colonies had to take it seriously and remain on guard. Whenever Vichy wanted to curry favor with the oppressors, it was free to carry out its threat.[22]

In the spring of 1941, the glittering German victories in Yugoslavia, Greece and the Western Desert persuaded the Vichy Government that the time to curry favor had come. Britain's collapse appeared near, and Darlan openly intended to make the most of it. Over Weygand's protests, he ordered the delivery of hundreds of trucks to Rommel's Nazi legions pressing toward Cairo and thousands of tons of petroleum to the Italian Navy. On the eleventh and twelfth of May, he met Hitler at Berchtesgaden. "My choice is made," Darlan told the Cabinet on his return. "I shall not allow myself to be deterred by the conditional offer of a shipload of wheat or a shipload of oil." In Berchtesgaden, Darlan had asked Hitler for admission to Nazism's New Order. Hitler, flushed with success, was now selective about the company he kept. Darlan was determined to show him the advantage of association with France.[23]

On May 15th, Pétain announced over the radio: "Frenchmen, you have learned of Admiral Darlan's talks with Hitler. I approved the principle of the meeting." Characteristically, he left himself an exit by endorsing a principle, rather than a specific promise. But Leahy reported after calling on the old man "the distinct impression that the Marshal has completely accepted the action of his Foreign Minister and that he is likely to approve any commitments that Darlan may make in the future."[24]

The dangers presented by a Franco-German entente caused Roosevelt such consternation that he declared a state of "Unlimited National Emergency." In a radio address on May 27, 1941, he said the Germans "have the armed power at any moment to occupy Spain and Portugal and that threat extends not only to French North Africa and the western end of the Mediterranean but also the Atlantic fortress of Dakar and to the island outposts of the New World." Roosevelt had a fixation on Dakar, which he had pointed out was only 1,700 miles from the bulge of Brazil, "less than from Washington to Denver—five hours for the latest type of bomber." The threat to Dakar gave Roosevelt reason to proclaim that "the war is approaching the brink of the Western Hemisphere itself. It is coming very close to home."[25]

But after giving the order to put guards aboard the French ships interned in American ports, he decided, in consultation with Hull, to remain faithful to his original French policy. His objective now was "to salvage whatever we can from Weygand's situation in Africa and from the Government at Vichy."[26] Only after Leahy reported that preparations were under way to reconquer Free French Africa did the Secretary of State consent to notify Vichy that such an attack would create a "most unfortunate impression." It was obvious he feared a more forthright warning would alienate Pétain.

Leahy's information had been accurate, for Darlan had instructed Weygand to prepare a strike to the south. Ambassador Halifax pleaded with Hull, as an aid to the defense of Free French Africa, to recognize the colonies as officially under Gaullist control. He asked the Secretary of State to grant de Gaulle the courtesies he accorded Weygand. Hull flatly refused. "If Weygand should stand up," he stated, "de Gaulle would have to become subordinate." But if Darlan gave the order to attack, would Weygand, loyal to Pétain, have become insubordinate? He would, at best, have resigned to leave his successor to lead the troops against Free France. America's indifference to Free French Africa, as Halifax pointed out, might well have been interpreted in Vichy as an invitation to invade. But the British Ambassador was told that if the policy toward de Gaulle were relaxed, "it would be difficult for the United States to maintain diplomatic relations with Vichy and, what was far more important, cooperative relations with authorities in North Africa." These goals, in the American view, justified its abandonment of de Gaulle's colonial realm.[27]

While the State Department worried about compromising its courtship of Vichy, Pétain, paradoxically, was trying to decide whether to go to war against England. Late in May, 1941, Darlan negotiated an agreement, known as the Paris Protocols, which granted the Nazis extensive privileges in the Levant, Tunisia and West Africa. If Pétain ratified them, conflict with the British would inevitably follow. The old man, as usual, was reluctant to make a commitment. His collaborationist advisers insisted it was now or never. In exasperation, Pétain summoned Weygand from Algiers. From the second to the sixth of June, the General held the center of the stage in a venomous Cabinet debate. In the end, a majority voted to reject the Protocols, and the Marshal adopted the Cabinet decision. Darlan had lost his major bid for outright collaboration with the enemy, and France, by a narrow margin, averted the supreme disgrace of going to war against its former ally.

The reasons for the rejection of the Paris Protocols have never been clear. Hull, gloating over the decision, was convinced it was a direct consequence of his policy of "stiffening the Marshal's backbone." But he undoubtedly overestimated American influence in Vichy. The Paris Protocols called for a degree of servility which, perhaps, even Vichy did not possess. But most important, they required a sense of certainty that the Nazis would win the war, and, by this time, the Cabinet had received information that Germany was about to invade Russia. A new, complicating element was introduced into its calculations. This explains why Darlan, the master opportunist, did not put his full vigor into fighting for the pact he had negotiated. Pétain found it opportune to hold off a little longer before making an irreversible decision.[28]

Darlan, however, had already overextended himself in Syria, and there it was too late to turn back. He had presented the Germans with the use of military facilities to support an anti-British revolt in neighboring Iraq. British planes had begun bombing Syrian airfields in mid-May. Britain's Middle Eastern Command, its forces spread thinly throughout the theater, was reluctant to take military action, however. Vichy's army in Syria, made up of 30,000 experienced soldiers, was stronger than anything the British could muster. Churchill, nonetheless, would not tolerate Vichy's action and ordered his generals to seize Syria at once.

De Gaulle's Middle Eastern contingent of 6,000 men was the most logical and most available force to lead the attack. It had fought well in Ethiopia. For months it had waited for British permission to swoop down on Djibouti, Vichy's important Red Sea port, where de Gaulle hoped to rally a garrison of 10,000 tough colonial troops. But the British generals, already surfeited with enemies in the Mediterranean, chose neutrality instead, a decision that angered de Gaulle. He saw in it a British plot to assure its own postwar hegemony in the Middle East. Only Catroux's restraining influence kept him from issuing a grave challenge to Churchill. But when the Syrian plan was proposed, it presented a better chance to increase the Gaullist dominions.[29]

Some British generals feared that the Free French presence would provoke Vichy's defenders, as it apparently had at Dakar. But Britain, without other troops, had no choice. When, on June 8, 1941, the invaders crossed the frontier, they hoped that the Frenchmen in Syria would be as hospitable to them as to the Germans. Their orders were not to fire unless fired upon. They were disappointed. Vichy's soldiers proved at once that they were unabashed at killing either their own countrymen or Englishmen.

The French Army, under the command of General Henri Dentz, quickly brought the British-Free French columns to a halt and, after a week of bloody fighting, held them in deadlock. In Vichy, the reaction to the invasion was typically equivocal. Darlan sent off ships filled with fresh troops from France, which the Royal Navy successfully blocked. But he declined to enlarge the conflict by attacking the British elsewhere and he steadfastly refused Axis air and naval assistance. Even after Britain dispatched sufficient reinforcements to doom Dentz's defense, Darlan had his army fight on, as if his object were not to win but to demonstrate to Hitler that France would use its arms against its former ally. The cost was heavy—6,500 casualties on Vichy's side, 4,600 for the British and the Free French. It was not until July 12th that Dentz sued for an armistice. Thanks to Darlan, the fighting in Syria lasted almost as long as the war in France the year before.[30]

De Gaulle could now, for the first time, claim an important share in a military victory. But in his quest for spoils, the battle had just begun. De Gaulle insisted that the administration of Syria and Lebanon, French mandates under the League of Nations, be conferred unconditionally on Free France. It was more than Britain had pledged under the August 7th agreement. His demand also required Britain to go back on a commitment guaranteeing independence of the two Levantine states. De Gaulle declared that the British had no authority to make a commitment on what was French territory. France, he said, would grant independence to Syria and Lebanon, in its own good time. Free France alone, he said, possessed this authority.

De Gaulle also had plans to campaign energetically in Dentz's ranks to rally Vichy's men to his cause. The matter started badly, however, when the British acceded to Vichy's demand that the Gaullist rebels be excluded from the armistice negotiations. As soon as de Gaulle learned of this, he denounced the armistice agreement.

The friction increased when the British helped Dentz to keep de Gaulle's emissaries from talking to his troops. Finally, the British Army showed a reluctance to relinquish the administration of the newly occupied territories. De Gaulle was certain his suspicions of Britain's imperialistic intentions were now confirmed.

A few days after the armistice, de Gaulle arrived in Cairo and presented the British Minister of State, Sir Oliver Lyttelton, with an ultimatum. If, within three days, the British did not transfer control of Syria and Lebanon to the Free French, he declared, he would issue the order for his troops to take it. Then, to emphasize that his forces were free to obey him, he announced their withdrawal from British command. To Churchill, he wired that "the British attitude, in an affair vital to us, aggravates our difficulties and will have results that I consider deplorable from the point of view of the task that I have undertaken." Having notified the members of the Free French delegation in London of his challenge, he waited nervously, like a gambler at the table, for the adversary to turn over his cards.

Two days later the British replied by conceding that the Free French grievances were genuine. Lyttelton assured de Gaulle that his government had no designs on the Levant and consented to negotiate an "interpretation" of the armistice to satisfy the Free French claims.

De Gaulle, it appeared, had won, but not without giving his collaborators in London a terrible fright. The members of the Free French delegation were not accustomed to questioning their leader's decisions. They normally approached him with great caution. Threatened with the most serious crisis in the short history of Free France, however, they appealed to him for restraint:

We attach an essential importance to the British alliance [they wrote]. At a moment when Vichy's practices make the promise given to you by our allies in the agreement of August 7th to restore France in its grandeur and independence particularly precious and difficult to keep, we cannot, without incalculable risks, take the initiative in nullifying an agreement which is vital in its spirit as well as in its letter. . . . We would risk compromising the essential by acts of rupture.

Before he had time to reply, de Gaulle learned that the British military command had not kept the promises made to him at Cairo by the British Government. Arriving in Syria, he spurned the advice of the London delegation and resumed his bitter campaign. Unflinchingly he ordered his troops to take over the installations held by

British forces, using whatever means were necessary. Only then did the British proceed to withdraw.

His triumph came too late, however, to swell the Free French armed forces significantly. Before de Gaulle's agents could reach them, some of Dentz's units had already left Syria. Those that remained had been well indoctrinated against Free French enticements. Catroux, Larminat, de Gaulle himself and others had time for only hasty appeals while the ships that had arrived for repatriation waited in the harbor. In all, only about 6,000 men elected to join Free France. In conjunction with 14,000 Syrians and Lebanese soon put under arms, they constituted an important addition to the Gaullist army. But Free France was grieved to see almost 25,000 battle-hardened veterans slip through its fingers, many of them, as it happened, to fight against the Allies again.

To his Free French colleagues in London, de Gaulle dispatched a reproach for their lack of boldness.

I measured, better than anyone else [he wrote], the grave national and international consequences that could have resulted from a rupture between Free France and England. That is precisely why I had to bring England face to face with the consequences, in case she acted in an unacceptable manner toward us. . . . I understand that the British were irritated but that irritation is unimportant compared to our duty to France. In my judgment, the crisis has been salutary for our relations with England. Mr. Churchill will understand without doubt that he can only lean on something that offers resistance. . . .

In conclusion, I invite you to close ranks and to permit no suggestion that my conduct does not follow my policies exactly. Our grandeur and our force consists uniquely in the intransigence we show in defending the rights of France. We will need that intransigence until we cross the Rhine.[31]

Thus de Gaulle defined his code. Britain, in acceding to his demands in Syria, agreed, albeit resentfully, to accept that code. The United States firmly rejected it. The events of the year 1941 demonstrated that no matter how base Vichy's submission to Nazism, the United States could find nothing in common with Free France. Barely a passing thought, Hull concedes, was spent upon the Free French, even when relations with Vichy were bleakest. De Gaulle, in Hull's view, "showed few signs of political acumen, being more likely to go off on tangents." With great pride, the Secretary proclaimed, "the President and I were able to hew consistently to the line we early adopted." Nonetheless, it was clear at this point that Vichy was growing weaker, while de Gaulle was getting stronger. Despite ample warning, the American Government did not perceive that the longer it delayed coming to terms with Free France, the more difficult the final resolution would be. De Gaulle had set a rigid code for himself. So had Roosevelt. Ultimately, there had to be collision.

Hitler's invasion of the Soviet Union in June added an exciting new element to the drama that was being played. Its full impact was not quickly discernible, but signs appeared at once that the relative positions of Vichy and Free France would be altered. The most immediate consequence was the awakening of the French Left, particularly the Communist Party, which had hitherto been paralyzed by Moscow's alliance with Berlin. Each day, acts of violence in both the unoccupied and occupied zones disclosed deepening ferment. De Gaulle, who in the spring had bewailed French passivity, took encouragement from spreading resistance to the oppressor. Even Leahy acknowledged, for the first time, "conclusive evidence" of a small Gaullist underground in France.[32] The French nation, recovering from its stupor, was becoming interested in the war again.

Pétain took to the radio on August 12, 1941, to admit his troubles. "From several regions of France," he said, "I have sensed for some weeks the rising of an evil wind. Worry is winning minds and doubt is seizing souls. The authority of my government is being questioned."[33] Nine days later, a German officer in Paris became the French underground's first assassination victim. Two weeks later the second fell, and the Germans embarked on a vengeful program of shooting hostages. Vichy did nothing in reply. At one point, Pétain contemplated offering himself as a hostage, an act that would have assured his place in French history. Instead, he went on the radio and denounced the French assassins but remained silent about the German executioners. From that time on, Vichy's authority disintegrated rapidly.

De Gaulle had, in the meantime, stepped up his efforts to win a change of heart in Washington. Some time before, he had decided to try to modify what he called "the almost belligerent attitude of the United States." As inducements, he had his territories in Africa and in the Pacific, both with considerable strategic value. In June he sent René Pleven, whose mild manner was in contrast to his own austerity, on a special mission to Washington, to establish harmonious relations with the American Government.

Pleven found the Free French movement in low estate in the United States. He reported to de Gaulle that it was little known and much misunderstood by the public and the object of a powerful propaganda machine directed by Vichy. His evaluation, interestingly, was distinctly different from that of Hull, who contended that the popular appeal of Free France was built upon "pressure and propaganda on the part of de Gaulle's friends."[34] Pleven reported that a small Gaullist organization, under the direction of some members of the French colony in New York, had functioned since the early days of the war, without notable achievements. Vichy's policies, he said, exercised a disastrous influence on France's reputation in the country. "We must convince the Americans," he wrote to de Gaulle, "that Free France is the France they have loved."

The State Department refused to receive Pleven, despite the requests of Lord Halifax, who submitted communications as an intermediary for him. The rest of Washington was not as reserved. Pleven visited with Roosevelt's adviser, Harry Hopkins, Vice-President Henry Wallace, Secretary of War Henry Stimson, Secretary of the Navy Frank Knox and Secretary of the Treasury Henry Morgenthau. In his first weeks, he reported two concessions from the American Government: Red Cross authorization to provide medical supplies and War Department agreement to send an inspection team to Free French Africa. At the end of July, 1941, Pleven reported that the State Department, as its first friendly act, had consented to discussions in conjunction with the British on Free French participation in Lend-Lease. But, Pleven said, the invitation was contingent on his attending as an "expert," not as a "representative." The State Department, Pleven commented to de Gaulle, "remains extremely preoccupied with questions of procedure in order to give Vichy and Weygand no pretext for complaints."

De Gaulle replied to Pleven that he was pleased a military inspection team would visit the Free French colonies. But, he added petulantly, "we are not asking the United States for charity but for the means of fighting. . . . I do not accept that you, representing France, attend a three-way conference alone as an expert. You will attend with rights equal to the other participants or you will not attend." Thus the summer passed without further significant contact.

On September 11, 1941, de Gaulle notified his envoy of a possible break in the deadlock. The British, he said, had informed him of American plans to establish a chain of landing fields in the Pacific for ferrying heavy bombers. United States authorities, he wrote, were extremely interested in New Caledonia and the New Hebrides. De Gaulle gave Pleven instructions to grant the use of the islands for bases. But he directed him to use the negotiations to get as much recognition from the Americans as he could.

Hull had hinted at an improvement in the atmosphere on September 6th when he told a press conference that American relations with the Free French were "most cordial." Two weeks later, the State Department notified Pleven that it would accredit a Free French delegation without precise diplomatic status to serve as intermediary with the United States Government. On October 1st, Welles agreed to the first direct encounter between the State Department and Free France. Pleven, at their meeting, found him cold and unsympathetic, anxious to defend American policy as having the complete approval of the British. Welles, he said, was pessimistic about the future of the Vichy policy but would not contemplate further recognition of Free France. He rejected a request that the United States designate a representative to de Gaulle in London. Pleven was not satisfied with the discussion, but he understood that the fact that it was held meant progress.[35]

The fate of Colonel Harry Cunningham of the United States Army, head of the three-man American team touring Free French Africa, however, illustrated how insignificant that progress was. Cunningham made the mistake of thinking that his job, at least in part, consisted in making friends of the Free French. Wherever he and his partners went they were enthusiastically received and lavishly entertained. "The Mission brought a message of hope" to the French, said the American consul in Léopoldville. He reported that Cunningham, "a gentleman of the old school . . . struck exactly the right note and made his position solid from the start." But it was not the right note for Washington.

When Weygand complained about the activities of the Cunningham group, Hull at once became embarrassed. He sent an apologetic reply to Weygand and told him that "in no sense should they be considered a mission to General de Gaulle's territory and there is no change in the position of this government as regards the Free French movement." Welles gave Vichy's ambassador the same assurances when he called to protest. Still, the State Department wanted no mistake made about Cunningham's role. Hull saw to it that Cunningham was sent a stern warning to avoid publicity. Vichy, however, sensed that it had its quarry on the run. The Pétain Government, on November 19th, objected that "even though it lacked an official character . . . the unfriendly nature of the step was heightened by the participation in the mission of officers and officials who were on active duty." Clearly, Cunningham's days in Free French Africa were numbered.[36]

Vichy's reaction was all the more impudent for having occurred during one of the periodic crises that convulsed its relations with Washington. On November 18, 1941, over vigorous American protests, Weygand was dismissed. Coming on the eve of a long-awaited British offensive in Libya, it appeared to Churchill to presage a Nazi seizure of the North African colonies. When Leahy called on Pétain, whose authority was vanishing a little each day, the old man could only repeat his pathetic explanation: "I am a prisoner." Weygand's departure was the price Pétain paid for defeat of the Paris Protocols. It was Germany's minimum condition for his keeping Darlan in office rather than having him replaced by Laval. It meant that America's guarantee of French resistance to the Axis in North Africa, represented personally by Weygand, was presumably now nullified.

In Vichy, Leahy had at last had enough. The environment disgusted him and he yearned to go home. No longer was he prepared to apologize and defend. "This is an appropriate time to consider a complete revision of American policy," he wrote to Roosevelt. But Murphy, who had recently extended his campaign in North Africa's behalf to an appeal for arms, would not be deterred. He unhesitatingly reaffirmed his endorsement of shipments of food and fuel. "The local reaction," he wrote to Hull, "is in part—if the Americans abandon us, there is nothing else to do but depend on the other side." Once again, the United States acquiesced to this blackmail. The State Department, after a brief suspension, ordered the resumption of aid. Leahy was also overruled and directed to stay at his post.[37]

On December 7th, Japan attacked Pearl Harbor and brought the United States formally into the war. It was a great milestone in the long struggle. Four days later Germany and Italy declared war. Vichy took for granted that its game with Washington was now up.

The Germans had, after all, demanded an end to relations with Moscow when they invaded the Soviet Union. They were expected now to insist on a rupture with the United States. And if Germany did not take the initiative, Vichy believed the United States would. But, inexplicably, Germany made no such demand. And Washington hesitated only momentarily. The day after the Japanese attack, the United States Navy seized the liner *Normandie* and the other French ships tied up in American ports. But, on December 14th, Leahy gave the Marshal a message from Roosevelt reaffirming the *status quo* in North Africa and in the French Antilles. "It is my continuing hope," said Roosevelt, "that the traditional relations of close and understanding friendship between the peoples of our two countries which have existed for so long a time can be maintained without change." That day, Leahy noted in his diary that the President seemed to be trying once again to strengthen Pétain against German pressure "and in my opinion it will have no useful effect." Pearl Harbor, strangely, had virtually no effect on the official American attitude toward France.[38]

De Gaulle, too, expected belligerence to change the American outlook. To display his solidarity, he offered to establish a "Lafayette Escadrille" of French fliers, to return the service American pilots performed for France during World War I. The Air Force, unmoved by the sentiment, turned the offer down as technically unfeasible.[39] It did not take de Gaulle much longer to recognize that the wooing of Vichy, despite Pearl Harbor, continued undiminished.

Angry and perplexed, de Gaulle recorded his feelings in a brief letter to the Prime Minister:

> I am fearful of the mistaken impression that this sort of public preference accorded by the Government of the United States to those responsible for capitulation and guilty of collaboration will produce on opinion, in the forces and the territories of Free France as well as in still unliberated France itself.
>
> It does not seem right to me that, in war, the prize should be awarded to the apostles of dishonor.[40]

As if to emphasize its rejection, the United States terminated the Cunningham mission to Free French Africa in mid-December. A week later, Welles turned down a plea by Lord Halifax that the State Department show more sympathy to the Free French. Welles wrote of their conversation:

As the British Ambassador well knew, this government had been moving heaven and earth to keep on close terms with the Vichy Government. . . .

I said that I was unable to see that the Free French movement at the present moment had anything very much to commend it from the practical standpoint. I said unfortunately there were no outstanding men with qualities of leadership and of initiative directing the Free French movement and providing that kind of inspiration to free men, both in France and in other parts of the world, to join in a movement against their German oppressors. I said . . . I could not see that either General de Gaulle or his associates provided any rallying point for French patriotism.

For all of these reasons I felt it was wiser . . . for the two governments . . . to pursue their respective courses until and unless existing conditions changed.[41]

Enlarging the Breach

December, 1941–July, 1942

I N 1938, IN *La France et son armée*, de Gaulle wrote:

France was made by blows of the sword. Our fathers entered history with the blade of Brennus. It was Roman arms that brought civilization to them. Thanks to the ax of Clovis, the *patrie* became conscious of itself again after the fall of the Empire. The *fleur de lys*, symbol of national unity, is nothing but the image of a three-speared javelin.

But if force is necessary to build a state, the endeavors of war are justifiable only in terms of policy. As long as the country was covered by feudal underbrush, much blood was spilled on sterile sand. From the day that the union of a strong government and a solid army was achieved, France was once again on her feet.[1]

Thus de Gaulle explained his understanding of the relation between the scepter and the sword. Politician and soldier, each in a different realm, functioned in behalf of a common national objective. This objective determined the government's policies and gave the army its mission. Only this goal gave meaning to war and justified the sacrifices it required. War, to him, was inseparable from policy.

As de Gaulle determined it, the goal of Free France was to preserve the sovereignty of the French nation and restore the French state. From the first days of dissidence, he rejected the contention that his role was simply to rally Frenchmen to battle. If his movement, no matter how much it helped to win the war, failed in its responsibility to France, his efforts would have been in vain. Free France functioned to serve neither England nor the United States.

74

De Gaulle would fight within an alliance led by England and the
United States but only if it was clearly recognized that he acted to
achieve the objectives of France.

The American Government took a contrasting view. Roosevelt
believed that war had put a moratorium on politics. Had he intended
this to mean domestic politics alone, his position would have been
understandable. But he extended the principle to include international politics, an entirely different matter. Roosevelt believed that
once war began, a nation had no right to a policy other than achieving the quickest, easiest, cheapest victory. There was ample time, in
his view, to deal with national interests after victory.

De Gaulle and Roosevelt thus looked upon the war from vastly
divergent perspectives. It means that they brought to each problem a
totally dissimilar set of premises. It portended that every difference
could turn into crisis.

Had either of these men been less egocentric, he might have
understood the other. Roosevelt, the mightier of the two, had little
to lose by giving de Gaulle's motivation some sympathetic reflection. Instead, he interpreted de Gaulle at his worst, as petty and
self-serving, a chauvinist, anxious to seize and retain absolute power.
He closed his mind to the notion of de Gaulle as the gallant defender
of French honor, who had risked all for his country's sovereignty
and dignity. De Gaulle, in return, regarded Roosevelt as supercilious
and patronizing, scornful of a great nation, anxious to play God with
France's future. He left no room for understanding Roosevelt as a
single-minded warrior and idealist. The blindness each man suffered
toward the character of the other served to compound the difficulties
created by their inherent political differences.

The natural friction might have been reduced by a judicious chief
of the Free French delegation in Washington. Pleven, who labored
tirelessly but softly, had made an excellent impression. But the man
de Gaulle sent to replace him as head of the permanent mission was
Adrien Tixier, who more faithfully mirrored the personality of his
leader. A tough and devoted Gaullist, Tixier was irascible, sarcastic
and rude. Though he worked hard, he was no man for the tortuous
processes of diplomacy. Tixier, by alienating the very Americans he
needed to please, did not serve de Gaulle well.[2]

Nor did de Gaulle evoke any sympathy from the American Government when he acted to delegate some of his absolute power over

the Free French movement. In September, 1941, de Gaulle replaced the informal directorate that had been administering Free France by a formal organ designated the French National Committee. A rudimentary cabinet in the parliamentary tradition, it represented a step along the path of "republican legality" that he had entered upon at Brazzaville. The Committee, he decreed, would be responsible for the "conditional exercise of public powers . . . because of the circumstances of war and until popular representation can be arranged to express the national will independently of the enemy." Though he was careful to retain the ultimate right of decision in his own hands, de Gaulle quite explicitly was planting the seed of a provisional government. The State Department expressed "appreciation" at being notified of the formation of the National Committee but pointed out, in the euphemistic language of diplomacy, that this was a matter of small concern, since the United States did not even recognize Free France as sovereign authority over its own colonies.[3]

The doctrine that the State Department had adopted to govern its relations with the various parts of the French Empire was known as "local authorities." It provided that the American Government would deal with whatever French administration exercised control over a given territory. It acknowledged the sovereignty of France, but in those colonies cut off from the central government it regarded that sovereignty as being in suspense. The "local authorities" doctrine subjected the Empire to transformation into a string of fiefdoms, each equal to the others in American eyes. "The policy of this government," the State Department said, ". . . is based upon the maintenance of the integrity of France and of the French Empire and of the *eventual* restoration of the complete independence of all French territories."[4]

The "local authorities" doctrine ran into direct conflict with de Gaulle's intention of acquiring active sovereignty so that all Frenchmen, on any French territory, would be brought back into the fight for France's liberation. He rejected "*eventual* restoration," based on the goodwill of another power. De Gaulle would have nothing of a policy that permitted Martinique, for example, to wait in comfortable neutrality while foreigners freed the homeland. The State Department, in all innocence, was persuaded that its policy guaranteed France against the designs of usurpers. It reflected Roosevelt's belief that France could be pulled back together in due course after the war. De Gaulle was convinced that it guaranteed France impotence, indignity and the undoing of the Empire bit by bit.

Despite the American attitude, the Soviet Union at once recognized de Gaulle and the National Committee as the sovereign authority over the territories they governed. Britain followed suit shortly afterward. They were joined by the end of the year by the governments-in-exile of Czechoslovakia, Poland, Greece, Yugoslavia, Holland and Norway.[5]

Yet Hull wrote to Roosevelt in May, 1942, as if he suddenly discovered that de Gaulle was trying secretly to set up an embryo state. "It is evident from numerous indications," he said, "that the Free French national commissioners who constitute the Committee and who have undertaken the functions of ministers are now endeavoring to create the future Government of France, and a political character is being sought for the committee." De Gaulle, of course, would have regarded Hull's analysis as completely accurate, though he would not have understood its tone of surprise. Hull, with Roosevelt's agreement, had his own ideas of what de Gaulle ought to be:

It was de Gaulle's constant insistence on political recognition . . . that excited so much suspicion against him [Hull wrote]. If he, as an Army general, had thrown himself wholeheartedly into the fight against the Axis in a military sense, if he had actually led French troops against the enemy wherever possible instead of spending most of his time in London, he could have rallied far more support to himself among the French and among the United Nations.[6]

Actually, some Frenchmen expressed the same feeling as Hull about de Gaulle. The Free French leader had only scorn for them. "They preferred to deliver to foreigners—whether Roosevelt, Churchill or Stalin—the future of France," he declared. Foreigners, he maintained, had no role to play in determining France's affairs. For de Gaulle, the future of France was a matter for Frenchmen alone to decide.

He was determined to prove this principle when, late in 1941, he ordered the Free French Navy to seize Saint-Pierre and Miquelon, a pair of bleak islands off Canada which had been French possessions since the seventeenth century. Under the nominal control of Admiral Robert, Governor of the Antilles, they were in fact ruled by a tyrant loyal to Vichy and detested by the local inhabitants. Sparsely populated, the islands had little to add to Free French strength. But,

on several occasions, they had demonstrated a sympathy for Free
France, and, militarily, they could be plucked from Vichy at little
risk. De Gaulle considered the matter an internal French affair. The
United States, conscious of its obligations to Vichy, did not. The
collision of wills over Saint-Pierre and Miquelon was to have reper-
cussions which far surpassed the intrinsic importance of the islands.
The episode did lasting injury to the relations between the United
States and the Free French.

De Gaulle first wrote to Anthony Eden, the British Foreign Secretary, in October, 1941, for sanction to take Saint-Pierre and Miquelon. The British had long favored a Free French seizure and
raised no objection. But about the same time, Canadian interest in the
islands was aroused by a series of sinkings in nearby waters. Saint-
Pierre's radio transmitter, which served the local fishing fleet, could
have—but probably did not—broadcast data on Allied shipping. The
Canadians settled on a plan to present the Governor with an ultimatum, then occupy the islands if he rejected it. London, apprehensive
of a possible charge of British imperialism, still preferred the Free
French action. At British request, the Canadians agreed to put off a
decision until the United States was consulted. Meanwhile, de Gaulle
watched and waited.

The United States vigorously opposed both the Canadian and the
Free French approach. The State Department would consent to
nothing more forceful than economic pressure. Its aim was to persuade the Governor to accept Canadian supervisors of the radio
transmitter. Canada was not satisfied. Throughout November and
early December, desultory discussions were conducted in Washington without any real outcome.

On December 16th, a week after Pearl Harbor was attacked, Vice
Admiral Emile Muselier, commander in chief of the Free French
Naval Forces, arrived in Ottawa with orders from General de Gaulle
to proceed to Saint-Pierre and Miquelon. Muselier, a maverick sea-
man with no personal loyalty to his chief, immediately notified the
United States Minister in Canada, J. Pierrepont Moffat, and indicated he would not go through with the mission over American
objections. When Moffat told Roosevelt, he summarily vetoed the
undertaking. As a result, Muselier regretfully but quite explicitly concurred. While he was making preparations to return to London, he
received a wire from de Gaulle, who announced that the British had

informed him of the Canadian plan to neutralize the islands. "Proceed to the rallying of Saint-Pierre and Miquelon with your own means and without saying anything to foreigners," de Gaulle ordered. "I take complete responsibility for this operation."

Muselier commanded a submarine and three corvettes, which had until recently been on patrol duty along the Atlantic convoy routes. In midafternoon on December 24th, the State Department learned from its consul at Saint-Pierre, Maurice Pasquet, that Muselier's diminutive flotilla had entered the harbor and taken control of the islands without firing a shot. The next day, Christmas, the population turned out overwhelmingly to ratify the action in a plebiscite. Pasquet reported that Muselier was courteous and friendly and had indicated that the facilities of the islands would be made freely available to the Allies. Muselier asserted, Pasquet wrote, that he had personally opposed de Gaulle's decision to disregard the Allied governments but would defend the islands to the last man against any attempt by the United States, Canada or Vichy to retake them.

In a Christmas Day message, de Gaulle notified the inhabitants of "all the joy that the nation feels at seeing them liberated. Saint-Pierre and Miquelon valiantly return with us and with our brave allies to fight for the liberation of the *patrie* and the liberty of the world."

In Washington, Hull's sentiments were less exalted. He was, in fact, beside himself with rage at a betrayal he believed represented a conspiracy between Canada and the Free French. When Moffat assured him there had been no collusion, he would not be calmed. It was true that privately Ottawa maintained—in the words of one high official—that "it was a good thing the blister had broken, even in irregular fashion." But officially, Canada took the position that it was, as Moffat told Hull, "shocked and embarrassed by the action of Admiral Muselier." The Secretary of State demanded, as an expression of Canadian good faith, that the Ottawa government restore the *status quo* at once.

Hull remained on the long-distance telephone most of Christmas Day trying to force the Canadians to act. In contrast, Mackenzie King, the Canadian Prime Minister, was undisturbed by the Free French action and looked forward to a leisurely and pleasant Christmas dinner with friends. He had arranged, in any case, to leave for Washington that evening for a long-scheduled conference with

Roosevelt and Churchill. He was quite willing to consider the matter then. Hull, however, wanted it settled then and there.

It was clear to Moffat on Christmas afternoon that the Canadians would not rush to repudiate the Free French, especially since the British tacitly supported de Gaulle's orders. When Hull announced that he would issue a public statement to pressure the Canadians, Moffat pleaded with him not to do so. The Secretary of State nonetheless proceeded to write the communiqué. It was not in the best tradition of American diplomacy.

Our preliminary reports [it said] show that the action taken by three so-called Free French ships at St. Pierre-Miquelon was an arbitrary action contrary to the agreement of all parties concerned and certainly without prior knowledge or consent in any sense of the U. S. government.

This government has inquired of the Canadian government as to the steps that government is prepared to take to restore the *status quo* of these islands.

That night, Moffat delivered the news that King, who insisted he was not the party to any such "agreement" with the United States, was now so angry that he was determined to do nothing. The communiqué, Moffat said, had so stirred up the Canadians that they were airing every repressed grievance they could find in retaliation.

But Canadian diplomats were not the only ones infuriated by the Secretary of State's ill-chosen remarks. The American public, starved for good news since Pearl Harbor, was delighted by the Free French audacity, however trivial within the general framework of Allied military actions. Editors took the "so-called Free French" phrase and mischievously turned it back on Hull so that it emerged in print as the "so-called State Department" and the "so-called Secretary of State." Hull, whose many years in politics had not taught him to tolerate criticism, became even more enraged.

The Vichy French, in fact, were probably the only ones whom the Secretary of State had made happy. Pétain's Foreign Minister thanked Hull for his statement and for the steps the American Government was taking to restore Vichy's control of the islands. But, conspicuously, the Vichy Government refrained from offering any concessions in return for American assistance.

The day after Christmas, Hull called in the British Ambassador and submitted a compromise offer. He proposed that arrangements be made through Admiral Robert in Martinique to permit a small

Canadian commission to supervise operation of the radio station at Saint-Pierre. The British would then persuade the Free French to evacuate the islands, with a friendly communiqué as a face-saving measure. Conscious of Hull's deep feelings, Halifax made no challenge to the proposal. But he did comment before he departed that, in his government's view, nothing should be done by any of the Allies to upset the *fait accompli.*

Churchill, whom chance found in Washington when the pressure was most intense, personally assumed de Gaulle's defense. He undertook the task without enthusiasm because he risked provoking the President, but he was loyal to de Gaulle. "Your having broken away from agreement about Saint Pierre and Miquelon," he wired to de Gaulle, "raised a storm which might have been serious had I not been on the spot to speak to the President. Undoubtedly the result of your activities there has been to make things more difficult with the United States and has in fact prevented some favourable developments from occurring. I am always doing my best in all our interests." Churchill's presence undoubtedly acted as a restraint on Roosevelt and kept him from playing a more active role in the affair. Churchill said in his *Memoirs* that the dispute had no effect on his overall discussions with the President. But he resented de Gaulle for it, as he always did when the Free French leader caused him difficulties with his chief ally and supporter.

Roosevelt backed Hull's action but he, too, recognized that the incident had been handled clumsily. The "so-called" remark annoyed him, not out of concern for the Free French but because of its effect on public opinion. It took Roosevelt only a short time to see that the matter had been blown completely out of proportion. But he seemed at a loss on how to terminate it. "The President in our daily talks," Churchill wrote, "seemed to me to shrug his shoulders over the whole affair."

When Halifax called on December 29th, Hull once again denounced the Free French and compared their action with Nazi and Japanese aggression. He said the matter was not an internal French matter, since de Gaulle was not recognized in the Western Hemisphere. He called it a violation of the Monroe Doctrine, a repudiation of the Good Neighbor Policy and a provocation to war in American waters between Vichy and de Gaulle. Furthermore, Hull predicted that, unless de Gaulle was driven out of the islands, "Leahy and all other Americans, including Murphy, who have been working in North Africa with such splendid results . . . would all be booted out by the Vichy government."

To add a new dimension on to the Secretary's frustration, Vichy rejected his compromise proposal and announced it would accept nothing less than full restoration of the *status quo ante*. When the Vichy Ambassador, Gaston Henry-Haye, whom Hull found obnoxious under the best of circumstances, called with the message from his government, the two men engaged in a heated dialogue. Finally, the harassed Hull reported:

I interrupted him to say that when I am being subjected to every sort of abuse even in this country in an effort to safeguard the whole situation by friendly and amicable settlement, just and fair to all, the only thing I received by way of a reply was a stump speech from the Ambassador about the greatness of the French nation.

Early in the New Year, the State Department notified de Gaulle that Hull had meant no offense by his "so-called" remark but was only betraying his surprise, in view of Muselier's pledge, at learning the ships were Free French. Despite this friendly overture, de Gaulle did not retreat from his firm stand. Contemplating the episode from London with both amusement and apprehension, he was determined to reject any proposal that limited his sovereignty over the island. When Eden, in an effort to make him more tractable, warned of a possible American attack, de Gaulle replied that such a move would have "the gravest possible consequences." Though Hull maintained the pressure, Roosevelt was obviously losing interest in face of the ridicule the American position evoked. On January 12th, de Gaulle wired Muselier, "We are entering in the last phase of this affair, which has had the immense advantage of bringing to the public stage Washington's inadmissible arrangement with Vichy for the neutralization of the French empire."

After Churchill, at the end of 1941, delivered an electrifying speech at Ottawa censuring Vichy and extolling de Gaulle, it became obvious that any American move against the islands would be interpreted as a challenge to the British. To Roosevelt, Saint-Pierre and Miquelon were not worth it. He dispatched a discreet memorandum to his Secretary of State directing him to keep cool and make no further statements on the subject. Hull was now beaten. Events had isolated him not only from the Free French but also from Churchill, from Vichy and from Roosevelt himself. It was not until March 26th that he actually surrendered, when he told Pasquet, the bewildered consul at Saint-Pierre: "There is no reason why your personal relations with the Free French officials should not be maintained upon the most cordial basis."[7]

De Gaulle, with three corvettes and a submarine, had thus defied the most powerful alliance in history and emerged victorious. This was not a victory that was cheaply bought. Roosevelt was deeply angered that the United States had been outmaneuvered and made to look foolish by a band of renegades. "Do not play little tricks on big powers" is an old axiom of diplomacy. De Gaulle had disregarded the axiom and had to be prepared to pay the price.

The first bill fell due almost immediately after Saint-Pierre and Miquelon, when Roosevelt and Churchill were drawing up the United Nations Declaration. The British proposed the Free French as signatories. Roosevelt was ready to consent, but Hull strenuously objected. The technicality was raised that Free France, not a "nation," could not become a member of the United Nations. On January 1st, the Declaration was signed—without de Gaulle. Not until 1945 were the French finally invited to subscribe to the document.[8]

Pointe-Noire, a tiny port on the coast of Free French Equatorial Africa, was the focus of the next dispute. In February, 1942, the United States Army proposed to improve the landing facilities there for use as a relay point on the air route to Australia. The French National Committee at once approved the request, adding that, while no conditions were attached, it would be grateful for the delivery of eight transport aircraft. The Committee explained that its own planes were old and unsafe, and inadequate for flying the great distances between colonial cities. De Gaulle himself had nearly been killed in the crash of a Free French plane.

The Committee regarded the answer it received from the State Department as condescending at best. The note said that the use of Pointe-Noire was a matter of urgent military necessity, and, although serious consideration would be given to the Free French need, the American Government would not bargain for the site. As a result, De Gaulle changed his position at once. He contended that the United States Government had given him little enough demonstration of generosity. It was sufficiently insulting, he said, that the Americans chose to make use of the colonies without recognizing

Free France as a full ally in the war. He would not, he maintained, stand by while the Americans took over Pointe-Noire without assurances that he would get his airplanes.

The negotiations over the site dragged on for months over this trivial point. The French felt the United States wanted to reduce them to begging. De Gaulle maintained he would have given his full cooperation had the United States delivered a few planes instead of thrusting the burden of good faith on Free France. To assert his presence, he forced American negotiators to haggle for whatever French assistance they wanted. Finally, the Army changed its plans and transferred some of its intended activities from Pointe-Noire to other African sites. When the French ultimately received the planes, the base was put into operation. But, for most of a year, mutual distrust generated ill will, and Pointe-Noire, to the detriment of both sides, was never utilized to its fullest potential.[9]

The affair on New Caledonia was much rowdier. It began even before Pearl Harbor, when the Army, undertaking an eleventh-hour survey in quest of Pacific bases, landed a team on the island without any prior notification to its Free French commander, Admiral Thierry d'Argenlieu. Even the American consul on the island agreed that the Army had no excuse for overlooking such a customary civility, however innocent its intention. D'Argenlieu, a Carmelite monk in time of peace, was fierce, austere and no less jealous than de Gaulle of the rights claimed for France. He informed the Americans they could remain in New Caledonia but he would not allow them to undertake any activity without the consent of the French National Committee.

The United States Government reached an agreement with the Free French on January 15, 1942, and at once began building airfields. But the new facilities disturbed d'Argenlieu. They made New Caledonia a succulent military target for the Japanese, who were rampaging southward through the Pacific. In addition, he feared that a strong Vichy naval squadron stationed in Indochina might seize on the preoccupation of the other naval powers in the Pacific to reconquer his domain. American defenses of the island were scanty. More vexing to him was the refusal of the Americans, because of the War Department's attention to the "leakiness" stigma acquired at Dakar, to share their defensive schemes with him. D'Argenlieu was faced with a terrified civilian population he felt helpless to defend. What was more troublesome, he became convinced, watching installations grow, that the American Army was planning to snatch the island away from him.

At the beginning of March, General Alexander Patch arrived with the first contingent of troops to defend New Caledonia. Relations between the easygoing American and the tense Frenchman did not go well. As more soldiers reached the island, the French became aware that the Americans were disrupting the living patterns of the community, composed principally of descendants of an old penal colony. D'Argenlieu proceeded to become the center of a confused political storm, during which his authority was challenged by Henri Sautot, the civilian governor of the island and a more popular leader with the disoriented populace. Patch, unfortunately, made the mistake of siding with Sautot. In London, de Gaulle backed the Admiral and reaffirmed his duty to keep Americans out of French affairs.

The political contest reached its climax at the very moment that the Battle of the Coral Sea was determining whether the Japanese would reach New Caledonia and Australia. Sautot had rejected de Gaulle's order to return to London, and the colony was in ferment. On the night of May 5th, d'Argenlieu put his rival and a handful of dissidents on a small communications ship and sent them off to exile on a distant island. When Patch learned of the action, which he described to Washington as "devious, surreptitious and unknown to me," he instructed d'Argenlieu to bring the ship back. The Admiral, of course, refused categorically. When disorders followed, Patch seriously contemplated locking up d'Argenlieu and declaring martial law. But the Free French chief made certain concessions to popular demands, and calm was restored to the colony.

From London, de Gaulle wired both d'Argenlieu and Patch to show restraint in the face of the approaching enemy. According to an American liaison report from London, de Gaulle was irate at Patch for meddling in New Caledonian politics but was anxious to establish decent relations between the two commanders. A few days later, the Battle of the Coral Sea was won and the South Pacific delivered from any immediate threat. D'Argenlieu and Patch proceeded to conclude a satisfactory working agreement that lasted until de Gaulle, to the Americans' relief, ordered the Admiral back to London in September. The crisis was thus resolved, but only after each side found ample new evidence to support its contention that the other could not be trusted.[10]

In May, 1942, the British invasion of Madagascar brought the Free

French face to face once more with Allied indifference to the rights they claimed in behalf of France. De Gaulle had proposed shortly after Pearl Harbor that a Free French expedition be sent to seize the island. Churchill recognized that as long as Vichy controlled Madagascar, which lay athwart the British supply line to India, it might fall into Japanese hands. But the Prime Minister, after giving the subject some consideration, ruled against a Free French attack. There is no evidence that Roosevelt ever said so, but Churchill undoubtedly recognized that the President would be opposed to such a plan. Churchill decided to say nothing to the Free French but to proceed with preparations for an invasion that would be all British.

While the expedition was being readied, Vichy put on one of its periodic demonstrations of impotence before Nazi pressure. Late in April, Pétain dismissed Darlan as the head of government and replaced him with Pierre Laval. Darlan remained *dauphin* and retained important powers as commander in chief, but he was finished as Vichy's principal policy maker. Laval, dedicated to earning France a place in Hitler's European structure, was now the major force in the Pétain Government.

The change was too much for even Roosevelt to tolerate, and he summoned Leahy home. Roosevelt denounced the Vichy move in a "fireside chat" to the country. But when Churchill asked him to send American warships into the Mediterranean to intimidate Pétain during the Madagascar landings, the President declined on the grounds that he could not risk his diplomatic advantages at Vichy. He sent a warning to the Pétain Government in Britain's behalf, but, beyond the symbolic penalty of the Ambassador's recall, he did nothing in response to Laval's assumption of power to revise his policy of solicitude toward Vichy.

Churchill, meanwhile, by limiting the Madagascar expedition to Englishmen, hoped he had at last found the formula for persuading Frenchmen not to resist. The landings caught the garrison by surprise, and the initial response was encouraging. But from Vichy Darlan ordered full-scale resistance. "Do not forget," he wired to his forces, "that the British betrayed us in Flanders, that they treacherously attacked us at Mers el-Kébir, Dakar and Syria, that they are assassinating civilians in the home territory [through aerial bombardment] and that they have sought to starve women and children in Djibouti." The French soldiers responded by fighting as fiercely and as skillfully as their comrades had in Syria and at Dakar.[11]

De Gaulle was equally surprised when he learned of the Madagascar landings. He concluded at once that another major colonial holding was being wrenched from his grasp. A communiqué from the State Department added to his rage and frustration. "The United States and Great Britain," it declared, "are in accord that Madagascar will, of course, he restored to France *after the war or at any time the occupation of Madagascar is no longer essential to the common cause of the United Nations.*"* The words seemed quite clearly to mean that the island would be neutralized for the duration of hostilities, either under British rule or, through the "local authorities" doctrine, under some band of Frenchmen other than his own. De Gaulle went storming into Anthony Eden's office and demanded that Free France take over the administration of Madagascar to contribute its capacities to the war effort. Eden agreed that de Gaulle's argument was just. On May 13th, a week after the invasion, the Foreign Office announced that "it is the intention of His Majesty's Government that the Free French National Committee should play its due part in the administration of the liberated French territory, since the National Committee is cooperating with the United Nations as the representative of fighting France." Once more de Gaulle had won an important point against the will of the United States.[12]

The next day, de Gaulle wired Leclerc in Brazzaville instructions to prepare a team to take over the administration of Madagascar. The matter, however, did not go smoothly. Vichy's troops, having retreated into the interior, still occupied most of the island, and the British had no desire to pin down their own units in fruitless jungle fighting. Free France obviously had to wait until the British, in their own good time, decided to undertake a mopping-up operation. De Gaulle was irritated and he showed it.

On June 6th, he notified his principal collaborators around the world that he had received information indicating that Britain and the United States were planning operations to neutralize some of Vichy's holdings in Saharan Africa. To each of them he transmitted a solemn oath that "if my suspicions prove true, I will not agree to remain associated with the Anglo-Saxon powers." He would, he said, assemble his forces in the Free French territories and notify the world he had taken his stand against imperialism.

At the very moment he was threatening to break relations with the Allies, Free France was exulting in its greatest military triumph

* Author's italics.

of the war. Throughout the last days of May and the early days of June, the First Free French Brigade under General Joseph Koenig practically alone held up the German desert offensive in Libya by repeatedly beating back attacks by Rommel's Panzers on its position at Bir Hacheim. Rommel, in his memoirs, devoted page after page to extolling the Free French feat. Churchill was unstinting in his praise for the service of the indomitable brigade. For the French, their remarkable achievement was a deep source of pride, a restoration of the sheen on their tarnished military glory.[13]

As bitter irony, de Gaulle learned while the battle of Bir Hacheim was being fought that the United States Government had not invited Free French officers to participate in Memorial Day ceremonies in Washington. This was May 30, 1942, six months after Pearl Harbor. The military attachés representing Vichy, however, took a prominent part. De Gaulle was particularly stung by the contrast.

On June 10th, Churchill summoned the Free French leader for a talk on their Madagascar differences. Once again he assured de Gaulle that the British had no designs on the island or on any French territory, and he vowed that the Free French would administer Madagascar as soon as the remaining Vichy forces could be cleared out. De Gaulle, who entered the meeting skeptically, emerged satisfied. Churchill, he reported, had told him: "We will perhaps be in France next year. In any case, we will be there together. . . . I will not abandon you. You can count on me." A few days later, de Gaulle withdrew the warning of a possible rupture with the Allies and instructed the administrators of all his territories to resume normal relations with the British officials. Free France, he said, must now "re-create an impression of détente."[14]

The prospect of a return to France, raised by Churchill, did not take de Gaulle unawares. Some time before he had begun to turn his mind beyond the goal of restoration of the French state toward the future of the liberated country. His public addresses dwelled increasingly on the devotion of Free France to the principles of liberty, equality and fraternity. At one point, he announced his dedication to a "revolution, the greatest in her history, that France, betrayed by her ruling elite and her privileged classes, has begun to accomplish. . . ."[15]

But de Gaulle's political thinking was still too vague to be called a philosophy. He was still driven more by scorn for the Third Republic and hatred for Vichy than by any set of positive political ideas. He who, in his voluminous writings before the war, had thought much about power in the service of the nation had reflected little on politics in the service of the people. De Gaulle, perhaps, was still many years from full political maturity. But in these, the middle years of World War II, he began to recognize that the exercise of power could be directed not only toward the aspirations of France but also toward the wants of Frenchmen. Roosevelt and Hull would continue to interpret his motives as dictatorial. But his beliefs, as they emerged on the speaker's platform, lined up more on the democratic left than on the nondemocratic right. Partly to appeal to, partly under the influence of the Resistance, Free France took on the appearance of an antifascist movement. De Gaulle thus came more and more to be looked upon as the champion of republican virtue and revolutionary idealism.

To win the allegiance of the growing Resistance, however, ideology was not enough. De Gaulle also needed organization. From the first, the agents he sent into France were charged not only with acquiring intelligence but also with pressing the leadership of Free France on the underground networks. De Gaulle's political aims at times generated friction with British and American secret agencies, far beyond that which normally results from the competitiveness of clandestine organizations operating with similar objectives on the same terrain. Materially, the Free French were at a disadvantage in the competition because the Allies could offer clandestine units more money, guns and equipment. But de Gaulle, as a Frenchman, had an ideological advantage. In some measure, de Gaulle diverted criticism by separating his political from his military agents. But he openly admitted his political intentions. He regarded it as essential that the Resistance be welded into a force receptive to orders from a single source, expressive of the national will and fighting, within the framework of the Alliance, in behalf of France.

On the night of January 1, 1942, a young ex-prefect from Chartres named Jean Moulin, who had been captured and tortured by the Gestapo before escaping to London, was parachuted back into France. His mission was to bring about a union of the French Resistance. His instructions were to include all groups, no matter what their politics or their past, so long as they were willing to take direction from de Gaulle. Moulin possessed as his principal lever the disposition of whatever funds and equipment the Free French had available, including means of communication with London. He was also remarkably skillful, persuasive and courageous. Within a few months he had organized a Resistance Council in the unoccupied zone that publicly recognized de Gaulle's authority. From there, he moved on to Paris where, under the nose of the oppressor, he undertook his hair-raising efforts to fuse command of the Resistance into a single national directorate under Gaullist control.[16]

Capitalizing on the burgeoning underground activity in Metropolitan France, de Gaulle announced on Bastille Day, 1942, that Free France would henceforth be known as Fighting France (*la France Combattante*). He thereby sought to put the world on notice that his followers included not only Frenchmen fighting openly abroad but also the Frenchmen who were under German rule and who fought the enemy in secret. The British at once issued a declaration supporting Fighting France's authority over all Frenchmen contributing to the struggle against Nazism. The United States said nothing. But on July 14th, reviewing the parade in London to celebrate the French national holiday was General Dwight D. Eisenhower, commander of American forces in Europe. The American Army was seriously interested in the leadership de Gaulle claimed to exercise over the potential mass of partisans waiting behind the German lines on the European continent.

De Gaulle's growing esteem in France had not escaped American military strategists, who were impatient to send an army to the Continent. Throughout the early months of 1942, the high command in Washington argued for a concentration of forces in Britain to permit the earliest possible direct assault of Germany's European fortress. On the Continent alone, they contended, could the war be won, and to divert strength elsewhere merely delayed a showdown. The American strategic conception was supported by the Russians, who desperately sought relief from German pressure on their own front. But the British favored a prior confrontation with the Germans in the Mediterranean, on the grounds that defeat of the Nazi challenge in the south was a prerequisite to a cross-Channel attack. While the two strategies were debated throughout the spring, Washington at last moved to hedge its policy toward Vichy by granting certain concessions to please de Gaulle.

In April, 1942, the State Department established a consulate in Brazzaville, capital of Free French Africa. In May, the War Department agreed to accept a Free French mission in Washington to deal with de Gaulle's military problems. Late that month, the American Embassy in London initiated a series of friendly conversations with de Gaulle. In June, Roosevelt even talked of inviting him to Washington to try to iron out their differences. Though the idea came to nothing, the American Government did receive Emmanuel d'Astier de la Vigerie, leader of an important Resistance organization, who discussed clandestine operations at the War Department and made public appearances to influence opinion in behalf of France.

The most significant gesture was extended early in July, when it was announced simultaneously that the United States would, for the first time, accredit representatives to de Gaulle's National Committee in London and make Free France directly eligible for Lend-Lease. But to avoid any suggestion of political recognition, the United States chose its delegates from the Navy and the Army, rather than the State Department. In assigning Admiral Harold R. Stark and General Charles Bolte as liaison officers, the State Department could explain to Vichy that the move was a practical measure, undertaken for military reasons. The statement announcing the decision exalted Free France as a bearer of arms but dismissed its political pretensions. American diplomacy, even coming as a petitioner to de Gaulle, could not be divested of its habitual reserve.[17]

The State Department, in truth, was quite unhappy about the deviation from its rigorous anti-Gaullist policy. Consent to the departure had been given, it was clear, to please the Army. On May 8th, Welles, in an unusually candid moment, confided to Halifax, the British Ambassador, that in his view recognition of Free France "would exasperate French public opinion and strengthen the hand of the Germans." Seizing on reports of dissension within the French National Committee, Welles went on to say, rather wistfully, that from "knowledge of the situation in London and the United States . . . it was very clear to me that the Free French movement . . . was rapidly falling to pieces." Welles proposed, as the only salvation for Free France, a reorganization of the National Committee to divest de Gaulle of power, relieve itself of executive responsibility and become purely a consultative body for the Allied powers. Welles acknowledged to Halifax that he was not expressing official American policy but, as usual, his words could be taken as representative of the thinking not only of the State Department but of the President himself.[18]

De Gaulle, by contrast, was certain that the end of his ostracism by the United States meant the beginning of a new intimacy. He was elated by the recognition which had been granted him. "I think that the rest, by which I mean the representation of the general and permanent interests of France," he told Tixier, "must necessarily follow—on the condition that, beginning with what we have already achieved, we give to the government and to public opinion in the United States the habit of confronting us each time that one of these interests is in dispute." De Gaulle had already warned, somewhat ominously, that "Fighting France intends to march shoulder to shoulder with its allies, under the formal reservation that its allies march with Fighting France." His diplomatic success had intoxicated him. He was sure that he could drive a hard bargain.

Convinced now that the Allies were organizing to cross the Channel, de Gaulle drew up a bold program as the condition of his cooperation. On July 18, 1942, he told Tixier that he would conduct negotiations only on a government-to-government basis. He said that the Allies must agree, first, to his personal participation in planning the operation and, second, to deliver enough equipment to Fighting France to arm the Resistance and, without delay, rebuild the French Army. "If the Allies want to deal with us in this grave matter through little men who can see no further than the ends of their noses," he wrote, "or if they want to exploit for their own profit or waste in the confusion the resources of ardor that exist in France, then I will not associate myself with their enterprise." He clearly was deluding himself if he believed that the United States considered his services so important that it would agree to his conditions.

A few days later, de Gaulle wrote to Churchill: "As you know, the mass of Frenchmen, especially in the occupied territory, rely on me and on the French National Committee to prepare with the Allies the French effort in this new phase of the war and, at least at the beginning, to direct this effort. . . . General de Gaulle and the French National Committee are determined to bring about this participation on the largest possible scale. They are in a position to begin organizing this at the present time and then to direct it as it develops." He then made his demands of Churchill, which included, in addition to those he had outlined earlier, the concentration of all Fighting French forces in Britain to participate in the attack and the command of all Resistance units during operations. But before Churchill could reply to his proposals, de Gaulle's dream house had collapsed.[19]

On July 18th, the Chief of Staff of the United States Army, General George C. Marshall, and the Chief of Naval Operations, Admiral Ernest J. King, arrived in Britain with Harry Hopkins, President Roosevelt's most trusted adviser. Their assignment was to decide with the British the strategy for the remainder of 1942. Roosevelt, not committed to a single strategic idea, was determined to get American troops into action against the Germans by the end of the year. Unless the United States soon received a real taste of war, its good faith as an ally, he believed, would be in doubt. Marshall, while he vastly preferred the continental assault, recognized that across the Channel the Germans possessed forces stronger than the Allies could muster for at least a year. Churchill, meanwhile, kept pressing for action in the Mediterranean. The American chiefs, after a few days of discussion in London, conceded that the assault of Europe would have to be delayed.

De Gaulle, meanwhile, had been straining to see Marshall. He was fully aware that the presence of America's top strategists in London meant that a major decision was impending. He wanted to submit his own ideas and to get some notion of Allied intentions. He was particularly anxious for the United States to understand the potential contribution of Free France.

A meeting was at last arranged for July 23rd. De Gaulle apparently had expected a private audience with Marshall. He found himself, instead, also in the presence of King, Eisenhower and Mark Clark, Eisenhower's deputy. The cold politeness, which champagne did nothing to relieve, indicated to de Gaulle at once that something was amiss. After formal handshakes all around, Marshall delivered a routine eulogy on the Fighting French war effort. An embarrassed silence followed. Then de Gaulle volunteered some information about the forces he had ready to advance into Europe. He proceeded then to review Fighting French strength throughout the world. After another exchange of amenities and small talk, more silence ensued. De Gaulle then offered to deliver his views on a second front in Europe. The Americans listened courteously and added nothing. After the third conspicuous silence, de Gaulle got up, shook hands in the French manner with everyone present, thanked Marshall and King and walked out. The meeting had consumed an uncomfortable half hour.[20]

De Gaulle knew the game was up, though he was not informed

what the Allies had decided upon in place of the continental landings. The meeting with the Americans had told him that the courtship was over. The succeeding months would confirm it. Roosevelt
and Churchill had at last agreed on a major strategic move. The
Allied forces would undertake their 1942 offensive in French North
Africa. The code name for the operation was "Torch." De Gaulle's
Fighting French were to be excluded from it.

The Search for a Stand-In

July–November, 1942

THE DECISION to invade North Africa was based on the premise that the French would not resist. The Allied objective was not to tangle with Frenchmen but to drive the Germans from the southern shore of the Mediterranean. Vichy's control of the long coast from Tunisia to Morocco did the Allied cause no harm. But if the invasion provided the Germans with the opening to take over the Tunisian ports and thereby shorten their supply lines from Italy, it would actually serve to consolidate the Axis position in Africa. Only an Allied drive of sufficient dynamism to grab all of North Africa ahead of the Germans could justify the risks of the operation. The Allies could not afford to fight an extended battle on the African periphery when they could win the war only in the center, on the Continent itself. They particularly could not afford to waste time, men and lives fighting Frenchmen, who were not the enemy. To succeed, the invasion had to have, openly or not, the concurrence of the French.

Roosevelt and Churchill thought first of making a direct approach to Pétain, but after some reflection they agreed it would be too dangerous. The wily Marshal, while piously assuring the Allies of his sympathy, might very well decide to pass his information on to the Germans. The President and Prime Minister did not foreclose a later deal with Vichy. But, for the moment, they buried the idea of an explicit proposal.[1]

Because the success of Torch depended as much on political as military factors, Roosevelt, almost as a matter of course, assumed principal responsibility for its planning. His pursuit of Vichy, he believed, had assured him the confidence of Frenchmen generally. He felt particularly well placed for manipulating the men and factions upon whom acquiescence might depend. Roosevelt went about preparing for Torch not as if it was an act of war. He looked on it as a maneuver such as he might engage in to force a bill through an obstinate Congress. Roosevelt set out to execute Torch as if it were a political, not a military, undertaking.

The President was convinced that all Frenchmen, for historical reasons, possessed a sentimental attachment to the United States, which encompassed a recognition of its disinterestedness. He was confident that Frenchmen understood that he, the President, was one they could trust. However patronizing, he was quite sincere in believing that France ought to put its fate in his hands, where it would be safeguarded. Once he wrote to Leahy, "It is most important for the French government and the French people to realize that the President of the United States is about the best friend they have."[2] Although he had promised Pétain to respect French sovereignty in North Africa, he regarded the promise as irrelevant since the steps he was taking were for France's own good. Roosevelt deeply believed that the Frenchmen in North Africa would accept him as a savior and not fire on the American flag.

Churchill had a far less mystical approach and favored going ashore with his guns blazing. "I did not," he wrote in his *Memoirs*, "wholly share the American view that either they were so beloved by Vichy or we so hated as to make the difference between fighting and submission." He had no objection to Roosevelt's political maneuvering, on the condition that "the necessary forces were set in motion and the operation was not fatally restricted in its scope." But he warned Roosevelt that "if the political victory, for which I agree with you there is a good chance, should go amiss, a military disaster of very great consequences will supervene. We could have stormed Dakar in September, 1940, if we had not been cluttered up with preliminary conciliatory processes."[3]

Eisenhower and his staff were not happy with Roosevelt's assumptions, either. The Torch commander grumbled about "invading a neutral country to create a friend."[4] At one point, he gave the operation only a fifty-fifty chance of succeeding. Another time he lamented the "desperate nature" of the undertaking, "which depends only in minor degree upon professional preparation or on the wisdom of military decisions." As soldiers, Eisenhower and his staff would have preferred to rely less on political cunning and more on military strength.

Roosevelt's objective was to find a Frenchman who, by lending his name to Torch, would give to an act of aggression the appearance of an act of liberation. He recognized that Vichy might order its forces in North Africa to resist the landings. A Frenchman of great stature, he believed, could persuade the troops that it was in the interest of France to lay down its arms. Roosevelt set out, even before Torch had been decided, to find a Frenchman who could unify all Frenchmen under United States leadership.

He rejected de Gaulle at once. Churchill had maintained that "if . . . Vichy persists in collaboration with Germany and we have to fight our way into French North and West Africa, then the de Gaullists' movement must be aided and used to the full." But Roosevelt was certain that de Gaulle's presence among the invaders was a guarantee of fierce resistance. He had not only Syria and Dakar to support his contention. He had also reports from Murphy and his "vice-consuls" throughout the colonies. He had the opinion of Leahy, who, after leaving Vichy, had joined the President's personal staff at the White House. All of them assured Roosevelt that de Gaulle was detested by Frenchmen. Clearly, their information had come from sources loyal to Pétain. British intelligence, while conceding the hatred of the armed forces for de Gaulle, insisted that its data showed the mass of common people in North Africa sympathetic to him. But Roosevelt had no misgivings about the soundness of the decision. He had no intention of letting the presence of the Fighting French complicate the appeal of the United States among Frenchmen in the invasion area.[5]

After Pétain, it was predictable that Roosevelt's mind should have turned to Weygand, who, somehow, remained high in his esteem. For the New Year, 1942, Roosevelt sent the General a message at his home in Provence. "I . . . believe," he wrote, "that France cannot fail to recognize now and in the future what your contribution is and has been to its welfare and future greatness. . . . I am confident that in the difficult hours that lie ahead, your devotion to the best interests of your country will rise above any adverse circumstances."[6]

It was another of those letters that would have made Churchill choke. That very week the Prime Minister delivered his famous diatribe in Ottawa against the men of Vichy, with Weygand his principal target. "Their generals misled them," he declared of the French. "When I warned them that Britain would fight on alone whatever they did, their generals told their Prime Minister and his divided Cabinet, 'In three weeks England will have her neck wrung like a chicken.' Some chicken! Some neck." It was a significant measure of the distance that separated Roosevelt and Churchill on the subject of France that the President should be petitioning a man whom the Prime Minister held in such thorough contempt.

An official of the American Embassy in Vichy paid a secret visit to General Weygand on January 20, 1942. He asked Weygand whether he would accept command of the French forces in North Africa if the United States landed a substantial expeditionary army and pledged him full economic and military support. Weygand not only refused the offer flatly but rejected the embassy official's plea that the visit be kept confidential.[7]

A few days later, Leahy called on Pétain and reported that "it was evident the Marshal already had been informed of [the] conversation." Aware that the cat was out of the bag, Leahy asked Pétain his intentions in the event of a North African invasion. The Marshal replied that he would defend his territory against any foreign power. "Does that mean Americans?" the Ambassador asked. "It means anybody—including Americans," the old man answered sternly.[8]

After the rebuffs from Pétain and Weygand, the President had to resume his quest from the beginning. Earlier, American agents had flirted with General Fornel de la Laurencie, a member of Pétain's circle, who aspired to lead a clandestine government of the Resistance while, somehow, remaining loyal to the Marshal. There is evidence that large sums of money were turned over to Laurencie from secret American sources, but Frenchmen refused to take him seriously and his efforts collapsed.[9] Roosevelt personally favored finding some important figure from the Third Republic, on whose political views he could rely. But when Leahy contacted Edouard Herriot, the old Assembly president suggested that the Ambassador turn to de Gaulle.[10] In Washington, such anti-Gaullist Frenchmen as Alexis Léger, former secretary-general of the Foreign Ministry, and Camille Chautemps, the unctuous ex-premier, had the ear of the

State Department. Leahy, after his recall from Vichy, looked over General Robert Odic, former Air Force commander in North Africa. But none of the émigré Frenchmen in the United States possessed sufficient stature to be considered leaders. In North Africa, the tireless Murphy tried to suborn any prominent Frenchman who would listen to him. Once he wired Washington for $1 million to support an unnamed Army officer who claimed an organization of 26,000 men prepared to "liquidate" the old-line leadership and send sixteen divisions into battle at the side of the Allies. The claim was obviously preposterous, because North Africa did not have the manpower for sixteen divisions. But if his plans failed to materialize, Murphy did not become discouraged. It was on him that Roosevelt counted most heavily to find the Frenchman he wanted.[11]

On April 17th, General Henri Giraud, a fiery commander captured in the early stages of the Battle of France, escaped from a German prison and, a few days later, turned up in Vichy. Churchill at once wired to Roosevelt that "this man might play a decisive part in bringing about things of which you had hopes."[12] It was true that Giraud had a fighting spirit and wanted to get back into combat. He rejected Laval's plea that, to avoid German reprisals against France, he return to captivity. But Giraud did not take to rebellion lightly. He refused to deal with de Gaulle and, to please Pétain, he signed an oath of loyalty and obedience. In June, American agents succeeded in making contact with him to submit their highly secret proposals. Despite his oath, Giraud was receptive to the American overtures. But he stated that his cooperation was contingent on appropriate guarantees for France and on his own command of any forces invading French territory. Roosevelt was rapturous when he learned of the apparent success of the approach. Without paying particular attention to Giraud's terms, he was convinced he had found his man.

Confident that destiny had summoned him, Giraud now moved from Vichy to a small villa near Lyons and began drawing up plans for Europe's liberation, based on an American landing on France's Mediterranean coast. It was in this villa that he was visited by Jacques Lemaigre-Dubreuil, a North African businessman who was working actively with Murphy and a group of co-conspirators to assist an American invasion of North Africa. When Lemaigre-Dubreuil reported a successful meeting with Giraud to Algiers, both his fellow plotters and Murphy became enthusiastic. With Washington's concurrence, Murphy decided to take over negotiations from American agents on the Continent, using as his intermediary Lemaigre-Dubreuil, whose business frequently took him to the unoccupied zone of France. Murphy, like Roosevelt, recognized potential in Giraud but was equally cavalier about the conditions Giraud had set.

To the day he died, Giraud insisted that in August, 1942, he received a message from Washington announcing the acceptance of his terms. In his files has been found a curious document which did indeed promise him command of any invasion force. On it is the written notation "OK Roosevelt," but not in the President's script. No American has acknowledged knowing anything of the origin of this mysterious document. On the contrary, Murphy maintains not only that no commitment was made to Giraud but that no information of American intentions was transmitted to him. It was, in fact, to settle the very question of Giraud's relations to the invasion force that Murphy, in early September, left for London, where Eisenhower and his staff were working furiously to resolve the massive problems involved in realizing Torch.[13]

By September, Torch's planners fully recognized the risks of their operation. The French had a defending force of 180,000 men, half again more than the invaders. They had land-based planes which were superior to the Allies' carrier-based aircraft. They had prepared defenses, and, perhaps most important, they would not be taken by surprise because of the American determination to ask them in advance to lay down their arms. If the French found the attack overwhelming, they might be persuaded to surrender. But a weak invasion would only promote contempt and might encourage them to drive the invaders back into the sea.

General Marshall had considerable respect for the French fighting potential and was disinclined to take more chances with it than necessary. In August, he decided to cancel the landing planned for Algiers and limit his operations to Casablanca and Oran. He was particularly fearful that the Germans would swoop down on Africa through Spain to isolate a large Allied force inside the Mediterranean. Marshall was willing to ignore the need to get to Tunisia in a hurry out of concern for safeguarding his supply lines and his rear.

Churchill objected forcefully when he learned of Marshall's directive. Though the chief proponent of Torch, he reasoned that a timid thrust would tie down Anglo-American forces indefinitely in wasteful fighting. "It seems to me," he wrote to Roosevelt, "that the whole pith of the operation will be lost if we do not take Algiers as well as Oran on the first day. . . . Not to go east of Oran is making the enemy a present not only of Tunis but of Algiers."[14]

According to a schedule Roosevelt had conceived, United States forces would, with French acquiescence, consolidate their positions in the invasion area within a week. It would take the Germans, he estimated, two weeks to occupy Tunis. The Allied army would thus have a one-week margin to beat the Nazis to key Tunisian cities. Churchill argued that, strategically, there was a contradiction in this analysis. If Roosevelt was so sure that the French would not fight, why not be audacious and strike as far east as possible? If, on the other hand, it turned out that they did fight, why do battle for Casablanca and Oran when the meaningful objectives were hundreds of miles away? One British planner wanted to attack as far east as Bône while another advocated a strike from the island of Malta at Tunis itself. Roosevelt's generals did not concede the contradiction. What Churchill viewed as timidity they considered sound planning. Roosevelt himself was mesmerized by the belief that the operation would be a splendid success because Frenchmen would embrace his soldiers as they ran up on the beaches.

Roosevelt finally succumbed to Churchill's insistence, however, and, on September 3rd, restored the order for an assault on Algiers. But it was clear he considered the matter academic. "Our latest and best information from North Africa," he wrote sanguinely to the Prime Minister, "is as follows: an American expedition led in all three phases by American officers will meet little resistance from the French Army in Africa."[15]

Murphy, the chief purveyor of this information, arrived in London on September 16th. After leaving Algiers, he had first gone to Washington, where he learned the date of the landings and received his instructions for dealing with Giraud. Murphy cheered Eisenhower with his sweeping predictions of French cooperation. His forthright manner convinced the London planners that his reports were objective and accurate.

Nonetheless, Eisenhower's meeting with Murphy had disquieting overtones. The soldiers and civilians who worked closely with Murphy had made plans to neutralize French defenses through a series of carefully timed *coups*. Washington had encouraged these efforts as an added means of nullifying resistance. Disabling the coastal batteries at Casablanca, for instance, was a surer contribution to a bloodless landing than the proclamation of a dissident French general. But Murphy's orders were to withhold from the conspirators the date of the landings until twenty-four hours in advance. He saw no reason to protest. "It would be a simple matter," he breezily told Eisenhower, to say that the invasion was scheduled for February, then "to move forward the date later on." But the decision, in which Eisenhower also concurred, was, in fact, an irresponsible compromise. On the one hand, if there was fear of disclosure, twenty-four hours would have sufficed to alert hostile garrisons all along the coast. On the other, if the objective was to paralyze defenses, it was virtually impossible to mobilize a highly organized conspiracy in so little time.

Murphy's meetings, both in Washington and London, also failed to deal with Giraud's insistence upon command. The President had authorized Murphy to assure the General that France would be treated as an ally, that her prewar frontiers would be restored and that the French Army in North Africa would receive Lend-Lease supplies. He had no compunctions about guaranteeing the General that the Fighting French, whom Giraud opposed more for reasons of tactics than of principle, would not take part in the invasion. But he remained silent about Giraud's personal role. The fact that none of the invading forces was French made the General's demand clearly preposterous. But neither Murphy nor his chiefs in Washington, in the many months that had elapsed since the question was raised, ever bothered to come face to face with it. Giraud proceeded on the assumption that his condition had been met. The Americans acted as if the General could be humored into doing what they wanted without their taking seriously what he expected in return.[16]

When Murphy returned to Algiers in early October, prepared to seal the arrangement with Giraud, he found a new and upsetting factor thrust into the intrigue. In a secret interview to which he was summoned by the French Army's intelligence chief, Murphy learned that Vichy regarded Allied landings in North Africa as imminent. The Germans, Murphy was told, had also divined the intentions of the Allies and were preparing to beat them to their destination. The intelligence officer wanted to know if the United States would pay a price to obtain the assistance not only of the French Army but also of the French fleet. The price, he said, was support of the commander in chief of the French armed forces, the master opportunist, Admiral Jean François Darlan.

Though startled by the proposal, Murphy was convinced that it was genuine. He reported to Washington that his own information confirmed the contention that the Axis was preparing to attack the colonies. His own sources, he said, led him to believe that either a land army would cross the Libyan frontier into Tunisia or an air army would descend on the colonies by parachute. This alarming prospect, he declared, justified dealing with Darlan.[17]

When Eisenhower learned of the new development, he recognized at once a potential danger in trying to handle both Giraud and Darlan at once. He did not oppose profiting from what he believed the two could contribute—Giraud the Army, Darlan the Navy. But he urged choosing one or the other as chief collaborator to the invasion. He toyed with a formula to make Giraud the civil and military governor, Darlan the commander of any French forces in combat against the enemy. He even contemplated offering Darlan the post of Deputy Allied Commander-in-Chief once all Allied forces were ashore. Churchill apparently knew of his designs and raised no objections. It was clear that Darlan, despite his past, would be welcomed if he crossed the line into the Allied camp.

Giraud's principal supporter in Algiers, General Charles Mast, flew into a rage, however, when Murphy told him of Darlan's overtures. He bluntly rejected any collaboration between Giraud and the Admiral. Mast, a leader of the conspiratorial clique in the Army, insisted that Darlan's presence would add nothing to an Allied invasion. Mast maintained, Murphy told Eisenhower, that "Giraud's command will give us entry practically without firing a shot."[18]

Obviously abashed at the impact of his suggestion that Giraud's role be diminished, Murphy had now to restore himself to Mast's confidence. To demonstrate his good faith, he decided to lend his authority to a fantastic proposal. Mast wanted Eisenhower to send a team of officers under a senior general to a secret rendezvous on the Algerian coast to discuss prospects for the invasion. At Murphy's recommendation, Eisenhower agreed to just such a plan. The result was one of the most dramatic, most foolhardy, most meaningless exploits of the entire war.

Within hours, General Mark Clark, deputy commander of Torch, was en route to Algeria with four ranking officers. On October 22nd, after four days in planes, submarine and rubber boats, they made their way up the beach at Cherchel, ninety miles west of Algiers, where Murphy, Mast and several other conspirators waited in a villa. Their meeting lasted less than a day, a substantial part of which was spent in a wine cellar to elude suspicious French police. After giving up another day to high seas, the American officers returned in their boats to a waiting submarine, their lives spared but money and papers lost in the waves. They arrived back in England on October 25th.

The objective that might have justified the risks of the Cherchel conference has never been clear. Clark seems to have acquired useful intelligence data, but an officer of lesser rank or, for that matter, Murphy himself, who was free to communicate with London by courier or code, could have obtained the same information. It did not require the Deputy Commander of Torch to collect material that arrived far too late to influence the operation. But, more significantly, because Clark was specifically barred, on orders from Roosevelt, from discussing with the conspirators either Giraud's command or the role of Darlan, the major outstanding questions remained unsettled. Clark was also prohibited from telling Mast the date set for Torch. Though the first convoys were already at sea, he lied and said the United States would land 500,000 men some time during the following year. He even let Mast believe that serious consideration was being given Giraud's plan for attacking southern France. After the meeting, Mast and his men, on whom the success of Torch seemed in great measure to depend, were less prepared than before to provide vital assistance. The American command had only confused the preparations. On security grounds, the United States refused to put confidence in its French collaborators. Yet if Clark had been captured at Cherchel as he very nearly was, the security of Torch would have been compromised and, quite possibly, Torch itself wrecked.[19]

Even without mishap to General Clark, it was obvious the word was out that action was near in North Africa. Darlan and the Germans were not alone in speculating about Allied intentions. The press in both Britain and the United States spoke openly of an invasion. From as far away as Japan, there were whispers of it. Eisenhower was uncertain whether his enemies, to say nothing of his friends, had specific information or were shrewdly guessing. The prospect of a genuine "leak" filled the Allied command with apprehension.

The week before the troops were to land, Vichy's Ambassador, Henry-Haye, mentioned quite casually to Sumner Welles that he assumed reports of an attack he had heard were unfounded. Welles replied that "in times like these," it was impolitic to pay attention to all the rumors in circulation. Henry-Haye, Welles reported, went away looking satisfied.[20]

De Gaulle, too, knew that the Allies were about to land in North Africa, although he had received no official confirmation. The Dakar stigma convinced both Roosevelt and Marshall that it was unsafe to confide information to him. Marshall, in fact, proposed that the Fighting French periodically be fed false information on the chance that it might get to the Germans. Roosevelt thought it was a fine trick and gave his approval.[21]

Though de Gaulle was well aware that he had been thrust aside, he made no more effort to be accommodating than before. It was his conviction that ultimately the Allies would come to him to lead France through the liberation into the Allied camp. To demonstrate his indifference toward the feverish Allied activity in London, he spent most of the summer and fall touring Fighting French installations in Africa and the Middle East.

But in early October, alarmed by the signs that the United States was seeking new French leadership, he departed from his policy of aloofness. For a moment, he submerged his pride and composed a long letter to Roosevelt in what were for him warm and personal terms. It was unlike de Gaulle to ask for sympathy, even from the President of the United States. Perhaps he was frightened, for himself or for France, at the rumors of bargaining with such men as Darlan. In this letter he dropped his defenses and, without affectation or arrogance, tried to make Roosevelt understand what he sought for his movement and his country:

France is deeply sensitive to the humiliation that has been inflicted upon her and to the injustice of the fate which she has suffered. That is why France must, before the end of the war, take her place once more in the fight and, while waiting, reject the impression that she ever completely abandoned it. She must be conscious of having been one of the countries whose efforts led to victory. It is important for the war and essential for after the war.

If France, when liberated by the victory of the democracies, looks upon herself as a defeated nation, it is to be feared that her bitterness, her humiliation, her divisions, far from orienting her toward the democracies, will drive her to submitting to other influences. *You know which ones.* This is not an imaginary peril, for the social structure of our country will be more or less shaken from privation and plundering. . . . European reconstruction, even the global organization of the peace, would find themselves dangerously impaired. Victory must reconcile France with herself and with her friends but it will not be possible if she does not participate in it.

De Gaulle's words were not the kind that appealed to Roosevelt. De Gaulle admitted he was looking toward peace. Roosevelt looked only to the war. De Gaulle, for the first time, called attention to the threat of a Communist revolution. Roosevelt was not worried by such a threat. De Gaulle believed that a world organization needed a strong France to be viable. Roosevelt regarded France as a factor of no great consequence in maintaining order in the postwar world. De Gaulle pleaded for France's self-respect. Roosevelt regarded such a concern as vanity and was convinced that France would do better to place her future in his hands.

You will ask me [de Gaulle continued], why did you assign yourself this goal? And on what qualifications do you base it? It is true that at the time of the Vichy armistice I found myself in an unprecedented situation. Belonging to the last regular and independent government of the Third Republic, I had publicly declared myself in favor of keeping France in the war. The government which seized power in the nation's panic and despair ordered a cease-fire. Inside France and out, the elected bodies, the members of the government and the presidents of the assemblies either submitted or kept silent. If the President of the Republic, if the Parliament and its chiefs had appealed to the country to continue the fight, I would not even have thought of addressing the country in its name. On one occasion after another, politicians and high military leaders found themselves free to speak and to act, in North Africa, for example. At no time did they show either enough conviction or enough confidence in their own mandates to wage war. There is no doubt that the problem was an inner bankruptcy of the elite. In its mind, the French people has already drawn this conclusion. But whatever it was, I was alone. Should I have been silent? . . .

We are told that we must not play politics. If that means that it is not our role to perpetuate the partisan fights of yesterday or to dictate at some future time the institutions of the country, we have no need of such recommendations. It is our principle to abstain from such pretentions. But we do not retreat before the word "politics" if it means to draw together not a few troops but the whole French nation into the war effort, if it means to deal with our allies in the interests of France at the same time as we defend them, in behalf of France, against the enemy. In effect, who besides ourselves can represent these interests? Or should France remain silent on them? Or must the United Nations treat these matters with the men of Vichy to the degree and in the form that Mr. Hitler finds convenient? ...

Because unprecedented circumstances in our history have assigned us that task, does that mean, as some are saying abroad, that we think of imposing personal power on France? If we nourished base enough sentiments to try to steal the future liberty of the French people, we would be giving proof of a singular ignorance of our own people. . . . Tomorrow, after the odious experiment with personal power undertaken by Pétain, thanks to internal oppression and the connivance of the Germans, after the long and hard burden of the invasion, who would be foolish enough to imagine that he could establish and maintain in France a regime of personal power? Whatever services he might have rendered in the past, the dreamer who made such an attempt would find himself unanimously opposed.

It was in conclusion that de Gaulle gave expression to his apprehensions that Roosevelt contemplated dealing with his enemies:

I am told that men around you fear that in recognizing our existence you will compromise the possibility that certain elements, mostly military, who now take orders from the Vichy government will soon return to the war. But do you believe that in ignoring the Frenchmen who fight, in letting them become discouraged in isolation, that you will attract others into combat? On the contrary, France faces no little danger in the fact that her allies are causing her division by contributing to the formation of rival branches, one side neutralized by the Allies' own consent. In spite of the capitulation and the armistice, France retains powers in the world that must not be overlooked. It is essential to determine how she will return to the fight in the camp of the United Nations, while maintaining her values and her unity. Among the problems of the war, that is one of the most important. I ask you, therefore, to accept the idea of a general and forthright examination of the relations between the United States and Fighting France.[22]

De Gaulle's emissary deposited the letter with Welles, who had it translated and sent to the White House. The original and the translation remain to this day in Roosevelt's files. But the President did not answer it. He made no comment on it. There is, in fact, no evidence that he even read it. It was merely filed.[23]

In the State Department, Ray Atherton, acting chief of the Division of European Affairs, read it and concluded that it contained "very little meat." A strong backer of Hull in the Saint-Pierre and

Miquelon fight, Atherton was a vigorous spokesman for the anti-Gaullist group in the State Department. The analysis he submitted to Welles epitomized the feeling of that group:

Unhappily [he wrote], General de Gaulle seems to have no conception of the reasons for our relations with Vichy or that the United Nations have acquiesced in and benefitted from them or that our information from France thereby is possibly as good as his and we have been able to maintain our contacts with the French people both in unoccupied France and North Africa. The blindness of General de Gaulle is more tragic in view of the fact of our ever-increasing collaboration with him and that we have fully explained to his representatives here and even later obtained the agreement of many of them that our policy was based on the best hopes for preserving the French Empire. . . .
I fear General de Gaulle will blindly attempt to force himself and his Committee on the French people, by the foreign arms, which if acquiesced in could only lead to a postponement of the final reorganization of France.[24]

De Gaulle's transcendent effort to bridge the gap of misunderstanding thus lay demolished in Atherton's inelegant prose. It became further evidence that Roosevelt and de Gaulle were unable to communicate meaningfully with each other. It was de Gaulle's last attempt at intimacy. The distance between the two men was now greater than ever.

Churchill, meanwhile, became increasingly irritated by the American treatment of de Gaulle. Despite another flare-up between the British and the Fighting French in the Levant, he fought hard to win de Gaulle some compensation for being left out of Torch. On November 5th, three days before the scheduled landings, he wired the President that he would reveal the intentions of the Allies on the day preceding the invasion. "You will remember," he told the President, "that I have exchanged letters with him of a solemn kind in 1940 recognizing him as the leader of Free Frenchmen. I am confident his military honour can be trusted." He put Roosevelt on notice that he would tell de Gaulle the Fighting French had been banned from Torch at American insistence. Further, he said, he would announce immediately prior to the landings the appointment of a Gaullist official as governor-general of Madagascar. "This we have been keeping for a consolation prize," he told the President. "It will be a proof that we do not think of throwing over the Free French."

"I consider it inadvisable," Roosevelt answered, "for you to give de Gaulle any information in regard to 'Torch' until subsequent to a successful landing. You would then inform him that the American commander of an American expedition with my approval insisted on complete secrecy as a necessary safety precaution. De Gaulle's announcement on Friday of a Governor-General of Madagascar will not be of any assistance to 'Torch' and it should be sufficient at the present time to maintain his prestige with his followers."[25]

Churchill knew better than to challenge Roosevelt again and accepted as law his "advice" on delaying notification of de Gaulle. Significantly, Roosevelt was not in the least bothered by Churchill's desire to lay the blame for de Gaulle's mistreatment on the American doorstep. It was characteristic that he understood Churchill's desire to make amends only as a device "to maintain his [de Gaulle's] prestige with his followers." On the subject of de Gaulle, Churchill was clearly no more successful than the General himself in penetrating Roosevelt's fortress. While the Prime Minister worked to prevent Torch from undoing his years of nurturing Free France, Roosevelt looked forward to it as de Gaulle's passport to oblivion.

During these last days before Torch, the President and Murphy labored strenuously to consummate the schemes they believed would vindicate their strategy. Because Darlan had not followed up his earlier overtures, Giraud once again became their principal hope. But despite Roosevelt's confidence, Eisenhower remained apprehensive. At the end of October, he received the encouraging news that the British offensive at Alamein had sent Rommel's *Afrika Korps* into headlong flight across the desert. Churchill's chief military adviser, General Alan Brooke, noted in his diary that the victory "should put Spaniards and French in a better frame of mind to make 'Torch' a success." But at the same time Murphy wired to Washington that General Alphonse Juin, commander of the French Army in North Africa, had warned: "We should not make the mistake of attacking because he would be obliged to give orders to oppose our forces."[26]

Two weeks before Torch, while troopships steamed toward Gibraltar, Murphy notified Giraud through Lemaigre-Dubreuil that he was expected to leave France at once. Giraud, on the basis of the information given to Mast at Cherchel, still believed there would be no invasion before 1943. Unmoved by any feeling of urgency, he told Lemaigre-Dubreuil that, because of family matters, he would not be ready to leave before November 4th. It was not until the

night of November 2nd that Giraud learned the invasion in which he
was expected to play a vital role was to take place in North Africa
six days later.

Lemaigre-Dubreuil, indefatigable in the leadership he gave to the
conspiracy, was informed of the landings at the same time. He
proceeded to write a long melancholy letter to Murphy to express his chagrin. "I pass silently over the brutality of the action," he
said, "particularly painful to the wretched hearts of beaten Frenchmen. . . . Should I continue to associate myself with your efforts even
though your military command has just demonstrated to us a lack of
confidence totally unjustified after the meeting of October 22nd,
when our military experts were consulted on an operation which was
going to take place, which had in fact already been decided and
begun? Or should I halt my cooperation and admit that the Germans
will collaborate with French troops?" Lemaigre-Dubreuil conceded
that for him there was, despite his bitterness, only one decision,
which he had to make in the interests of France. He continued his
efforts, but it was with the feeling that he had been betrayed.

When Mast found out on October 29th not only that Torch was
imminent but that a submarine was already en route to Marseilles to
pick up Giraud, he was again outraged. To make matters worse,
Murphy still had not revealed the exact date. Mast declared that he
had been betrayed at Cherchel and that the United States was now
presenting both him and Giraud with an ultimatum. Only a gesture
of confidence, he declared, could restore the situation. He demanded
that Murphy delay the Torch landings for three weeks so that the
operation could be redirected toward Metropolitan France and
Giraud could get his organization in order.

Murphy, seeing his carefully laid plans verge on collapse, was
stricken with horror. Mast, in effect, was now asking the United
States to pay for the supercilious attitude it had adopted toward the
plotters. Having failed to anticipate the fury his deception would
generate, Murphy sought hurriedly to make amends. Rather than
force Mast to face up to the oncoming juggernaut, he agreed to try
to stop it. On October 31st, a fortnight after he told the President
that an Axis attack was impending, he changed his position and insisted that speed was less significant than a friendly overture toward
Giraud. He desperately urged Roosevelt to delay the landings to
meet Mast's demand. "I am convinced," Murphy wrote, "that without French Army cooperation and the danger of its active opposition

that if we do not have French command with us that Torch may fail." Murphy's was a solemn admission, made in a moment when reality had assailed his complacence, that Torch had been decided on dubious premises and planned with grievous flaws.

His plea was rejected a few days later. Murphy had no reason to believe that the wheels of such a complex and gigantic enterprise could at that late date have been reversed. "It is utterly impossible," said the message from Roosevelt, "to arrange for a delay of operation to which we are already committed. Therefore the decision of the President is that you will do your utmost to secure the understanding and cooperation of the French officials with whom you are now in contact. . . . It cannot be delayed. It must be executed. Therefore there can be no change in the plan as recommended by you." Roosevelt then emphasized once again that he would concede nothing to the French. "You will not divulge the date or location of landings to anybody," the message said, "until Eisenhower authorizes you to do so."[27]

Giraud, though resentful of the condescending attitude he encountered, consented to leave France and head for the Allied command post in Gibraltar. But unable, because of bad weather, to reach the submarine waiting for him on the fourth, he did not board until the fifth. At sea, he missed a rendezvous with an airplane because of a defective radio and was held up another day. It was not until late afternoon on November 7th, hours before the first troops were to go ashore, that Eisenhower welcomed him to Allied headquarters. In a few hours, the two men presumably were to bring to fruition the hopes for Torch that Giraud's advent had aroused.

Eisenhower at once produced a message he had prepared in Giraud's name for presentation to the French in North Africa. If Murphy's predictions were accurate, it was going to persuade an army to lay down its arms. The message said, in Giraud's behalf, "I resume my place of combat among you." It justified the Allied action as the only way to save the colonies from the Axis. Eisenhower's plan was, after successful landings, to have Giraud flown to Algiers, where he would take charge of France's contribution to the war against Germany.[28]

Giraud, however, had other ideas. To the complete dismay of the British and American officers gathered around him, he refused flatly to lend his name to the Allied enterprise unless he became its commander. Eisenhower was shocked at the demand, Giraud equally shocked at the refusal. Deep in the bowels of Gibraltar, Giraud maintained not only that he had been promised the post but that his own honor and that of France required it. At the same time, he declared that once in charge he would redirect the expedition according to his own plans to a landing on the French Riviera. Eisenhower regarded Giraud's position as absurd. As afternoon wore on into evening, he became convinced that Giraud had decided not to commit his prestige while the fate of Torch was in doubt, which was when he was needed, but after it had succeeded, when he would no longer be running a risk. Whatever the reasons, Murphy's failure to have made his terms absolutely clear to Giraud was now exacting its price. Well after midnight, as the first waves of soldiers approached the beaches, the General went to bed. "Giraud," he said, bidding Eisenhower goodnight, "will be a spectator in this affair."[29]

On the day Giraud left France, Murphy sent another frantic message to Roosevelt on an unexpected and vitally important development. "Admiral Darlan arrived in Algiers in greatest secrecy today," he said. Murphy explained that Darlan's son had been taken ill in Algiers and that the Admiral had flown to the city on an unannounced visit. It was still, however, three days till Torch. "Darlan's presence here on D-Day," Murphy wrote, "might be embarrassing but it is believed he will depart before then."

Darlan, however, did not depart. His son had contracted infantile paralysis, and the Admiral decided to remain on. To this day, the evidence is inconclusive whether he was in Algiers by chance or because he expected to meet the Allies there. The Admiral unquestionably knew of Allied designs, but Juin's remarks to Murphy suggest that he believed the Americans would act only in response to a Nazi initiative. Darlan himself always insisted that his presence had been fortuitous. But whether or not it was part of a plan did not matter. When the landings began in the early hours of November 8th, Darlan was on the scene, ready to play his part.[30]

De Gaulle at the same time was in London. The invasion was well under way when Churchill told him the news. De Gaulle's reaction was surprisingly mild. He had obviously steeled himself for the announcement and had somehow determined that his interests would be best served by taking it calmly. To the delight of Churchill, de Gaulle stated: "Nothing matters more today than to put a stop to the fighting. For the rest, we'll see about that afterwards."

Over the B.B.C. that night, de Gaulle gave one of his most inspiring speeches in support of Torch. "French commanders, soldiers, sailors, airmen, officials, French colonists of North Africa: Rise up," he declared. "Help our allies. Join them without reserve. The France which is fighting implores you. Do not worry about names or formulas. Only one thing counts, the welfare of our country." De Gaulle's words disclosed a confidence that his day as the great pivot of the French Empire would be not long in coming.[31]

The response in Vichy to Torch was quite different. Roosevelt had for weeks worked on a message to flatter Pétain into submitting to the invasion. He did not expect the Marshal's blessings. He would have been satisfied had Pétain refrained from stirring up the defenders. The first draft of the President's message was addressed to "my dear old friend" and, among obsequious comments, credited Pétain with having "of necessity" concluded the armistice of 1940. When Churchill read what the President had written, he balked. "Will you allow me to say," he wrote, "that your proposed message to Pétain seems too kind? . . . Of course, it is absolutely right to send him a friendly message but will you consider toning it down a bit?" Roosevelt consented and cleansed the final draft to meet Churchill's objections. Its key line, as it was sent to the Marshal, declared: "In the light of all the evidence of our enemy's intentions and plans, I have . . . decided to dispatch to North Africa powerful American armed forces to cooperate with the governing agencies of Algeria, Tunisia and Morocco in repelling this latest act in the long litany of German and Italian international crime."[32]

When the American chargé in Vichy arrived with the note in the early morning of November 8th, he found that Pétain had already been delivered a copy from a wireless intercept. The Marshal had his answer ready:

It is with stupor and grief that I learned during the night of the aggression of your troops against North Africa.

I have read your message. You invoke pretexts which nothing justifies. You attribute to your enemies intentions which have never been manifested in acts. I have always declared that we would defend our empire if it were attacked. You knew that we would defend it against any aggressor whoever he might be. You knew that I would keep my word.

In our misfortune I had, when requesting the Armistice, protected our Empire and it is you who, acting in the name of a country to which so many memories and ties bind us, have taken such a cruel initiative.

France and her honor are at stake.
We are attacked.
We shall defend ourselves. This is the order I am giving.[33]

In the early morning hours of November 8th, radio waves throbbed across North Africa with exciting and startling messages. Transmitters aboard American warships anchored near shore alternated the "Marseillaise" and "The Star Spangled Banner" with statements from General Eisenhower and President Roosevelt. "*J'ai conservé toute ma vie*," declared the President in his best French, "*une amitié profonde pour le peuple francais.*" The American radio carried a plea for peace.

But near dawn, the Vichy radio broke in with a message of war. Over and over, Pétain's words were showered on the soldiers and sailors sheltered behind their coastal defenses. They were the same words dispatched to Roosevelt. "We are attacked. We shall defend ourselves. That is the order I am giving."

The invasion had achieved complete tactical surprise. The Germans and Italians were fooled. The French, alerted by the radio, were astonished to see in the early dawn that Allied vessels actually stood within range of their guns while American soldiers waded through the surf. The advancing troops held their fire, but the French did not hesitate. Even before they heard the Marshal's order, the defenders reacted with the vigor and brutality of warriors. At Casablanca, Oran and Algiers, Americans found that Roosevelt was wrong. French guns were blazing and those who had hoped to be acclaimed as liberators were falling dead in the sand.[34]

Faulty Premises, Grievous Consequences

November–December, 1942

"E XISTING FRENCH SENTIMENT here does not remotely agree with prior calculations," Eisenhower wired back to Washington.[1] The master plan had gone awry. Nothing on the battlefield corresponded to Roosevelt's convictions or Murphy's prophecies.

In Oran, the chief of the conspiracy lost his nerve under the pressure of last-minute preparations, too late to be replaced. The underground's elaborate scheme to neutralize resistance to the invasion collapsed. Ridgeway Knight, the American vice-consul in the city, radioed Gibraltar as the soldiers came ashore that the plot had been abandoned and that the landing would meet a hostile reception.[2]

In Casablanca, a pro-Allied coup was executed shortly after midnight, when the American attack was considered imminent. Its leader, General Emile Béthouart, a hero of the battle of Norway, seized control of the Army headquarters in the city, while in Rabat, the capital of Morocco, his collaborators surrounded the home of Noguès, the resident-general. Orders were issued to Army units not to fire on the invaders. An approach was made to the Navy, in an effort to silence the big guns in Casablanca harbor. But hours passed and no invaders appeared. As the defenders stood impatiently by, reports affirmed the presence of the Allies in Oran and Algiers. Since French resistance there was fierce, the Casablanca garrison could react no less vigorously. Noguès, uncertain until then of the course he should take, turned the tables on Béthouart, had him arrested and

115

ordered French troops to defend against the enemy. It was not until daylight that the Americans reached the shore. The French, alert and ready, welcomed them with gunfire.[3]

But it was in Algiers, capital of North Africa, that the unforeseen gave way to the bizarre. Algiers possessed the key to the success or failure of the entire operation. Here was the headquarters of General Juin, commander of all North Africa's land forces. It was here that Murphy himself was the mastermind, working closely with Giraud's personal representative, General Mast, who led the conspiracy. Algiers was the city that was to have been delivered without a shot. But it was here that bungling and indecision led to days of fighting and, ultimately, to the failure of Torch to achieve its objective.

Shortly after midnight on November 8th, Murphy appeared at Juin's suburban residence and solemnly announced that an invasion which had the sanction of General Henri Giraud was in progress. Juin, startled, shrugged off Giraud's participation but conceded at once that an American success was vital to the salvation of France. Had circumstances been different, Juin, tough and practical, would have tried to end the fighting then and there. But in Algiers at that moment was his commander in chief, Admiral Darlan, without whose approval he could make no such decision. It was to Darlan then that Murphy had to deliver his petition.

While Murphy was rousing Darlan from his bed, Mast's operatives took over the city. They cut telephone and radio communications and put top municipal officials into custody. Irregulars surrounded Juin's residence and gave notice to the General that he was under house arrest. Mast himself, commander of the Algiers Division, ordered his troops to accept the Americans as friends. But Mast's men could not hold the city long without assistance. They needed the American Army and General Giraud, their designated leader, to sustain them. For hours they stood guard, waiting anxiously for the consummation of their coup.

Darlan arrived at Juin's villa in a nasty temper. He was more intent on denouncing Murphy for excluding him from the operation than in settling the dilemma at hand. Juin implored Darlan to give the order to stop the bloodshed. The General had already gone to the limit of his own authority by directing his commanders in the Algiers region to withdraw before the invaders. But Darlan had no such capacity for decision. He insisted he had to look to Pétain for instructions. Murphy, uncertain himself how to handle this plea, consented to let Darlan dispatch a message to Vichy.

But while the American and the two Frenchmen argued, French Army units had moved out of their barracks and, with little difficulty, sent Mast's lightly armed conspirators scurrying. At headquarters, a higher officer relieved Mast of his command and revoked his orders. A detachment of troops drove the partisans away from Juin's villa. It was now Murphy who was under house arrest. Although the Americans had landed, they were floundering about in confusion on the outskirts of the city. The conspiracy had been thwarted. The next move was Darlan's.[4]

Had Darlan been in Vichy when the Allies landed, under the influence of Pétain, it is quite likely he would have ordered unlimited resistance and been obeyed. Juin would probably have been helpless to reverse him. But in Algiers, Darlan was exposed to pressure from the Allied side. He perceived at once a shift in weight on the scale of power from the Axis to the Allied camp. But even as an opportunist, Darlan was not decisive. It was his nature to vacillate. He had too long taken into account Germany's capacity for reprisal to overlook it now. If Darlan were to wind up on the Allied side, he could only make up his mind in agonizing fashion, after he was certain he had extracted the maximum possible concession from both belligerents.

The fighting persisted in and around Algiers for hours after the landing, but, thanks to Juin, casualties were light. By late afternoon, the American columns had surrounded the city and were on the point of penetrating its final defenses. Juin at last persuaded Darlan to authorize a cease-fire. In the early evening, he and the American commander, General Charles Ryder, reached an agreement under which the French would retain their arms and their colors and retire to their barracks. By nightfall, though the killing continued at Casablanca and Oran, the battle of Algiers was over.[5]

The following day, November 9th, was marred by death and wasted opportunity. Darlan could not bring himself to make an irrevocable commitment. While tolerating the Americans in Algiers, he sent orders to his commanders in Tunisia to cooperate with the Germans to keep the Americans out. He maintained radio contact with Pétain, who he claimed secretly approved of the Allied venture, while at the same time the Marshal publicly spurred French soldiers on to fiercer resistance. Murphy, inexplicably, made no effort to press Darlan into stopping the bloodshed. Late in the day, Clark landed in Algiers, but he too failed to challenge Darlan. Giraud, on the scene several hours later, made no impact whatever and, in contrast to the tumultuous reception predicted for him, had to go into hiding to avoid arrest. Marshal Pétain, not General Giraud, was the name to which North Africa responded. It was clear that only Darlan, who exercised Pétain's vicariate, could end the folly of Frenchmen and Americans serving Germany by killing one another.[6]

The next morning, November 10th, Clark at last came face to face with the Admiral in a small room in the Hotel St. Georges. A platoon of American infantry stood guard outside the door. Before a tense, perspiring crowd of officers and diplomats from the two countries, Clark vowed to force Darlan to order an armistice at once. Aware that Torch was at the edge of disaster, he had made up his mind that the time for discretion had passed. Towering over the tiny, quivering Admiral, Clark declared menacingly that the alternatives were action or prison. Darlan, with incredible impudence, replied that he must await the outcome of a meeting that night between Hitler and Laval, presumably so that Pétain could then choose the side that made the better offer. Clark flew into a rage, but it was Juin who broke the deadlock by calling Darlan aside to lecture him sternly on the senselessness of the savagery that continued at the two remaining beachheads. Darlan finally relented. But, characteristically, his decision carried him only halfway to a definitive commitment. Darlan consented to order the troops to lay down their arms, but he refused to let them join the Allies in the attack against the Germans. Despite Juin's plea that neutrality would get France only the worst from both sides, Darlan would not be moved.[7]

Shortly after the order was issued, Pétain declared from Vichy that he had removed the Admiral from office, revoked the cease-fire and named General Noguès as his commander in North Africa. The moment Clark heard the news, he raced back to Darlan's side. The Admiral, obviously confounded by the disavowal, told Clark that he must cancel the armistice. But when the American General informed him that such a move would land him in a prison cell, Darlan thought better of his proposal. That night, after three days of heavy fighting, the cease-fire went into effect. France's soldiers, many still tortured by uncertainty of conscience, obeyed Darlan, for he assured them that his instructions corresponded to the *real* desires of Marshal Pétain.[8]

Once the fighting stopped at Casablanca and Oran, Vichy ceased to serve any purpose for the Nazis. In the early morning of November 11th, German columns crossed the demarcation line and occupied the remainder of France. Only one French general, Jean de Lattre de Tassigny, raised a hand against them, and he was thrown into jail by his own government. Vichy still exercised nominal control over the fleet, bobbing at anchor at Toulon, but with the Germans free to take unlimited reprisals it seemed unlikely the admirals would try to go over to the Allies. The Pétain Government was now, in every sense, a German captive. Pétain himself, pathetically dressed in the uniform he wore at Verdun in 1916, received the Wehrmacht's representative with a feeble protest. But he had long before lost his spirit to resist and supinely consented to do the bidding of his captors.

Darlan seized on the German action with some relief. At midday on the eleventh, he announced that with Pétain's secret sanction, transmitted to him by naval code, he had taken it upon himself to exercise the powers of government in the Marshal's name. Pétain, he explained, was a prisoner of the Nazis and no longer free to act. On the basis of this reasoning, Darlan at last ended the equivocation and declared that France's enemy was Germany. The French Army in North Africa, he announced, would rejoin the war on the side of the Allies to fight for the liberation of France. Such, he declared, was the real desire of Pétain.

Unpersuaded about Pétain's endorsement, several generals refused to accept Darlan's command. For a few hours, the Nazis could with impunity have occupied all of eastern Algeria because the Marshal had publicly ordered the Army to cooperate with Germany. Only under severe pressure from Juin, the most clearheaded of the North African leaders, did these generals abandon their plan to welcome the Nazis and consent to direct French forces toward Tunisia.

In Tunisia itself, the outcome was less favorable. The Germans had begun flying troops into the Tunis-Bizerte area, the key strategic sector, almost immediately after the first Torch landings. In contrast to Roosevelt's prediction that they would need two weeks to mobilize, they had within a few days built up a substantial enough force to block any quick Allied stab at the major Tunisian ports. The

French could have prevented them. But a profusion of contradictory orders arrived from Vichy and Algiers. Juin, in Darlan's name, demanded resistance, while Pétain insisted on surrender. Each commander, bewildered spectator of a grim farce, had no alternative but to choose for himself whether he would obey a captive head of state or the commander in chief who claimed to speak for him. The governor-general, Admiral Jean-Pierre Estéva, and the naval commander, Admiral Louis Derrien, chose to follow Pétain. Only the Army chief, General Barré, Juin's friend, opted for Darlan, but he was too weak to challenge the Germans alone. Instead, he withdrew his 9,000-man force into the mountains west of Tunis, where he waited for the Allied columns to come to his support. On the plains, Frenchmen stood by as if paralyzed while the Germans assembled a powerful army in their midst.

Had Eisenhower chosen an audacious course, he would have dispatched commandos and parachute troops to Tunisia during the first few days. He would have beaten the Germans there and, in the opinion of some, rallied the French garrison. But the stubborn defense at Casablanca and Oran made him abandon just such a plan. He was unwilling to gamble on sustaining a force across the narrow desert and mountain roads that linked Algiers through unfriendly countryside with Tunis and Bizerte hundreds of miles away. The British general, Kenneth Anderson, on his own showed considerable daring by pushing off from Algiers before he was certain of stability in his rear. One column went overland, while separate contingents were sent by sea as far as Bougie and Bône. Anderson's forces probably prevented the Germans from driving into eastern Algeria. But they arrived too late and in too little strength to win a quick victory in Tunisia, where it counted most.

With French and Allied caissons rumbling side by side toward the front, Clark had successfully resolved the highest priority problem that faced the Allied command. Next in line was the question of how North Africa was to be governed. As a matter of principle, the United States had decided that the French colonies were not to be treated as conquered provinces but as friendly territories. Roosevelt had made an explicit promise to Giraud that the United States would not interfere in domestic affairs in North Africa. In practical terms, Eisenhower's command did not have the organization or the personnel to establish a military government. But as it was made

De Gaulle, seen here as colonel of a tank unit, was named commander of a hastily organized armored division during the Battle of France in May, 1940. His division, heavily outgunned by the German panzers, "temporarily checked the German spearhead, inflicted severe losses in men and equipment and barely missed driving the Nazis out of their beachhead on the southern bank of the (Somme) river. But his cause was hopeless. . . ."

De Gaulle, as an infantry captain, poses shortly after winning his first citation for bravery in 1915. In March, 1916, he was wounded for the second time in World War I and cited again. The citation signed by his commander, General Henri Philippe Pétain, said he "inspired his men to a furious assault and a savage hand-to-hand battle," before he was knocked unconscious and taken prisoner by the enemy.

De Gaulle and Madame de Gaulle relax in the garden of their country home near London in 1940. "Jealous of his privacy, de Gaulle hardly ever allowed his role as public figure to interfere with his role as husband and father. The style de Gaulle adopted as Free French leader was in distinct contrast to the unpretentious quality of his private life."

De Gaulle exchanges a salute with a member of the Free French forces as he leaves Carlton Gardens, his headquarters in London in 1940. Always austere, de Gaulle showed toward his followers, according to a loyal colleague, "something of the style one has for an old domestic whom one sometimes treats rudely but like a member of the family."

De Gaulle, standing in front of General Edgard de Larminat, reviews a parade at Brazzaville in the Congo, capital of Free French Africa. It was at Brazzaville in October, 1940, that de Gaulle issued the Manifesto in which he declared: "There exists no longer a truly French government. . . . It is necessary . . . for a new power to assume the burden of directing the French war effort. Events impose this sacred duty upon me. I shall not fail to discharge it. I will exercise my powers in the name of France. . . ."

Roosevelt greets Adrien Tixier, de Gaulle's representative in Washington, at a reception in his White House office in 1942. Tixier, who lost his left arm in World War I, suffered constantly from his wounds. "A tough and devoted Gaullist, Tixier was irascible, sarcastic and rude. Though he worked hard, he was no man for the tortuous processes of diplomacy. Tixier, by alienating the very Americans he needed to please, did not serve de Gaulle well."

(Harris & Ewing)

De Gaulle flying on an inspection tour of Free French Africa in 1942. The French National Committee sought American transports for these tours because "its own planes were old and unsafe and inadequate for flying the great distances between colonial cities. De Gaulle himself had nearly been killed in a crash of a Free French plane."

With Roosevelt looking on, de Gaulle and General Henri Giraud engage in the celebrated handshake that closed the Casablanca Conference on January 24, 1943. "Later, Roosevelt claimed he had tricked de Gaulle into this public handshake. De Gaulle's cool demeanor, which had not abandoned him before, seems to belie the claim. But, in creating the impression of an agreement between the two generals, Roosevelt played a cruel trick on Frenchmen everywhere and on the world." (*Wide World*)

De Gaulle chats with American ambassador John Winant in front of Buckingham Palace in London on United Nations Day, June 14, 1942. Because the Allies were then contemplating an invasion of France, where de Gaulle was known to have considerable following, "Washington at last moved to hedge its policy toward Vichy by granting certain concessions to please de Gaulle. . . . The American embassy in London initiated a series of friendly conversations. . . . The State Department, in truth, was quite unhappy about the deviation from its rigorous anti-Gaullist policy. Consent to the departure had been given, it was clear, to please the Army."

De Gaulle, with Giraud, reviews troops at the airport in Algiers on May 30, 1943. "... Giraud had forced him to land at an isolated airfield ..., where crowds were unlikely to gather. But a guard of honor saluted him ... and Giraud was there with Catroux to meet him." Characteristically, De Gaulle noted in his *Memoirs* "the contrast with his arrival in Casablanca four months before."

De Gaulle returns to the soil of Metropolitan France for the first time in nearly four years. On June 14, 1944, five days after D-Day, he went ashore with the men he had assigned to establish his rule. The tall officer with his back to the camera is François Coulet, de Gaulle's Regional Commissioner, who was to assure Gaullist authority in Normandy. General Bernard Montgomery, commander of the beachhead, "was delighted to have de Gaulle make a try at running the liberated territory. With official acquiescence, de Gaulle thus took the first step in his master plan to exercise dominion over France."

De Gaulle and General Alphonse Juin, his commander in Italy, meet with French officers near the front in the spring of 1944. "Juin's Expeditionary Corps in Italy, grown to nearly five divisions, in early May led the offensive to take Rome. The theater commander, General Harold Alexander, reported that French troops 'drove like the wind' and exploited their successes 'possibly quicker than United States or British troops.'"

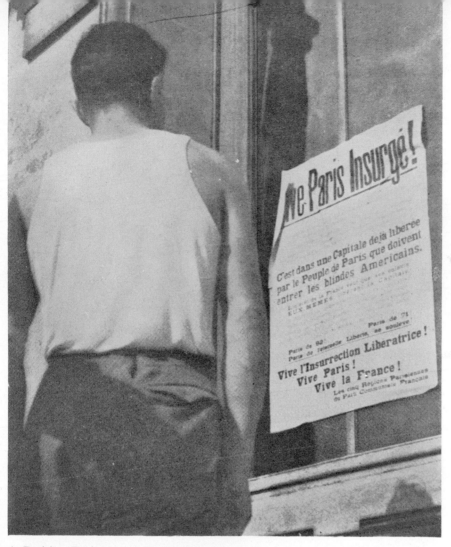

A Parisian Resistant reads a call to insurrection against the Germans posted by the Communist Party in mid-August, 1944. "It is a Capital already liberated by the People of Paris," says the notice, "that the American tanks must enter." De Gaulle opposed mass insurrection. "The cunning game he played with the Communists required him, on the one hand, to encourage popular activity against the Germans but, on the other, to avert the kind of general disorder which could destroy all authority and facilitate Communist seizure of control."

Opposite, top. De Gaulle greets the liberated population of Bayeux, Normandy, on June 14, 1944. "His return to his native soil evoked the deepest expressions of emotion wherever he went. Emerging from the ruins of their homes and public buildings, the traditionally lethargic Normans thronged excitedly around him. . . . Even the most skeptical observer did not doubt the sincerity of his welcome or its meaning as a popular endorsement."

Opposite, bottom. While Secretary of State Cordell Hull and Mrs. Anna Boettinger, the President's daughter, look on, Roosevelt welcomes de Gaulle to the White House for the first time on July 6, 1944. "After a round of introductions, Roosevelt led de Gaulle and his guests to the south veranda, where Mrs. Roosevelt served tea. The pleasant tone was a remarkable improvement over their previous encounter at Casablanca. . . . Hull, whose attitude had scarcely changed since St. Pierre and Miquelon, conceded that the general 'went out of his way to be agreeable.'"

De Gaulle and Eisenhower meet at SHAEF headquarters in August, 1944. "Eisenhower had delayed a decision on taking Paris. He had hoped he might by-pass it to avoid the burden its provisioning would put on his supply lines. Unsure of German intentions, he did not want to fight a battle inside the city. But de Gaulle was willing to risk warfare and even some damage. He pleaded with Eisenhower to send forces to take the capital at once."

De Gaulle reviews the terms of the German surrender of Paris with General Jacques Leclerc, the French commander whose division liberated the city on August 25, 1944. "De Gaulle, having spent the night in the Presidential chateau at Rambouillet, entered the jubilant city in mid-afternoon of the day of liberation. His objectives were clear. His program had been thought out with care. . . . De Gaulle went first to the Montparnasse Station, where he congratulated Leclerc on his victory, then reprimanded him for sharing the surrender with the Resistance chiefs. . . . De Gaulle's esteem for the Resistance was great. But it did not diminish his determination to acknowledge to no one a share in the prerogatives of the state."

De Gaulle leads a great parade of celebration from the Arc de Triomphe down the Champs Elysées on the day after the liberation of Paris, August 26, 1944. On his right is Georges Bidault, president of the National Resistance Council. On his left is Alexandre Parodi, who served as his delegate to the Council. Behind him, partially obscured, is General Pierre Koenig on his right. Leclerc and Juin are beside Koenig, to de Gaulle's left. "The parade was a tonic that Paris, enfeebled by four years of occupation, badly needed. It was an explosion of rejoicing and national fervor. It represented the redemption of de Gaulle. It was his moment of popular triumph."

French troops cross into Austria as conquerors during the final offensive action of the war. "The First French Army had penetrated to the Danube at Ulm and deep into the Austrian Tyrols. . . . When the Third Reich capitulated in a little red schoolhouse in Reims on May 7th, France was represented. . . . France, defeated and humbled in 1940, the only country that had surrendered to Hitler, had somehow emerged triumphant. . . . De Gaulle achieved that, almost alone. While the world sneered at a dishonored country, he asserted the premise that France was not beaten and brought it to reality."

Prior page, top. De Gaulle emerges from the Church of Notre Dame, where a special service was conducted after the liberation parade. Shots had rung out as he entered the Church. De Gaulle, however, "continued inside, ostensibly unperturbed. But . . . more shots sounded. In an exhibition of cool courage, de Gaulle paid no attention to them. He remained seated in his pew. . . . De Gaulle, in his memoirs, maintained that this was the final attempt by extremist leaders, presumably Communists, to trigger an insurrection. . . . De Gaulle determined to disband the partisan armies as fast as possible."

Prior page, bottom. Churchill and de Gaulle conduct one of their informal talks during the Prime Minister's visit to France on Armistice Day, November 11, 1944. "De Gaulle found that with Churchill, unlike Roosevelt, he could probe the most . . . sensitive areas of their relationship and could expect candid answers. . . . Churchill and de Gaulle, at their Armistice Day conference, established a united front against Roosevelt's postwar designs."

clear from the outset and became progressively more evident, Roosevelt did not mean precisely what he said in committing the United States to dealing with France as a liberated friend. He did not intend giving the French freedom to run their affairs as they chose. Rather, he intended having the French run their affairs in a manner he considered satisfactory. Roosevelt's conception of liberation included American supervision of French administration. For the moment, this conception engendered no conflict with the French. Darlan and the men around him were too bewildered by the dazzling events of the previous days to raise serious objections.

Clark convoked the French leadership on the afternoon of November 12th to negotiate an agreement on civil administration. He was quite willing to have the French themselves determine the nature and membership of their governing organization. His only condition was that they had to include Giraud, which showed astonishing loyalty in view of Giraud's failure during the period of the landings. But Noguès, who claimed Pétain's mantle on the basis of the decree issued two days before at Vichy, sneered at Giraud as a rebel and a traitor. It was for Juin to remind his colleagues that failure to settle their differences in the Allies' favor would mean American military government and the end of French sovereignty in the colonies. This was the argument that persuaded Noguès to relinquish his mandate to Darlan and the entire assemblage to accept Giraud into the inner circle.

The next day, Admiral Darlan took on the title of High Commissioner and assumed the civil powers in North Africa. Giraud was named commander in chief of French forces, with Juin his deputy in charge of ground troops. In what had already become a ritual, it was announced that a secret telegram had been received from Pétain. The Marshal, it was declared, had ratified the Darlan appointment and absolved all officers of their personal oath of fidelity to him.

Clark and Darlan then proceeded to draw up an agreement setting out the relationship between the Allied forces and the French administration. It was, by any standards, a conqueror's bargain. The United States made no concessions to French sovereignty. Darlan, though acknowledged as High Commissioner, was denied the status of political recognition. The United States promised "to liberate France and to restore integrally the French Empire," but Eisenhower subsequently interpreted these as "purposes commonly agreed upon" rather than national commitments. Juridically, the Clark-Darlan Agreement was nothing more than a military pact, made for the convenience of the field commander. Though it left the French few independent prerogatives, it confirmed as chief officeholder Admiral Jean François Darlan, *capitulard*, collaborationist and former would-be member of the Nazi New Order.[9]

After confirming the arrangement, Eisenhower wired to the President:

Completely understand the bewilderment in London and Washington, because of the turn that negotiations with French North Africans have taken. . . . The name of Marshal Pétain is something to conjure with here. Everyone attempts to create the impression that he lives and acts under the shadow of the Marshal's figure. Civil governors, military leaders and naval commanders agree that only one man has an obvious right to assume the Marshal's mantle in North Africa. He is Darlan. Even Giraud, who has been our trusted adviser and staunch friend since early conferences succeeded in bringing him down to earth, recognizes this overriding consideration and has modified his own intentions accordingly. . . . It is important that no precipitate action at home upset the equilibrium we have been able to maintain.[10]

But at home there was clamor for precipitate action as soon as it was learned that Darlan had emerged as top man in Algiers. Those who believed that the North African prize should go to Germany's foes were staggered to see it won by one of Nazism's staunchest friends. Roosevelt's liberal backers vociferously decried what was quickly designated the "Darlan deal." The Government might have attracted less abuse had not Hull chosen to gloat over the outcome of Torch as vindication of his Vichy diplomacy. "The French people," he declared, "will continue, I am sure, to be grateful to us for our policies." But the uproar stirred by American support of the Darlan deal made Saint-Pierre and Miquelon look like a quiet affair, indeed.[11]

General Marshall was so concerned lest the tempest upset the uneasy stability in North Africa that he took the unprecedented step of imploring editors and broadcasters to refrain from criticism. "In any discussion of the current political situation in North Africa," he said in a confidential message to the press, "the War Department requests that it be borne in mind that the prime consideration of General Eisenhower at the moment is the immediate defeat of the Axis forces now in that area, at the minimum cost of American lives. . . . Conclusions as to the advisability of political adjustments might well be deferred until this has been completed." The denunciation of the North African action voiced by Jean Baubé, de Gaulle's press representative in Washington, was, as a result, suppressed by more than one American newspaper.[12]

De Gaulle, exhilarated during the opening hours of Torch, turned progressively more wrathful as events unfolded. He at first planned to send a mission to Algiers for the purpose, he told Churchill, of "mutual exchange of views and information." But his objective clearly was to win control for himself in the confusion. "The Americans," he wrote on November 10th, "have taken Giraud over with the idea that the announcement of his name would make the walls of Jericho fall down. . . . His agreement to accept powers from the Americans . . . is inadmissible for Frenchmen, whether Vichyite or Gaullist." A day later, angry at the intrigue in Algiers but still optimistic, he wrote, "It's not very pretty. I think that before long the retching will take place and we will emerge as the only capable and worthy organization." But when it became clear that the Vichy regime, reincarnated in Darlan, had been solidly established, de Gaulle took a different view. Cancelling his proposed mission to North Africa, he determined to have nothing whatever to do with those he regarded as his own enemies and the enemies of France.

A week after Torch, de Gaulle called on Stark and presented him with a one-sentence note. "The United States," he said, "can pay traitors but not with the honor of France." Stark was so angry at the words that he refused to accept the letter. De Gaulle, after some reflection, consented to withdraw it. But a few days later, an almost identical version appeared mysteriously in the newspapers, leaving no doubt in the public mind about the Fighting French opinion of America's leadership in North Africa.[13]

De Gaulle showed no mercy in interpreting the American action. He questioned its military premises. He was contemptuous of its political short-sightedness. He feared for its impact on the France of the future. Most significantly, he impugned its motives as part of a design for American hegemony in the postwar world. In a letter to Tixier, his Washington representative, he lamented:

Darlan . . . can return to France at the moment of victory with, practically speaking, the only French army in existence and perpetuate the Vichy regime. *"Maréchal, nous voilà."* Pétain thus has, with Laval on the one hand and Darlan on the other, a foot in each camp.

I fear that this arrangement is not completely disagreeable to certain parties in the United States which are playing for a new Europe to oppose the Soviet Union and even England. These arrangements might for the time being appear profitable to the Americans. But they will end by the democracies, in the moral sense, losing the war. I do not share President Roosevelt's opinion when he explains that it is a question of avoiding bloodshed and implies thereby that anything goes.

As for myself, I will not lend myself, either directly or indirectly, to this sickening saga. What remains of the honor of France will stay intact in my hands.[14]

But de Gaulle, in his understandable bitterness, did Roosevelt an injustice in suggesting that he was insensitive to the immorality of the Darlan deal. The President was not happy with the arrangement, even if he sanctioned it on military grounds. On November 16th, Roosevelt notified Eisenhower that the policy of the United States Government was:

1. That we do not trust Darlan. 2. That it is impossible to keep a collaborator of Hitler and one whom we believe to be a fascist in civil power any longer than is absolutely necessary. 3. His movements should be watched carefully and his communications supervised.[15]

Roosevelt's pragmatism in using Darlan was characteristic of him. What was unusual was his defensiveness in bringing it to the public. For years, he had suffered in silence over his Vichy policy, reasoning that a public explanation might destroy it. But he obviously was so sensitive about the Darlan deal that he could not resist fighting back. Admiral Leahy and the State Department objected that an apology would jeopardize the advantages the United States gained from the arrangement. Nonetheless, Roosevelt on November 16th released a statement to the press:

I have accepted General Eisenhower's political arrangements made for the time being in Northern and Western Africa. I thoroughly understand and approve the feelings in the United States and Great Britain and among all the other United Nations that in view of the history of the past two years no permanent arrangement should be made with Admiral Darlan. People in the United States likewise would never understand the recognition of a reconstituting of the Vichy government in France or in any French territory. We are opposed to Frenchmen who support Hitler and the Axis. No one in our Army has any authority to discuss the future government of France or the French Empire. The future French Government will be established, not by any individual in Metropolitan France or overseas, but by the French people themselves after they have been set free by the victory of the United Nations. The present temporary arrangement in North and West Africa is only a temporary expedient, justified solely by the stress of battle.[16]

From the beginning, Roosevelt was dissatisfied with Darlan's way of running North Africa. Having borne more than two years of reproach for his Vichy policy, the President wanted now to make a clean break with the past. Roosevelt felt responsible for bringing liberal rule to lands he considered under his aegis, both for its own sake and to disarm his critics at home. He was disturbed that, under Darlan, the atmosphere and the laws of Vichy were perpetuated in Algiers.

Eisenhower did not quarrel with Roosevelt's objectives but, having a war to fight, chose not to challenge Darlan's claim that disruption of the *status quo* created the risk of disorder. Murphy, whom Roosevelt had elevated in rank despite the fiasco he made of his responsibilities in Torch, continued to identify himself with the Vichyites and was indifferent to reform. Eisenhower's generals— Patton in Morocco and Fredendall in Oran—had become so friendly with the local French leadership that they opposed any change. The consequence was that anti-Semitic measures enacted under the Nazi influence remained in force. Civil liberties were restricted. Most irritating, soldiers and civilians who had assisted the Allies during Torch still suffered discrimination. Many, like Béthouart, continued to languish in jails, though Darlan himself, as soon as he had been sure of succeeding, did precisely what they had done. On November 24th, Eisenhower tried to reassure Washington by reporting that "Darlan has stated to me that he will conduct the affairs of North Africa on a liberal and enlightened basis." But well into December, Roosevelt could not detect signs of any substantial change.[17]

The President was also alarmed by Darlan's energy in seeking to extend and preserve his rule. He vetoed Darlan's proposal to designate himself the repository of French sovereignty "in the absence of the head of state who is a prisoner." He refused to authorize Darlan to notify French representatives abroad that he had assumed responsibility for the Empire in Pétain's name. Leahy, among others, objected vigorously to the President's restrictions, on the grounds that alienation of the Admiral might cost American lives. Roosevelt answered Leahy by saying: "I am a pig-headed Dutchman, Bill, and I have made up my mind about this. We are going ahead with it and you can't change my mind."[18]

Darlan was uneasy at not having Roosevelt's confidence. He was deeply hurt by the "temporary expedient" statement, which had unquestionably undermined his authority. Though he was often denounced at Vichy, he had felt in command under Pétain. Under Roosevelt, he and those around him knew his regime was insecure.

Late in November, Darlan sent a rather pathetic letter to Eisenhower, defending his behavior. "Information coming from various sources," he wrote, "tends to substantiate the view that I am only a lemon which the Americans will drop after they have squeezed it dry." He claimed that he had conducted himself since Torch out of pure patriotism alone. "I did not act through pride, ambition or calculation but because the position which I occupied in my country made it my duty to act. When the integrity of France's sovereignty is an accomplished fact—and I hope it will be in the least possible time—it is my firm intention to return to private life and to end my days, in the course of which I have ardently served my country, in retirement." He sent a similar letter to Churchill, which defended in greater detail his actions beginning with the armistice of 1940. But he failed to evoke a sympathetic response from any quarter.[19]

Had Darlan succeeded in rallying the fleet, the Allies might have looked on him differently. He tried, but his admirals scorned his appeals. The finale was appropriately ignominious. After the Germans crossed into the unoccupied zone, the fleet remained at its moorings, its officers paralyzed by an inability to distinguish between the virtues of discipline and patriotism. Before dawn on November 25th, German soldiers raced to the water's edge at Toulon. They were in time only to be witness to the suicide. In all, 177 ships were scuttled, including three battleships, seven cruisers, thirty destroyers and sixteen submarines. Vichy at last retired from the stage of history. The long courtship was over, with both suitors rebuffed. The order of Darlan, Admiral of the fleet, who long before had told his men to sink their ships rather than give them up, was obeyed. The order of Darlan, High Commissioner in North Africa, who called his men back to war, was ignored. The dead hand of Vichy had won over the beckoning hand of Algiers.[20]

Darlan did score a victory when French West Africa rallied to the Allies at the end of November, but Roosevelt chose to give the credit to Boisson, the fanatical old soldier who had driven the British and Free French away from Dakar in 1940. Boisson added an army of 50,000 men to the fight against the Axis. With the casuistry that had become standard for reformed Vichyites, he proclaimed that he was "certain that in [joining Darlan] we were remaining true to the oath which we have given to the Marshal. . . . Long live the Marshal!" Eisenhower was relieved not to have to divert resources to take Dakar. Roosevelt reveled in the decision, for to him Dakar, "on the brink of the Western Hemisphere," was the symbol of the danger the war meant to the United States.[21]

To Churchill, the fiction of Pétain's authority which mesmerized the North African administration was a source of political trouble. Though Churchill defended the wisdom of the United States in dealing with "that rogue Darlan," he had to contend with public opinion at home. In a speech to the House of Commons, he tried jest to turn away the wrath generated by the transfer of the Vichy estate to Algiers.

It is in accordance with orders and authority transmitted or declared to be transmitted by Marshal Pétain [he said] that the French troops in Northwest Africa have pointed and fired their rifles against the Germans and Italians instead of continuing to point and fire their rifles against the British and Americans. . . . All this is done in the sacred name of the Marshal, and when the Marshal bleats over the telephone orders to the contrary and deprives Darlan of his nationality the Admiral rests comfortably upon the fact or fiction—it does not much matter which—that the Marshal is acting under the duress of the invading Hun and that he, Darlan, is still carrying out his true wishes. In fact, if Admiral Darlan had to shoot Marshal Pétain, he would no doubt do it in Marshal Pétain's name.[22]

Eisenhower's dissatisfaction with Darlan was based on the continuing political and administrative disarray in Algiers. In his memoirs, he affirmed that Darlan always kept his promises to the Allies. But, Eisenhower complained, "the tangled political situation kept worrying us; it was difficult to pierce the web of intrigue, misinformation, misunderstanding and burning prejudice that surrounded even the minor elements of the whole problem. . . . Politics, economy, fighting—all were inextricably mixed up and confused with the other. . . His mannerisms and personality did not inspire confidence and in view of his reputation we were always uneasy in dealing with him."[23]

Unfortunately, Eisenhower was not satisfied with Giraud, either, though he recognized and admired his fighting spirit. The American found Giraud seriously lacking in organizational and administrative ability. As early as November 20th, Eisenhower cabled Washington that the French Army was making "a real contribution," and, as the weeks passed, his esteem for its combative qualities grew. But Giraud became an obstacle to coordinated action by his haughty refusal to accept orders from a British general, which was aggravated by his persistence in requesting appointment to the supreme command himself. Eisenhower was further irritated by Giraud's relentless demands for equipment, which were untempered by any sympathy for the Allies' enormous supply problems. Giraud was a fighter. He wanted the French in battle. But his indifference to the problems that the commander of a large modern army must face became an American burden.[24]

Exasperated that he had to spend more time in Algiers than on the battlefield, Eisenhower found himself desperately anxious for relief. The President personally favored increasing Murphy's control by such devices as the right of veto or the power to make specific demands on the French administration. Murphy, though not averse to more personal authority, adopted Darlan's suggestion to bring Marcel Peyrouton, a former member of the Pétain Cabinet to Algiers, to profit from his long experience as a colonial administrator. Peyrouton was in Buenos Aires, where he had settled down after quitting as Pétain's Ambassador to Argentina. Even Hull, who was notably indifferent to purging Vichyites, had the good sense to warn Murphy that the recommendation had dangerous political connotations. But Hull consented when Murphy pleaded military need. Eisenhower was far too preoccupied with the sputtering Allied offensive in Tunisia to question Murphy's judgment. His objective was, whenever possible, to let Algiers take care of itself.[25]

Eisenhower's irritation with the French leadership in North Africa provided the opening wedge for Roosevelt's temporary rehabilitation of de Gaulle. "In regard to de Gaulle," Roosevelt had told Churchill shortly after Torch, "I have hitherto enjoyed a quiet satisfaction in leaving him in your hands. Apparently I have now acquired a similar problem in brother Giraud. . . . We must remember that there is also a cat-fight in progress between Giraud and Darlan. . . . The principal thought to be driven home to all three of these prima donnas is that the situation is today solely in the military field."[26] His concern for military affairs finally led Roosevelt to reconsider de Gaulle. It was ironic that the Fighting French leader was to gain status in Washington because of Roosevelt's distaste for the alternatives he had himself created.

A few weeks after Torch, Marshall circulated a letter advising an immediate change in policy toward Fighting French representatives in Washington. "In the past," he said, "we have always been fearful of their looseness of talk, in addition to the diplomatic involvements. It seems to me that we should now change our tune, our courtesies and so forth." Assistant Secretary of War John J. McCloy pointed out that "they represent a strong body of French opinion and resistance which we may need some day as much as we need Darlan's assistance today." Even Leahy, who had always denounced the Gaullists, told the President that "we should not be placed in the position of abandoning the Fighting French. Final arrangements with Darlan should, therefore, include collaboration with them in some manner."

Roosevelt, for the moment at least, was willing to go along with a policy of keeping all French channels open, so that at the appropriate time he could choose the one that suited him best.[27]

On November 20th, Roosevelt received André Philip, a special emissary from de Gaulle, and Tixier, the Fighting French representative in Washington. Philip and Tixier had been making the rounds at the State Department to press the demand that a unified French authority be created to exercise sovereignty over the Empire pending the liberation of France. They found no satisfaction anywhere, for their objective was the antithesis of Roosevelt's. Their meeting with the President changed nothing in his attitude. Roosevelt was irritated, because at no time during the fifty minutes of their talk did the Frenchmen express any appreciation of the American action in North Africa. On the contrary, Philip and Tixier bitterly protested when the President, according to Welles's account, said that "so long as the United States was the occupying power in North Africa, the final decision would be reached solely by the occupying power." Unlike the Frenchmen, Roosevelt saw no contradiction in his contention that the United States had *liberated* North Africa and, at the same time, *ruled* it. Philip's indignation broke to the surface when Roosevelt told him that until all of France was freed, "the sole decision as to what, if any, Frenchmen would administer the liberated territory was a matter solely for this government to determine." Philip responded irascibly that Fighting France would never permit any liberated French town, village or farmhouse to be administered by foreign powers. Convinced by now that Roosevelt intended to support the Vichy administration, he declared menacingly: "We are not a colony. The American army will never make us accept the authority of traitors." The meeting demonstrated that de Gaulle would not forego what he regarded as essential and what the United States Government considered unacceptable.

The meeting, however, had one positive result. Roosevelt said that he wanted de Gaulle to come to the United States so that the two of them could sit down to iron out their differences. It is not clear who first proposed the visit. Roosevelt apparently confirmed what Philip and Tixier had discussed earlier at the State Department. The issue was important, for later there was a clash on whether the visit that finally took place was by Roosevelt's invitation or de Gaulle's request. Whatever the case, two days after the encounter, Welles notified the French delegation that the General would be welcome at the White House any time before December 15th or after January 8, 1943. From the President's remarks, it is plain he looked forward to exercising his charm on de Gaulle, whom he was sure he could persuade to his point of view.[28]

The mess in Algiers had put Eisenhower on de Gaulle's side. His own aim, Eisenhower wrote, "was to promote an eventual union between the local French administration and the de Gaulle forces in London." He called it "a difficult but necessary development." Eisenhower even forbade Darlan's propagandists to berate de Gaulle, in the hope of encouraging union, although the Fighting French observed no such limitation. Eisenhower was convinced that de Gaulle's presence in Algiers would go far toward solving his problems.

In mid-December, Eisenhower consented to let de Gaulle send a special mission to Algiers, despite the warning from Roosevelt and Leahy that its aim would be to stir up trouble for Darlan. In Eisenhower's view, de Gaulle was simply resurrecting the proposal for a fact-finding mission he had made shortly after Torch, before Darlan took over. It suggested to him that de Gaulle was once again willing to consider unity. On December 20th, General François d'Astier de la Vigerie, brother of the resistance leader who had toured the United States earlier in the year, arrived in Algiers. In seeking an opening to achieve French unity, his objective corresponded with Eisenhower's. But more precisely, his quest was for a means for de Gaulle to wrest the leadership of the principal French war effort from Darlan's hands. Roosevelt and Leahy were right in contending that his real goal was to make trouble.

Darlan would have arrested d'Astier on his arrival had not Eisenhower intervened. The two Frenchmen met face to face only because of Eisenhower's insistence and merely exchanged recriminations before separating. Of his meeting with Giraud, d'Astier reported better results, for Giraud did not share Darlan's fundamental antipathy to de Gaulle. D'Astier spent most of his time, however, assessing the strength of de Gaulle's following in North Africa and in seeking to spur its growth. After four days, even Eisenhower agreed that d'Astier's presence was provocative. When Darlan ordered him to leave, Eisenhower raised no objection. D'Astier took off for London early on December 24th.[29]

A few hours later, as Darlan entered his office in the Palais d'Eté, he was shot dead. A young man named Fernand Bonnier de la Chapelle fired two shots at point-blank range, which killed the Admiral almost at once. Clark clamped down rigid censorship over the city the moment he learned of the assassination. In case the act was part of some grand plan, he alerted Allied troops. But, though it was later rumored that Murphy and others were the targets of an assassins' ring, nothing more happened to upset the quiet of Christmas Eve.

Bonnier de la Chapelle, who was twenty years old, was among those who had participated in the abortive coup in Algiers on the night the Americans landed. Like others, he had become disgusted with a liberation that had promised to banish fascism but had instead consolidated it. If he was part of a larger conspiracy, no one has ever learned with whom he plotted and to what end. Pétain's agents accused the British. The British accused the Axis. Giraud suggested it might have been the Gaullists, and, indeed, d'Astier's activities threw considerable suspicion in that direction. De Gaulle, in his *Memoirs*, hints that Giraud was somehow involved, particularly since accounts of the military trial were suppressed. Bonnier's associates were known to be monarchists, but though the Count of Paris was among those openly aspiring to Darlan's power no proof was ever discovered to implicate him. Bonnier himself at first spoke confidently of important friends who would come forth to save him. None did. He was tried on Christmas Day and in the name of the Marshal executed the next morning.

Darlan's funeral was attended by appropriate French and American dignitaries. In both Washington and Algiers, kindly if modest eulogies were spoken about him. But, in reality, Darlan went virtually unmourned. By the time of his death, he had outlived his usefulness, both to the United States and to France. He knew it himself and so did all of Algiers. In Churchill's words, "he went forward through two years of worrying and ignominious office to a violent death, a dishonored grave and a name long to be execrated by the French Navy and the nation he had hitherto served so well."[30] Though the public posture of the Allied leadership was shock, the assassination was in reality a stroke of good luck. Few spoke as candidly about it as Clark in his memoirs:

Admiral Darlan's death was, to me, an act of Providence. It is too bad that he went that way, but, strategically speaking, his removal from the scene was like the lancing of a troublesome boil. He had served his purpose, and his death solved what could have been the very difficult problem of what to do with him in the future.[31]

On the day Darlan died, Eisenhower, slogging through the mud on the Tunisian front, made the decision to abandon the Allied army's offensive operations until spring. The Germans, profiting from the terrain and their greater experience, had succeeded in blocking the route to Tunis and Bizerte. The Allied attempt to win North Africa quickly had failed. Thanks to Darlan, the Allies, with the French at their side, were fighting Germans in the Tunisian hills when they might, with the French against them, still have been fighting in the Algerian desert. Darlan had saved the Allies from disaster. But his three days of vacillation had kept them from victory. Torch had relieved pressure on the Russians in some small measure. But much more significantly, it had given Germany another whole year to pursue conquest in the East. As long as the Nazis held off the Allies in peripheral theaters, Russia had to wait for a second front. With the Allies fighting in Africa throughout much of 1943, they could not get to central Europe before the spring of 1944. The crucial days lost during Torch cost the Allies an entire year in their quest for the decisive battle that would bring Nazism to defeat.[32]

Eisenhower turned his jeep around on Christmas Eve and, through the rain and sleet, took the long road back to Algiers. With Darlan dead, everything had changed. Giraud, along with the men of Vichy who had surrounded the Admiral, waited anxiously to learn what orders he would give. In London, de Gaulle waited too, his trip to Washington having been abruptly cancelled because, the President said, "of the unsettled situation in North Africa." For all those who detested Vichy and the principles for which it stood, Darlan's death ended a chapter of history. It now seemed like the time for a fresh start.[33]

SEVEN

The President Picks His Frenchman

January, 1943

Eisenhower arrived back in Algiers on Christmas Day, 1942, after thirty hours of relentless driving. He faced a dangerous hiatus of power created by the death of Darlan. The French, leaderless, looked to him for guidance. He knew he could not be indifferent to the succession. Nonetheless, he wrote in his memoirs, "My headquarters was still in no position to sponsor a puppet government. Such a resort to Nazi methods would have been a . . . serious violation of the principles for which we were fighting." Even more important, he was acutely aware how useful the French had become as allies and considered it imperative that they not be alienated by the imposition of American rule. Waiting on his desk when he entered his office, however, was a telegram from Marshall. "President desires," it said, "that no announcement be made reference Darlan's successor without reference here." The message clearly meant that Roosevelt expected to have the final say, regardless of the desires of Eisenhower or the French.[1]

Either Béthouart or Mast would have been an ideal choice. Both were capable and loyal. But among the French, they continued to be treated as outcasts as a consequence of their actions on November 8th. Eisenhower had insisted on their return to appropriate duty and the restoration of their rank. But neither could exercise effective command because of the intense disapproval felt for them by their fellow officers.

Giraud was next in line. Eisenhower had serious reservations about his leadership capacity. He obviously lacked not only ability but also taste for coping with the problems of government. But Americans could trust him more than the others and he was, after all, a fighter. If he was indifferent to the uses of political power, so much the better, since Roosevelt preferred it that way. He was not a man who would challenge the President's plans for determining the future of France.

The Imperial Council, a body created by Darlan and composed of the men who accepted his direction, met in Algiers on December 27th. Its dominant member was Noguès, the devious Resident-General of Morocco, who was, through the Vichy hierarchy, the logical successor to the Admiral. In French eyes, Noguès had the advantage of being able to preserve the fiction of a legitimacy that descended from Pétain. Giraud himself acknowledged the preeminence of this claim. He also recognized that Noguès, philosophical heir to Darlan, would not upset the Vichyite orientation of the Algiers administration. But Noguès, whom Eisenhower detested, understood that he was unacceptable to the United States and prudently withdrew from competition. After hours of debate, Darlan's entourage produced what was expected of them. To Giraud, the rebel, the Imperial Council passed the mantle of leadership. On him was bestowed the exalted title Military and Civil Commander in Chief. The principal departure from the reign of Darlan was that he did not receive his mandate "in the name of the Marshal." The French thus discreetly bowed to the United States in selecting Giraud and in foregoing the fictitious authority of Pétain. But by resorting to the authority of the Imperial Council, they succeeded in retaining the appearance of legality that they considered indispensable.[2]

Giraud proved to be not quite as pliant as the Americans had hoped. Even if he was himself unconcerned about matters of sovereignty, he was under the influence of Lemaigre-Dubreuil, who, since the eve of Torch, had burned with resentment at the American indifference to what he regarded as French prerogatives. Eisenhower notes in his memoirs, with some displeasure, that Giraud's first request after promotion to his new post was that the United States "cease treating North Africa as a conquered territory and treat it more as an ally, which it was trying to become." Lemaigre-Dubreuil himself flew to Washington at the end of December to argue for authorization to establish a provisional government to manage French resistance efforts. He contended that further recognition would strengthen Giraud's hand in future negotiations with the Gaullists. His arguments proved fruitless. His persistence, however, demonstrated that the Algerians, apart from the desires of Giraud himself, did not regard the matter as settled.[3]

Roosevelt considered the position he took on French sovereignty both logical and fair. He denied that he was usurping the sovereignty of the French people, as de Gaulle and now Giraud maintained. He insisted, in fact, that he was its principal guardian. Any recognition of a provisional government, he believed, would prejudice the rights of the French people to select a government freely after the war. "The United States government," he wrote to Eisenhower, "has no intention of disregarding the sovereignty of the French people by attempting to predetermine the choice they will eventually have to make in the selection of a leader." Shortly afterward, he prepared a memorandum which stated that "the Government of the United States will not accord recognition to any provisional government of France, no matter how constituted and no matter where constituted, until the French people have themselves been afforded the opportunity freely to select such a government." He adopted the argument that French sovereignty was for the time being in suspense. Until it could be restored to the French people, he regarded it as his responsibility to make decisions on France's behalf.

Roosevelt, near the end of 1942, also became more forthright in avowing that the United States regarded North Africa as being under military occupation. He was so irritated by Lemaigre-Dubreuil and Giraud, as well as by de Gaulle's propaganda from London, that he notified Churchill that "in the final analysis" the French had to do what Eisenhower demanded of them. His note, which Churchill forwarded to Algiers, declared menacingly that if Eisenhower was unable to handle Giraud, "I will soon find out about it." Roosevelt, though there remained some equivocation in his own mind, had come up strongly for the view that North Africa had been conquered, not liberated.[4]

Eisenhower became alarmed when he received the President's note from Churchill. Gingerly, he expressed his anxiety to Marshall:

We have learned that in some quarters at home there is an apparent conviction that we are in North Africa as an occupying, powerful, conquering army fully capable of carrying out our military missions and, if need be, of controlling the population by force. As a result of this conviction it appears to be assumed that we are in a position to deal with the French on the basis of giving orders and compelling compliance. I am writing . . . with the request that when opportunity arises you do what you can to correct or soften this view, at least to the extent that during ensuing critical weeks we do not receive any arbitrary instructions which might precipitate a military crisis. I know that you . . . are aware of the extent to which we are dependent upon active cooperation of the French. . . . The immediate effect of non-cooperation now would be catastrophic. . . . This matter is purely military.[5]

Churchill was not happy either with the way Roosevelt was handling matters in North Africa. Just a few days after Torch, he had warned Roosevelt that "you and I ought to avoid at all costs the creation of rival French émigré governments, each favored by one of us." To him, Darlan's death had been the providential opportunity to solve the problem of French factionalism once and for all. He was angry when the Americans settled on Giraud without consulting him, although he ratified the decision when faced with the *fait accompli*. He let Roosevelt know that he considered Giraud's selection a missed opportunity to create "some French nucleus, solid and united, to work with." But it was precisely because Roosevelt was uninterested in any "French nucleus" that the two rival émigré governments had come into being.[6]

De Gaulle made an attempt to establish relations with Giraud as soon as he received the news of Darlan's death. He proposed an immediate meeting, either in Algeria or Gaullist Chad, to establish a "provisional central authority." Giraud, now bearer of the title of Military and Civil Commander in Chief, had little need of de Gaulle, however, and was cool to the proposal. He authorized the Fighting French leader to send an emissary to negotiate collaboration between the two rival French armies—his own and de Gaulle's—but he said the atmosphere in Algiers was "for the moment, unfavorable to a personal conversation between us." When de Gaulle pressed him, Giraud said that "prior engagements" occupied his time until the end of January. De Gaulle was infuriated and sent back a stinging letter charging that Giraud's inaction was "a disappointment to the French people and harmful to our country." The same week, he issued a fiery public statement intended to put pressure on Giraud. The Military and Civil Commander in Chief, however, remained unmoved.[7]

De Gaulle's campaign against Giraud succeeded only in further alienating the United States and stirring up trouble for the British. Undersecretary Welles summoned Tixier to say that the American Government disapproved of de Gaulle's political pressure. Hull called in the British Minister to chide him on London's failure to restrain de Gaulle. "I insist," Hull said, "that where there is a plain and palpable interference with the prosecution of the North African campaign by pure brazen politics it is high time, in my opinion, that this should receive the serious attention of the British government." Neither Churchill nor de Gaulle, however, agreed that the effort to achieve unification interfered with Eisenhower's military operations. Both, in fact, argued that French unification had sound military, as well as political, justification. The British persisted in submitting new ideas to the State Department for a de Gaulle-Giraud settlement, which merely aggravated the friction. At last it became obvious even to Roosevelt that Churchill was quite serious. The Prime Minister seemed quite willing to risk discord with the United States to reach a satisfactory solution to the French problem.[8]

To resolve the irritant, Roosevelt first decided to renew the plan to have de Gaulle come to the United States. On January 11th, he instructed Welles to tell Tixier that the President would like to see de Gaulle in Washington at the end of the month.[9] But a few days later, Roosevelt left for a meeting with Churchill at Casablanca. He had invited Giraud, on the grounds that discussion with the French commander would fit within the military framework he had pre-scribed for the meeting, but he told Churchill he did not want de Gaulle present. When he reached Casablanca on January 14th, how-ever, the President changed his mind and accepted Churchill's con-tention that the circumstances were propitious for settling the matter then and there.

Roosevelt arrived at Casablanca in a buoyant mood. He and the Prime Minister, surrounded by dozens of aides, were quartered sumptuously behind barbed wire in the elegant villas and hotels of Anfa, Casablanca's finest suburb. Ringing the principals at all times were countless security agents, who created, for the casual members of the party, the atmosphere of a plush prison. But within the com-pound, Roosevelt, basking in the hot African sun, established a vaca-tion-like atmosphere. He seemed determined to enjoy the respite from his Washington cares. He was not well disposed to having anyone disturb his pleasures.[10]

Churchill first tried to summon de Gaulle on January 16th. His invitation was polite, almost deferential. Aware of de Gaulle's sensibilities, he promised "complete discretion" for a discussion between Frenchmen, uninterrupted by the intrusions of foreigners.

"As you know," de Gaulle answered testily, "I have telegraphed Giraud several times since Christmas to urge him to meet me. I much appreciate the sentiments which inspire your message and I thank you warmly. Let me say to you, nonetheless, that the atmosphere of a high level Allied conference around Giraud-de Gaulle conversations and, in addition, the suddenness with which the conversations were proposed, do not appear to be the most favorable conditions for an effective agreement. Simple and direct talks between French leaders would be, in my opinion, more appropriate for negotiating a useful arrangement."

At the same time he sent a cryptic message to Giraud to emphasize that a meeting between them was no one's business but their own, and certainly not the business of Roosevelt and Churchill. "Remember," he said, "that I remain ready to meet you on French territory, between Frenchmen, where and when you choose."[11]

At Anfa, however, Giraud enjoyed being the focus of attention. He met with the British and American military staffs, to whom he outlined his aspirations for the organization of a 300,000-man French army of twelve divisions. He also conferred with Roosevelt. Harry Hopkins wrote of the meeting:

The President laid out to Giraud in a masterful fashion his concept of French resistance, emphasizing the fighting. I gained a very favorable impression of Giraud. . . . Had a feeling that *he had made up his mind that he was going to do whatever the President wanted** in Africa. . . . Giraud laid out his problems, which his aide had previously told me, and the President settled them all to Giraud's complete satisfaction, but on the sovereignty point he was adamant and insisted that Giraud, at the moment, act only as a representative in North Africa. . . . On the whole I thought it was a very satisfactory conference and I am sure that Giraud and the President have mutual confidence in each other.

But Hopkins misinterpreted the conversation. Roosevelt had received an unfavorable report on Giraud from Eisenhower and had made up his mind that the Frenchman needed some assistance. "It appears," he cabled back to Hull in Washington, "that we must get a civilian into the administrative picture here. Apparently Giraud lacks

* Author's italics.

administrative ability and the French army officers will not recognize
de Gaulle's authority." It thus seems that Roosevelt, though he
acknowledged Eisenhower's need for help, did not agree that de
Gaulle would be the best choice to provide it. He was willing to go
along with Eisenhower and Churchill far enough to examine de
Gaulle firsthand, but he did not prepare himself for acceptance.[12]

Roosevelt seemed almost delighted that Churchill could not get de
Gaulle to Anfa. The terms in which the President explained the
situation to Hull suggest that he found the Prime Minister's predica-
ment rather funny. "We produced the bridegroom, General Giraud,
who cooperated very nicely on the proposed nuptials," he wrote,
"and was prepared to go through with it on our terms, I am sure.
Our friends, however, could not produce de Gaulle, the tempera-
mental bride. She has become quite high-hat about the whole affair
and doesn't wish to see either of us, and shows no intention of getting into bed with Giraud. We intend to do the best we can under
these circumstances, and I believe can turn something fairly good
from it all. Giraud seems to me to be a man who wants to fight and is
really not greatly interested in civil matters." Though Roosevelt
found some amusement in telling Hull the story in stag-party fashion,
he still had not solved the serious problem of administration in Algiers.

His own choice for reinforcing Giraud, he told Hull, was Jean
Monnet, the French banker, industrialist and armament expert.
Monnet, since the Armistice, had not identified himself with any
French faction but had independently given his talents to the Allies.
In that role, he had become a valuable adviser on armament matters.
Hull, however, thought he was sympathetic to de Gaulle. Any man
the United States selects, he said, must be beyond reproach in his
"integrity and loyalty to all the best elements in France." His defini-
tion of "the best elements in France," of course, excluded de Gaulle.[13]

Paradoxically, the man whose integrity satisfied Hull was Marcel
Peyrouton, about whose Vichy associations he had himself given a
warning only a month before. Peyrouton, at Murphy's insistence,
was en route from Buenos Aires to Algiers when Darlan was killed.
Welles, out of caution, immediately canceled the authorization for
Peyrouton's trip. It left the former Vichy minister stranded in Rio
de Janeiro, where newsmen discovered him, learned his destination
and spread the word that the Americans had picked him for an important post in Algiers. Despite the fury the Peyrouton plan ignited,

Hull overruled Welles on the grounds that military priorities deprived the State Department of any veto over Eisenhower's decisions. Again the State Department became the target of critics throughout the country for its apparent inability to abandon its predilections for Vichy. On January 19th, while Roosevelt and Churchill were still at Anfa, Peyrouton's appointment as Governor-General of Algeria was announced. His presence immediately rendered the difficult problem of cleansing North Africa of Vichy's influence enormously more complex.[14]

The day the appointment was announced, de Gaulle received an angry message from Churchill in London. The Prime Minister, nettled by the President's constant reminders that he could not produce the "bride," was determined to get de Gaulle to Casablanca, no matter what the cost. He wrote to de Gaulle:

We are about to make arrangements for North Africa, on which we should have been glad to consult you, but which must otherwise be made in your absence. . . . The fact that you have refused to come to the meeting proposed will, in my opinion, be almost universally censured by public opinion and serve as a complete answer to any complaints. There can, of course, be no question of your being invited to visit the United States in the near future if you reject the President's invitation now. My attempt to bridge the difficulties which have existed between your movement and the United States will have definitely failed. I should certainly not be able to renew my exertions in this direction while you remain the leader of your movement. The position of His Majesty's Government towards your movement while you remain at its head will also require to be reviewed. If with your eyes open you reject this unique opportunity we shall endeavour to get on as well as we can without you. The door is still open.[15]

Churchill's words were not those of a chief advocate. He was by now infuriated with de Gaulle, for the stubbornness he had shown and the embarrassment he had caused. Churchill was quite prepared to carry out his threats.

De Gaulle could not have mistaken Churchill's meaning. But it still took pressure from the French National Committee to make him change his mind. Grumbling, he agreed at last to go to Casablanca. Unwilling to rush his departure, it was not until two days later that he arrived. Characteristically, he complained of being received at the airport without military honors. Instead of the conciliatory Catroux, whom Churchill had asked him to bring, de Gaulle was accompanied by d'Argenlieu, who had been wounded at Dakar, and Hettier de Boislambert, who had recently escaped from a Vichy prison. The significance of their presence was evident. Despite Churchill's threats, de Gaulle was saying that he had not come to Casablanca to compromise the integrity of Fighting France.

Giraud, who did not go to the airport, waited for de Gaulle at his villa. When the two men came face to face for the first time, de Gaulle unceremoniously snapped, "What's this all about? I proposed four times that we get together and it is in this compound, surrounded by barbed wire, in the midst of strangers, that I have to meet you? Doesn't it seem to you that there is something wrong from the point of view of the nation?" Giraud saw nothing wrong. The Anfa conference was proceeding to his satisfaction. He had no incentive to make concessions to the Fighting French. During their lunch, de Gaulle made clear that he would have nothing to do with a regime that made use of figures so prominently identified with Vichy as Noguès and Peyrouton. Giraud defended them vigorously on the grounds of their capacity. For himself, he said, he gave no thought to politics. His only goal was to fight. The two generals parted coolly but amicably. They had met, at last, but remained locked in disagreement.[16]

Later that day, de Gaulle and Churchill held an unfriendly meeting. The Prime Minister insisted that if necessary he would break with the Fighting French. De Gaulle maintained that Fighting France would rather go down with honor than be stained by an alliance with Vichy. De Gaulle reported in his *Memoirs* that Churchill proposed the establishment of a French triumvirate, composed of Giraud, himself and some undesignated third Frenchman. De Gaulle said he rejected outright any discussion of sovereign French matters with Churchill and chose to quit the encounter.

Late that night, after returning from dinner with the Sultan of Morocco, Roosevelt summoned de Gaulle to his villa. It was the first time the two men had come face to face. Churchill reported later that "the President was attracted by the spiritual look in his eyes."[17] De Gaulle had nothing quite so positive to say of the meeting. A "strange atmosphere" permeated it, he wrote, largely as a result of the bodyguards and other eavesdroppers imperfectly hidden behind the window drapes. Taking note of the President's distrust, Hopkins said de Gaulle was covered by machine guns throughout the entire meeting.

De Gaulle has written in his *Memoirs* that Roosevelt opened the visit amicably by suggesting that the two sit side by side on a couch. The President then proceeded, he reported, to try to persuade him more with charm than with argument to his own point of view, although he never let it be forgotten that he possessed the power to impose his will. De Gaulle complained that Roosevelt was interested only in talking, not in listening. He wanted to make Roosevelt understand him, but he had little opportunity to lay out his own position. Both men, de Gaulle related, were careful to say nothing that might offend the other and precipitate a clash. But he made it clear that the meeting had little impact on either of them.[18]

De Gaulle and Giraud met again the following day and, once more, exchanged only remonstrances. De Gaulle reproached Giraud for retaining his command through a chain of authority that began with Pétain. He censured Giraud for having once given Pétain an oath of allegiance, which could not be lightly forgiven. De Gaulle proposed setting up a government in Algiers under his own leadership, which would deny any legitimacy to Vichy, dispose of anyone associated with Vichy, and under which Giraud would become commander in chief of French armies. Giraud pointed out to de Gaulle that he already commanded a substantial army which would soon reach 300,000 men, while Fighting France had only two small divisions. This was the measure of strength that Giraud understood. All de Gaulle had to support a claim to power, he said, was a "right of anteriority," which Giraud did not find very compelling. Giraud repeated Churchill's proposal for a triumvirate, but in it he proposed to hold virtually all the power. Once again the two generals broke off their talks without any narrowing of their differences.[19]

Giraud, in the last days of the Casablanca conference, was much more interested in sealing his bargain with the United States on the rearmament of his fighting forces than in reaching an understanding with de Gaulle on a political coalition. In collaboration with Robert Murphy, Giraud drafted a memorandum formally noting certain promises made to him by the American generals there. It provided that the French would receive "by priority" the most modern material for an army of three armored and eight motorized divisions and an air force of a thousand planes. It declared also that Roosevelt, Churchill and Giraud recognized "that it was to their common interest for all the French fighting against Germany to be reunited under one authority and that every facility would be given to General Giraud in order to bring about this reunion." With commitments such as these, Giraud would have the army he wanted and more political power than he needed. It would virtually foreclose any growth of the Fighting French movement.

But shortly before the Anfa conference was to close, Lemaigre-Dubreuil arrived from Washington and insisted that the memorandum was not enough. Having pleaded the case for political recognition for weeks at the State Department, he saw the opportunity now to settle the matter with Roosevelt. Giraud was reluctant to risk his military advantages by pursuing his political interests, but Lemaigre-Dubreuil, whose outlook on French sovereignty was close to de Gaulle's, persuaded the General to make the attempt. He handed Giraud a second memorandum, which Giraud agreed to submit to Roosevelt.

The memorandum specified that the Torch invasion was an act of liberation, undertaken at the demand of the French themselves. It reaffirmed the validity of the promises made to Giraud through Murphy on the eve of the landings. It acknowledged that France, because of the German occupation, was temporarily without a government. But, most importantly, it declared that: "In the interests of the French people, in order to safeguard France's past, her present and her future, the Government of the United States and the Government of Great Britain recognize in the Commander in Chief, with his headquarters at Algiers, the right and duty of preserving all French interests in the military, economic, financial and moral plane. They bind themselves to aid him by all the means in their power until the day when, in complete freedom, the French people and the French nation shall be able to designate their regular government." In short, the memorandum made Giraud the trustee of the French nation, and, in effect, put in his hands the attributes of French sovereignty that de Gaulle so desperately sought.[20]

Roosevelt, by now, had ceased to find the French situation funny. He was determined not to leave Casablanca without some semblance of an agreement between the two generals. He was irritated at what he considered impudence on de Gaulle's part in refusing to enter into the relaxed, compliant spirit of the conference. To settle the matter, Roosevelt had remained at Casablanca several more days than he had intended. He did not plan to go home admitting failure.

On the night of January 23rd, Roosevelt and Churchill drew up a communiqué to which they asked the two generals to subscribe. It was so inoffensive, in their view, that neither could object. But de Gaulle did object. He insisted he would not sign an "Anglo-Saxon" document that would deceive the world into believing that an agreement had been reached between him and Giraud. Roosevelt, irate at de Gaulle, assigned him to Churchill the next morning for further persuasion. He had let the Prime Minister know that he regarded de Gaulle as a British satellite whom Churchill was responsible for bringing to order.

That morning, the President was in the mood to strike a mortal blow at de Gaulle. When Giraud appeared for a final formal call, the opportunity suddenly presented itself. The General casually handed his two memoranda—his own on the American pledge to equip his army and Lemaigre-Dubreuil's on French politics—to the President. Somewhat to his astonishment, Roosevelt signed them both at once, barely glancing at either.

The act the President committed was one of enormous irresponsibility. He had made important commitments, for which both the United States and Britain were liable, yet Churchill was not even present. Hopkins, inaccurately, noted in his diaries that "Giraud wanted a confirmation on supplying his army but the President referred him to Eisenhower." This may have been Roosevelt's explanation to Hopkins. The only point that the President referred to Eisenhower was a shipping schedule for supplying North Africa with civilian goods. Secretary of War Stimson and General Marshall knew nothing of the agreement until Giraud's representative in Washington, ten days later, gave them a copy. Hull subsequently told Stimson that it was an agreement "signed over a drink," a characterization which Roosevelt accepted—though the papers were signed before noon—and which he laughed about. But, however inconsequential Roosevelt considered the documents, Giraud believed he had the pledged word of the President of the United States. He was convinced he had the contracts which assured his dominance, both military and political, until France was liberated.[21]

Shortly after the signing, Churchill returned with de Gaulle to the President's villa, where photographers and war correspondents waited for the press conference that was to close the Anfa meeting. The two men had reached an understanding about a communiqué, as a consequence of what de Gaulle described as "our bitterest encounter" of the entire war. De Gaulle promised Roosevelt, whom he

found still amiable and smiling, that he would meet with Giraud later
to draw up between them a brief statement for the press. Roosevelt,
de Gaulle said, gave the appearance of being satisfied. In this atmosphere, Roosevelt asked de Gaulle if he would consent to being photo-
graphed with Giraud. De Gaulle said he had no objection.

The President and the Prime Minister, along with the two French
generals, proceeded to the garden where the cameramen waited.
They took seats with Giraud on the right, followed in order by
Roosevelt, de Gaulle and Churchill. At a signal, the photographers
began snapping. Then Roosevelt asked de Gaulle and Giraud if they
would shake hands for the photographers. Both generals stood up
as the cameras recorded one of the historic pictures of the war.
Later, Roosevelt claimed he had tricked de Gaulle into this public
handshake. De Gaulle's cool demeanor, which had not abandoned
him before, seems to belie the claim. But, in creating the impression
of an agreement between the two generals, Roosevelt played a cruel
trick on Frenchmen everywhere and on the world.

Before leaving Casablanca, de Gaulle and Giraud met and prepared their communiqué. It could hardly have said less. In full, it read:

We have seen each other. We have discussed. We have affirmed our
complete agreement that the goal to be reached is the liberation of France
and the triumph of human liberty by the total defeat of the enemy. This
goal will be achieved by the union in the war of all Frenchmen fighting
side by side with their allies.[22]

But little as it was, it was friendly and left the door open for
further negotiations in behalf of French unity. De Gaulle and
Giraud had concurred on the desirability of union. They agreed to
establish a permanent liaison between them to exploit any possibility
of achieving it.

Over the succeeding weeks, Roosevelt vented his bitterness at the
Fighting French leader by telling the story of the Casablanca conference over and over again at de Gaulle's expense. Roosevelt's narra-
tions were more than embellished. They were, in many cases, grossly
inaccurate.

The President's most famous story, by the testimony of his loyal
friend Harry Hopkins, was pure fiction. Its origin was in a remark
by Harold Macmillan, Churchill's political adviser, that de Gaulle
proposed that he be the Clemenceau—the head of government—
while Giraud be the Foch—the commander in chief—of the French

effort in World War II. Hopkins wrote that Roosevelt altered the story so that "at the first conference de Gaulle compared himself to Clemenceau, while at the next conference he indicated that Joan of Arc was perhaps more his prototype." Two weeks after he returned from Casablanca, Roosevelt wrote to his son John that the conference "was really a great success and only General de Gaulle was a thoroughly bad boy. The day he arrived he thought he was Joan of Arc and the following day he thought he was Clemenceau." By the time Hull got around to relating the story in his *Memoirs*, the President had said that "de Gaulle, walking up to him rather stiffly, remarked, 'I am Joan of Arc. I am Clemenceau.'" "As the President told the story," Hopkins admitted, "I have no doubt it took on more authenticity and finally came to be accepted as fact." It was widely circulated in American newspapers and magazines. When de Gaulle heard the story, it simply added to Casablanca's heritage of animosity.[23]

But de Gaulle did not regard Casablanca as a disaster for his cause. He had gone there with the intention of proving his independence and he had succeeded. In reporting to his colleagues on his conversations with Roosevelt, he said, "I have the impression that he discovered what Fighting France is." Somewhat equivocally he added: "that can have important consequences later."[24] He had also taken the measure of Giraud at Casablanca. He left convinced that, however modest his accomplishments there, the resources of Fighting France gave him the ultimate advantage. Few would have agreed with de Gaulle at the end of January, 1943, that the odds of the game were in his favor.

Giraud, by all outward signs, was the major victor at Casablanca. The Allies had acknowledged his supremacy, both military and political, in the most important segment of the French Empire and, presumably for the future, in France itself. They had promised to build the army he commanded into a large and powerful force. They made a commitment to assist him to consolidate his political leadership. He seemed destined to return to France as the savior. In Algiers, the controlled press trumpeted his companionship at Casablanca with Roosevelt and Churchill, barely mentioning the presence of de Gaulle.

EIGHT

The Ideological Wedge

January–June, 1943

AFTER CASABLANCA, de Gaulle was not as weak as Roosevelt believed nor Giraud as strong. Independently of the United States, de Gaulle had steadily buttressed the position of Fighting France. His power was by no means as visible as Giraud's but it was firmly rooted and free to grow. Though the deadlock between the two Generals continued, de Gaulle was convinced that time was working in his favor. While waiting for a showdown he was certain would come, he passed up no opportunity to acquire advantages. Despite the setbacks that had begun with Torch, Fighting France displayed unremitting vigor.

At the end of November, 1942, the Fighting French destroyer *Léopard* appeared at the island of Réunion in the Indian Ocean and, after silencing a hostile shore battery, rallied the colony. It was de Gaulle's first territorial gain since Saint-Pierre and Miquelon, almost a year before.

Two weeks later, the Madagascar dispute was at last resolved with an agreement between Eden and de Gaulle setting the terms of Fighting French administration of the island. In announcing the accession of Madagascar, de Gaulle praised the "complete loyalty . . . of our old and good ally England." Half of the officers, two thirds of the noncommissioned officers and all of the men in the Madagascar garrison elected to continue fighting as Gaullists. The rest went to North Africa to enlist with Giraud.

148

In late December, de Gaulle renewed his bid to the British to sanction a move against French Somaliland, Vichy's last colony in the Middle East. The port city of Djibouti, the capital, remained important to Allied strategy. The colony had been weakened by Vichy's loss of Madagascar, its principal source of supply. Both the armed forces and the civilian population, demoralized by Pétain's impotence and de Gaulle's propaganda, seemed ready to give in. The State Department protested that possible bloodshed between Frenchmen might somehow upset the equilibrium in North Africa. But the British this time rejected the American contention. On December 28th, a Fighting French detachment crossed the Somali frontier by train from Addis Ababa. Djibouti fell without firing a shot. The garrison of 8,000 men, which de Gaulle had coveted since the lean days of 1940, rallied unanimously to Fighting France.[1]

Leclerc, the young general who had been building an army in Central Africa, had meanwhile begun his legendary dash from Fort Lamy to the Mediterranean Sea. Leclerc had planned the operation for more than a year. Driving from one oasis to the next, he pressed the Italians backward through the desert. His column quickly took possession of all of southern Libya. Over the objections of the British, Leclerc established a Fighting French military government in the conquered territory, the first of the war in an Axis province. Thirty-nine days after leaving Chad, the column made contact with Montgomery's Eighth Army on the coast at Tripoli. Leclerc had swept clean the British left flank. More important, he had enraptured a dejected and uncertain French people with a daring military exploit.

General Larminat's Fighting French forces, serving under Montgomery, were waiting for Leclerc when he arrived at the Mediterranean. They had fought well against Rommel at Alamein but, having suffered heavy losses, were withdrawn from the line to reorganize and refit. At the beginning of the New Year they were joined by the Djibouti elements, which strengthened the force sufficiently to permit its reorganization as the First Free French Division. Still in reserve, the Division followed the British eastward, impatient to reenter the fight as soon as the Germans stopped fleeing in order to give battle.[2]

As his military enterprises prospered, de Gaulle stepped up the clandestine campaign to establish his ascendancy in Metropolitan France. In February, 1943, Jean Moulin returned from the Conti-

nent to report progress in the effort to unify the Resistance. De
Gaulle, anxious to enlarge his base of support, directed Moulin
henceforth to solicit the allegiance not only of Resistance groups but
of the Third Republic's old political parties as well. The decision,
made with misgivings, was one of de Gaulle's most controversial, for
it compromised his determination to give a fresh start to postwar
French politics. But under pressure from Giraud and the United
States, he chose to forego the luxury of distant reform in the hope of
profiting from the ferment in the established parties. When Moulin
was dropped back into France a few weeks later, he carried instructions to found a Council of the Resistance to "form the embryo of a
nationally elected body that will act as political advisor to General
de Gaulle on his arrival in France." De Gaulle was not thinking of a
parliament to take power on liberation. His objective was to organize
and focus a maximum of national support in behalf of Fighting
France.[3]

Giraud, meanwhile, contributed to de Gaulle's strength by retaining his identification with Vichy, which was by now thoroughly
discredited. His most prominent followers were Noguès, Boisson and
Peyrouton, all popularly linked with Pétain. Like Darlan, Giraud
was indifferent to the repeal of the authoritarian and anti-Semitic
measures enacted under Nazi influence. He had ceased to act in
Vichy's name, but he still accepted it as the legitimate source of his
authority. This association with the Vichy regime inevitably weakened his claim to be a vigorous enemy of Nazi occupation and oppression.

Though the policy of the White House was meant to encourage
republicanism, Roosevelt was badly served in its execution by his
principal agent in North Africa, Robert Murphy. No liberal democrat
himself, Murphy was committed to the men in Algiers who wore the
Vichy stamp. Those with whom he had conspired before Torch were
Vichyites by sympathy. Those with whom he worked after Torch
were of Vichyite mentality. Only by purging the men on whom he
had so long depended could Murphy have promoted a vigorous republican policy. But he was too deeply involved with the *status quo*
himself to put real effort into disrupting it. Since Giraud leaned
heavily on Murphy, events were allowed to drift.[4]

In contrast to Murphy's apathy, Churchill was by design out to
undermine Giraud. When the Prime Minister learned of the com-

mitments Roosevelt had made at Casablanca, he made up his mind to modify them. His own motivation was concern for de Gaulle, despite their fierce clash at Casablanca. His generals were cool to Giraud because the pledge to rebuild the French Army could only be met by depriving British forces of weapons. On February 5th, returning from an inspection tour of the Middle East, Churchill appeared unannounced in Algiers and declared his intention to transform the Anfa agreement to suit his own aims.

Churchill managed to persuade both Giraud and Murphy of the need to revise the pact. His easy success is explainable only by Giraud's lack of interest and discernment, particularly toward Roosevelt's political pledges. By the time Lemaigre-Dubreuil protested to Giraud, it was already too late. Churchill managed to diminish Allied recognition of Giraud's authority from "all French interests" to North and West Africa alone. On the military side, he reduced French rearmament from first priority to "that priority which . . . may be determined by the Combined Chiefs of Staff," a body over which he exercised considerable influence. When the changes reached the State Department, Hull endorsed them and forwarded them to Roosevelt. The President not only sanctioned them but indicated that they coincided with what he had intended in the first place.[5]

Giraud's prestige had also slipped with the Army, whose support he needed most, because of the failure of the United States to deliver equipment that had been pledged at Anfa. The promise of new arms was supposed to buoy the spirit of his troops. For a while it did, but though they fought gallantly, they repeatedly fell back with heavy losses because of insufficient and antiquated matériel. Eisenhower recognized that morale could be restored only by bringing French armament into line with that of neighboring British and American units. Giraud was understandably vexed. By contrast, de Gaulle's troops had been outfitted by the British with the most modern weapons. Giraud was fully aware that without better performance from the Americans his ability to retain the loyalty of his army was in danger.

When Eisenhower notified Marshall that "I have here to face the insinuation that we are not straight-forward, that we are long on promises and short on performance," he received immediate action. Over British objections, Marshall ordered the organization of a special convoy to carry enough equipment for two infantry divisions and several armored units. But the convoy was a stopgap measure. The President still had to establish a long-range rearmament policy, either in conformity with his Anfa pledges or apart from them.

Murphy, too, was alarmed by the state of the French Army. His own prestige was involved, since it was he who wrote the letters on the eve of Torch promising rearmament to Giraud. On February 20th, he told the President that the French were beginning to feel "hoodwinked." They read of the prodigious American production effort, he said, and could not understand their being deprived of a share. Giraud, he wrote, considered himself the victim of "opposition if not deception."

Roosevelt's reply to this candid message was rapid and angry. He denied that he had ever agreed to more than "the principle of rearmament." His assertion was at best a curious interpretation of the clauses to which he agreed at Anfa. But it did not satisfy him merely to challenge the validity of the French claim. He felt compelled to add haughtily: "Tell your friends in North Africa that they ought not to act like children. They must take prompt steps to deny the silly rumors that they have been let down. . . . They must remain calm and sensible."[6]

Roosevelt knew, however, that he had to do something about the bad situation in North Africa. His solution was to send Jean Monnet to Algiers to stand by Giraud. Monnet, who first arrived in the United States in 1938 to promote the production of aircraft that France could buy, had become a close friend and adviser to Harry Hopkins. Brilliant and sophisticated, moving quietly in the most influential Washington circles, he had won high esteem for his advice on armaments problems. Hull suspected him of secret Gaullist sympathies. But Hopkins persuaded the President that Monnet's technical knowledge, combined with his liberal convictions, would make him the ideal influence on Giraud. When he turned up in Algiers, it was unclear whether he was responsible to the President, Giraud or simply to France and himself. But in his possession were letters from Hopkins to Eisenhower and Murphy, requesting full cooperation in Roosevelt's name.[7]

Giraud was convinced that Monnet held the key to Roosevelt's storehouse of arms. The General, Monnet said, suffered from his reputation in the United States as a reactionary and an anti-Semite.

He could expect guns and tanks only by establishing a democratic regime in Algiers. But much as Giraud wanted the arms, he found the proposed transformation distressing. Not only was he a sincere authoritarian but he depended heavily on Vichy disciples. Monnet, in constant consultation with Murphy, was unyielding. He insisted that Giraud face the alternatives. Giraud finally did. One by one, he dropped Lemaigre-Dubreuil, Peyrouton and the other ex-Vichyites from his circle of intimate advisers. With a shrug, Giraud resolved that if Roosevelt wanted democracy, he would become a democrat.

On March 14th, Giraud recited a speech written by Monnet in which he affirmed his belief in liberal democratic principles. Although he boasted later that he had softened Monnet's text, he rejected last-minute entreaties from the Vichyites to discard it altogether. "Paris was worth a mass," he wrote in his memoirs. "This armament was worth a speech." Giraud declared a conviction in the French people's right of self-government and promised the abrogation of the laws of Vichy. The climax of the speech was an appeal for unity, which included a generous reference to de Gaulle. It was a new element injected into a stalemate, a herald of significant change.[8]

It had certainly not been Roosevelt's plan in sending Monnet to Algiers to facilitate de Gaulle's ascent to power. It was, nonetheless, almost inevitable this should happen once Giraud deserted his old friends from Vichy in the quest of new ones from the republic. De Gaulle had long before established himself as the leader of French republican elements. Stubbornly Roosevelt, who favored the republican cause, refused to recognize him as its champion. Because he distrusted de Gaulle, Roosevelt backed an antirepublican. It was not that he trusted Giraud as much as his own ability to manage Giraud, to make him look and act republican. But the result of the March 14th speech was that the Vichyites fled Giraud without the republicans rallying around him. Before long, it became evident that Roosevelt was left with a candidate who had isolated himself from any support but that of the President of the United States. The President, at the same time, had, by embracing Giraud, alienated from himself the very French elements he wanted to please and encourage. The major advantage on March 14th went to de Gaulle.

Giraud was nonetheless convinced that the speech had substantially strengthened his hand. The press in the United States and Britain had responded enthusiastically. Churchill had noted his approval, and Hull, defensive as usual, asserted that Giraud had now vindicated the confidence placed in him. Once again at Monnet's urging, Giraud made his move. He sent an invitation to de Gaulle to meet him in Algiers to organize French unity.

De Gaulle, who vouchsafed that the speech marked "in many respects, great progress toward the doctrine of Fighting France," sensed better than anyone that he had his rival on the run. He declared now that he would meet Giraud only on certain conditions, the principal one being an agreement that any body they created together must exercise the sovereign powers of France. But on March 28th, he received word from General Catroux in Algiers that "Giraud has shown himself still attached to the concept of a provisional central power that he defined at Anfa." Catroux actually pleaded with de Gaulle to begin the bargaining on the basis of Giraud's terms. De Gaulle, however, resolutely rejected consideration of a system which would not be heir to the basic principles and the defiant spirit of Free France.[9]

In London, Churchill was impatient to get the question of unity settled so that it would cease being an issue between him and Roosevelt. After Giraud's speech, he told the House of Commons that "it now appears that no question of principle divides these two bodies of Frenchmen." But in a meeting at Downing Street on April 2nd, de Gaulle told the Prime Minister that the latest proposals were no better than those made to him at Casablanca. While Churchill listened angrily, de Gaulle vowed not to go to Algiers until an accord based on French national sovereignty was assured.[10]

Roosevelt did not deviate from the conviction that the French must not be permitted to set up a sovereign government in Algiers. He proposed as his model the experience of the thirteen American colonies, which, he said, had no common authority during the Revolutionary War other than Washington, a military chief. In mid-February, he told a news conference: "As to the future of France, I think everybody is agreed that we must not influence by act or deed today—by recognizing this, that or the other individual as to what the future has got to be. . . . That is why you have got the great efforts of de Gaulle to be recognized. . . . Nobody is going to do that because it would give an unfair advantage. Giraud wants to be recognized as the representative of France all over the world. I said no. That will give you an unfair advantage. Let France choose her own government. In the meanwhile, run your own bailiwick, wherever you happen to be." Roosevelt realized that it might be necessary at some point for Allied armies to enforce this policy of giving no political faction unfair advantage. It did not upset him that a foreign force, however friendly, might be required to impose rules on the French. He remained confident that the French, suspicious of their own generals, would appreciate that in total disinterestedness he would do what was best for them.[11]

De Gaulle did not share the benevolent interpretation that Roosevelt put on his own intentions. "From the time that America went to war," he wrote in his *Memoirs*, "Roosevelt made up his mind that the peace had to be an American peace, that it belonged to him to dictate its organization, that the states swept away in the struggle be submitted to his judgment, that in particular France had to have him for a savior and arbiter." De Gaulle, without misrepresenting Roosevelt's objectives, revised the diagnosis of their psychological origin. Were Roosevelt a leader given to introspection, he would probably have conceded that de Gaulle was not being unjust.[12]

In a new set of proposals he offered on April 1st, Giraud remained attached to Roosevelt's position on sovereignty, though he met many other Fighting French conditions. But to de Gaulle, establishing the sovereignty of the body directing the French liberation movement was the most important condition of all. The source of sovereignty, far from being a theoretical consideration, to him had practical application of enormous consequence.

Without sovereignty, a French central body could not claim to be the government of France at the time of the liberation. It would then be up to the Allies to determine France's rulers. Roosevelt might select the Allied high command. Or he might choose Vichy, in its original or some Darlan-like form. De Gaulle insisted that Frenchmen had to determine the rulers of France. He would not consent to leave it to foreigners.

Equally important, a central body without sovereignty could not exercise control over the French Army. De Gaulle had demonstrated many times his commitment to the doctrine that the Army was an instrument of national policy. He had written about it as early as 1924 in *La Discorde chez l'ennemi*.[13] Without a government empowered to set military policy, Giraud, as commander in chief, would be free to run the Army independently, with direction only from Allied headquarters. Insistence on sovereignty was not merely a trick to maneuver Giraud out of power. De Gaulle believed that it was not up to Giraud, Roosevelt, Allied headquarters or the French Army to make decisions for France. That was the responsibility of the French state.

While the two generals argued, their relative strength was being tested in arenas around the world. In a series of encounters, demeaning to France and distracting to the conduct of the war, each side sought to improve its bargaining position. While the struggle for unity approached its climax in the spring of 1943, new animosity between Frenchmen as well as between the French and their allies was being generated far from the focus of battle in Algiers.

When in mid-March the Vichyite administration in French Guiana, a South American jungle colony, was overthrown in a *coup d'état*, the State Department did not hesitate to enter the race for control in Giraud's behalf. Welles categorically refused transportation to the representative de Gaulle selected to send from Washington, while he authorized an immediate air flight to Giraud's man. De Gaulle countered by dispatching a second representative from London on a British plane, but when his man reached the Caribbean island of Trinidad the State Department stepped in again and effectively blocked him from going farther. Meanwhile, the United States furnished a plane to Giraud to transport a new governor from North Africa to Guiana. Giraud thus won a victory in the Guiana affair, but it was with American means, not his own.[14]

The State Department exercised similar restraint when de Gaulle proposed sending a mission to Martinique to persuade Admiral Robert to surrender authority. Of all France's colonies, Robert's in the Caribbean were the only ones still loyal to Vichy. At the end of April, 1943—a year and a half after Pearl Harbor—the United States at last withdrew its recognition of Martinique's Vichy tie and ended the guarantees of neutrality that had been in force since the war began. Robert, meanwhile, was being subjected to severe pressure from local Gaullist sympathizers, both civilian and military. Isolated and harassed, upset by the coup in Guiana, he was clearly disposed to give way. But the State Department wanted Giraud to share in the selection of a replacement. Because the two French factions could not agree on a candidate, many more months passed before the islands rallied to the Allied cause.[15]

Far more bitter, however, was the struggle in which the prize was not colonies but the personal allegiance of men. On land and sea, the banners of Giraud and de Gaulle summoned Frenchmen to the fight against the Axis. Giraud offered partnership in a solid, substantial military force. De Gaulle offered identification with the steadfast refusal to be beaten. The contest proved to be uneven. Free France had penetrated the soul of a people who wanted only to expunge their defeat. Uncommitted Frenchmen chose de Gaulle in far greater numbers. More imposing was the decision of the many who deserted the Giraudist camp to give their allegiance to Fighting France.

In February, 1943, the battleship *Richelieu*, still under the officers whose only battle had been against the English at Dakar, arrived in New York for repairs. During March and April, dozens of sailors jumped ship to enlist with the Fighting French. Soon their action spread to the crews of several French merchantmen docked in New York harbor. At Giraud's request, Roosevelt declared the men deserters, claiming that they had changed flags for higher pay and other inducements. De Gaulle, protesting vigorously, denied the charge. He refused not only to return the sailors but to discourage further defections. Despite American complaints, desertions from the *Richelieu* continued, until they finally numbered in the hundreds.

Across the Atlantic in the Scottish port of Greenock, a half-dozen French merchantmen were immobilized by the defection of almost all their sailors. At the end of March, 1943, a detachment of American Marines boarded the French ship *Jamaïque* to prevent an impending mass desertion. De Gaulle brought the matter before Admiral Stark in London in violent fashion and delayed the sailing of the *Jamaïque* for several weeks. But when she finally left port, from her mast flew the Cross of Lorraine of Fighting France.[16]

Even more acrimonious was the struggle on land, which began when the Fighting French contingents under Larminat and Leclerc moved into position in Tunisia not far from Giraud's army. As the combined Allied forces compressed the Germans and Italians into a progressively smaller pocket around Tunis and Bizerte, it became clear that these Fighting French units, veterans of Bir Hacheim and the dash from Chad, were the darlings of the battle line. The civilian population they liberated from the Axis greeted them with an enthusiasm that Giraud's men never evoked. Starting with a trickle, Giraud's soldiers deserted to the Fighting French. Gradually the pace increased until, to Giraud's dismay, his men were going over by hundreds at a time.[17]

Even in triumph the Fighting French did not let Giraud forget that they regarded themselves as ascendant. In early May, a few days after the final victory in Tunisia, Roosevelt wired Giraud his congratulations on the "brilliant contribution of the French forces under your command." He wired nothing to de Gaulle. But in the victory parade through Tunis, Leclerc and Larminat refused to share honors with their French comrades from Algiers. As Eisenhower and Giraud watched from the reviewing stand, the soldiers of Fighting France marched apart, as if to dramatize de Gaulle's refusal to yield to the Frenchmen who came late to the struggle for France's liberation.[18]

After the Tunisian victory both de Gaulle and Giraud felt the pressure for French unity intensify. The pause between campaigns, with no battle as distraction, seemed the ideal moment. Continued factional strife was destructive and demeaning. Both de Gaulle and Giraud recognized that if they did not now resolve their differences, France itself would pay.

Of the two generals, Giraud still appeared in the favored position. He had won the credit for the French contribution to the victory in Tunisia. His army was being fitted with the best American equipment. He had at last been promised, in unequivocal fashion, the weapons for eleven first-rate divisions. In mid-May, he won command of the French naval squadron long immobilized at Alexandria by a persistent loyalty to Vichy. Materially at least, Giraud since Casablanca had widened his margin of superiority over de Gaulle.[19]

But every defection to Fighting France testified to the compelling quality of de Gaulle's claim of moral preponderance. After the Tunisian battle, entire units with their commanders enlisted under the Cross of Lorraine. On the first day after the liberation, 412 recruits in one Tunisian city signed up with de Gaulle, while Giraud attracted only four. Manifestations in de Gaulle's favor increased throughout the colonies. Eisenhower himself noticed that de Gaulle's popularity was growing. Public opinion, intangible but nonetheless potent, was by all measure on de Gaulle's side.[20]

Juin, whose leadership in battle had evoked admiration from the Allies, was among those who gradually shifted his loyalty from Giraud to de Gaulle. Though a classmate of de Gaulle's at Saint-Cyr, he had throughout the early years of the war been indifferent to the

Free French movement. He alone of the Algiers circle had been hospitable to Giraud in the days after Torch. Giraud was his battlefield commander. But in writing he now referred to Giraud as "that devil of a man . . . always afraid someone will foul up his nest." Juin looked to de Gaulle's strength to replace the vacillation and inefficiency in Giraud.[21]

From a prison in France further evidence emerged of de Gaulle's esteem. Edouard Herriot, president of the Third Republic's Chamber of Deputies, wrote: "I am ready to enter any movement or government presided over by General de Gaulle, whom I consider the only man capable of realizing the union of the immense majority of Frenchmen. . . . In my view, General Giraud's qualities are not political but military." Herriot was the man even Roosevelt regarded as the incarnation of French republicanism.[22]

Most persuasive of all was the message de Gaulle received on May 15th from Jean Moulin. Long awaited, it was the announcement of Moulin's success in uniting the Resistance. "All the movements and parties of the Resistance of the northern zone and the southern zone on the eve of General de Gaulle's departure for Algeria renews to him as well as to the French National Committee the assurance of their total attachment to the principles that they represent. . . . They must not, without violently offending French opinion, abandon a fragment." A few days later, the National Resistance Council met for the first time under Moulin's direction. De Gaulle was now confident that the great outburst of energy represented by the Resistance was overwhelmingly behind him.[23]

By late May, 1943, Giraud and de Gaulle had agreed that a meeting must no longer be deferred. Giraud had been pushed closer and closer to de Gaulle's terms by Monnet, whom the persuasive Catroux effectively seconded. De Gaulle, also under the pressure of Catroux, declared himself sufficiently satisfied with the concessions he received to settle the outstanding differences face to face. The tireless work of the intermediaries had brought the generals to the threshold of accord.

Giraud and de Gaulle had concurred in the formation of a single body to incorporate the administration in Algiers and the direction of Fighting France into a united French effort in behalf of liberation. Giraud, in his correspondence, referred to it as a "committee." De Gaulle, who intended it as a government, called it simply an "organism." The two thus remained apart on the sovereignty of this central body, but they were able to reach agreement on its form. Each general was to become co-president and alternately conduct meetings; they would each appoint two members and ultimately, by joint consent, enlarge membership to suit their need; both pledged, on liberation, to surrender authority to an elected assembly. For the moment they left silent the relationship of the body to the Vichy regime and the men still in office who had served it.

The last squabble between them was over the site of their meeting. It almost wrecked arrangements. De Gaulle, conscious of the usefulness of popular support, insisted on Algiers itself. Giraud wanted to meet in some small provincial city. De Gaulle won. "I plan to arrive in Algiers at the end of this week," he wrote to Giraud on May 25th, "and am looking forward to collaborating directly with you in the service of France."[24]

On the day de Gaulle left London, Churchill, who had watched the rigorous bargaining impatiently, was with Roosevelt in Washington, exchanging fulminations about the Fighting French leader. Frank Knox, the Secretary of the Navy, reported ominously that after one "frank discussion . . . the de Gaulle matter . . . came very close to a radical solution." He added that "everyone . . . who has had much to do with de Gaulle finally came to the same conclusion—that he is a prima donna of the first water, with no real capacity for statesmanship." Churchill confirmed in his own account of the meeting that the President pressed vigorously for action to curb de Gaulle. The "radical solution" to which Knox referred was Roosevelt's contention that the British should cut off de Gaulle's access to funds. Churchill admitted being "most indignant" with the General, since "I felt that our continued support might lead to an estrangement between the British and the United States government." He maintained that he seriously considered breaking relations with "this most difficult man." But he decided against any action until he learned the results of the negotiations with Giraud.[25]

De Gaulle reached Algiers at noon on May 30, 1943. To his displeasure, Giraud had forced him to land at an isolated airfield, distant from the city, where crowds and the press were unlikely to gather. But a guard of honor saluted him as he stepped from the plane and Giraud was there with Catroux to greet him. Behind them were British and American officers of high rank. It was characteristic that de Gaulle should have taken note in his *Memoirs* of the contrast with his arrival in Casablanca four months before, when he felt he was being received by strangers in a foreign land.

The two generals went directly from the airport to the Palais d'Eté, seat of the Giraud administration, where a festive lunch had been prepared. De Gaulle had brought a team of six advisers with him from London. Giraud was surrounded by his own counselors, who included Monnet and General Alphonse Georges, a favorite of Churchill's whom the British had recently helped to escape from France. The atmosphere was affable. But it was clear, de Gaulle reported, that everyone present tacitly acknowledged they were divided into two contending camps.

In midafternoon, de Gaulle's placing of a wreath at the foot of the war monument became the occasion for the Gaullists in the city to emerge for a massive expression of feeling. Even Giraud acknowledged that the manifestation was tremendous. He himself had never been the object of such fervor. It confirmed de Gaulle's claim of a strong foundation of sympathy concealed beneath Giraud's military facade.

De Gaulle paid no calls on Allied dignitaries that day. It was part of his plan to ignore Eisenhower, who he believed ought to call on him, the symbol of French sovereignty. De Gaulle had not, however, set out his course for dealing with Winston Churchill, who had flown secretly to Algiers to be on hand for what he, like Roosevelt, had begun to call the "Giraud-de Gaulle wedding." Churchill, never one to miss a good show, had even summoned Eden to join him. De Gaulle, having insisted on a meeting that was exclusively French, was angry at Churchill's tasteless intrusion. Certain of Eisenhower's esteem, he was also confident of Eisenhower's discretion. But he was suspicious of Churchill and regarded his presence as an irritating distraction.[26]

De Gaulle took the offensive against Giraud as soon as their first meeting opened the following morning. He insisted that one man could not be both co-president and commander in chief, and proposed that Giraud choose between them. He demanded an end to equivocation about the powers of the central body, which he said must exercise the attributes of a sovereign state. Among them he specified the power to establish military policy. Finally, he called for the immediate dismissal of Peyrouton, Boisson and Noguès, along with other officials in positions of authority who remained as vestiges of the Pétain era.

Giraud rejected all of de Gaulle's demands. As he saw it, surrender of the co-presidency would have betrayed his own interest; his opposition to sovereignty, that of Roosevelt; and the dismissals from office, those of the men of Vichy who had remained faithful to him. Inside the meeting room, the pressure became intense when Monnet, avowing himself a nonpartisan, switched to de Gaulle's side on the issue of the purge, leaving Giraud only Georges's support. But the day ended without progress toward the resolution of differences.

Later, de Gaulle telegraphed an order to the National Committee in London. His instructions were to concentrate propaganda on the elimination of the Vichyites from the Algiers administration. That is the point, he said, on which Giraud is most vulnerable.[27]

The next day, Algiers was in turmoil. Larminat, apparently on his own responsibility, had dispatched several thousand men to the city from their camp near Tripoli. Their purpose was uncertain, but, had it been as innocent as he maintained, their presence would still have been provocative. Giraud aggravated matters by his curious choice of a deputy to keep order. It was Admiral Emile Muselier, hero of Saint-Pierre and Miquelon and a bitter foe of de Gaulle since his ouster from the National Committee during a sectarian struggle in 1942. Muselier, whose aims had always been dubious, had transformed Algiers into a bristling fortress. With each side accusing the other of planning a *putsch*, the heralded conference between the two generals threatened to turn into a fiasco. De Gaulle added to the confusion by publicly denouncing Giraud during the afternoon at a press conference. Fearful of serious trouble, the Allied command alerted British and American troops. But the crisis ended as mysteriously as it began. Larminat pulled back his soldiers. Muselier relaxed his defenses. Each side now confronted the other more sternly than before, but by the end of the next day Algiers was quiet again.[28]

The major break in the deadlock occurred on the night of June 1st, when de Gaulle, to his surprise, received a letter from Marcel Peyrouton. It was addressed to General de Gaulle in his capacity as "President of the Executive Committee." In it, Peyrouton announced his resignation as Governor-general of Algeria and requested assignment in his reserve rank as an officer in the colonial infantry. De Gaulle, fully aware that there was no "Executive Committee" and that he was certainly not its president, hastily accepted the resignation and assigned Peyrouton to a Fighting French unit in the Levant. Without wasting a minute, he made copies of both letters, which he sent to Giraud and the press. Unknown to de Gaulle, Peyrouton had addressed an almost identical resignation to Giraud, who meanwhile was trying to persuade him to stay. But by now the news was out and the world had been told that de Gaulle had won an important round in his battle. Giraud took some small satisfaction in changing Peyrouton's assignment to one of his own units in Morocco. The resignation, however, was irrevocable. De Gaulle had behaved most unethically, but as a consequence one of the best-known Vichyites was gone.

When Catroux learned in the morning what had happened, he stormed angrily into de Gaulle's quarters. In an unusual turnabout, Catroux charged de Gaulle with stupidity, unreasonableness and usurpation. De Gaulle sought meekly to defend his action as being in the best interests of France. Unwilling to accept the excuse, Catroux stalked out and, a short while later, sent in his resignation as a member of the National Committee. But de Gaulle maintained his composure. However grave his fault, he refused to take the resignation seriously. Catroux simmered for many hours more but the next day was back on duty for de Gaulle.[20]

When deliberations resumed on the morning of June 3rd, the contest between the two generals was all but over. De Gaulle walked into the room at 10 A.M., a set of written proposals in his hand. By noon, the seven men of the council were ready to announce the establishment of the French Committee of National Liberation. De Gaulle had correctly calculated the sequence of the battle. Once Giraud's front was pierced by Peyrouton's departure, his flanks simply rolled up. Giraud agreed that Noguès and Boisson would be replaced. He surrendered completely on the issue of sovereignty. Though he retained both the co-presidency of the Committee and command of the armed forces, it was implicit that the Committee had the power to enforce its will over him. De Gaulle, as a concession, consented to have the body go by the name of "Committee," but he acquired for it the attributes of a government. Unity had at last been achieved and, as he had predicted, on de Gaulle's terms.

The French Committee of National Liberation, said the declaration issued that day,

... is the central French power. As a consequence, the Committee directs the French effort in the war in all its forms and in all places. It exercises French sovereignty over all territories placed outside the power of the enemy. It assures the management and defense of all French interests in the world. It assumes the authority over the territories and the military forces—land, naval and air—which have until now been under the direction of the French National Committee and the Civil and Military Commander in Chief. . . . The Committee pledges solemnly to reestablish all French liberties, the laws of the Republic and the Republican regime and to destroy completely the regime of tyranny and personal power imposed on the country today.[30]

Giraud had sacrificed every major issue but the one he regarded as essential. He remained commander in chief of the armed forces. He was also, to be sure, co-president, but this was an office which, apart from prestige, had little meaning to him. Giraud did not understand that in conceding sovereignty to the Committee, he acknowledged its power to divest him of authority by majority vote. He thought that in arguing against sovereignty and in behalf of the Vichyites, he had been doing his duty to Roosevelt and his supporters in Algiers. He did not realize that, far more important, he was defending his own sources of strength. "When the general looks at you with those eyes of a porcelain cat," Monnet once said of him, "he comprehends nothing."[31] Abandoned by Monnet and Peyrouton, Giraud was left alone with principles to which he was indifferent and which he did not understand. Tired of haggling, he found it easier to give in. He thought he had salvaged the Army, which was to him all that mattered. He was unaware of the flimsy thread on which his authority hung.

But de Gaulle, even in success, was not satisfied. He found it unbearable to share the presidency with Giraud. In his view, acknowledging Giraud as an equal compromised the principles of Free France. Furthermore, he regarded Giraud as totally unqualified for the office. De Gaulle was repelled by the inherent contradiction in Giraud's dual capacity. He was determined to give the Committee the logical form of a government, as well as its attributes, which included the reduction of the commander in chief to a position of subordination. "I believe, in all good conscience, that we did not have the right to refuse that mediocre compromise," he wrote to his colleagues in London. "Everyone looks on it simply as a step." He clearly considered the agreement as a wedge to his total domination of the Committee and the united liberation movement.[32]

The next day de Gaulle, in the company of other members of the Committee, finally consented to have lunch with Churchill. De Gaulle wrote in his *Memoirs* that the Prime Minister denied that his purpose for being in Algiers was to interfere in French affairs, though he admitted that "there would have been measures we'd have had to take if some brutal jolt had taken place, if, for example, in a single gulp you had devoured Giraud." Churchill may have made the remark humorously, but de Gaulle knew he was not joking. De Gaulle was far too cunning, however, to offer Roosevelt a pretext for intervention by devouring Giraud in a single gulp—when he could achieve his purpose nibble by nibble. Though Churchill and de Gaulle were dueling, the Prime Minister, in a note to Roosevelt, was able to report that the atmosphere of the luncheon was "most friendly."[33]

Churchill tried to assure Roosevelt that the prospects were good for a harmonious relationship between the Allies and the French Committee. "If de Gaulle should prove violent or unreasonable," he told the President, "he will be in a minority of five to two, and possibly completely isolated." It is doubtful that he was convinced of the accuracy of his own arithmetic, since Georges was the only vote on which Giraud could unquestionably count. Nonetheless, he announced that he intended transferring at once his relations with the Fighting French to the French Committee of National Liberation. "The Committee," he said, "is a collective authority with which in my opinion we can safely work."[34]

Washington received the news with considerably more reserve. Hull wrote that when he and Roosevelt learned of the formation of the French Committee they reluctantly "decided to accept this development, regardless of the tactics of pressure used by de Gaulle." On June 9th, the State Department issued a statement welcoming the establishment of the Committee and commenting on the "spirit of sacrifice," presumably Giraud's, that made unity possible. But during the following week, Roosevelt refused to include France in the celebration of United Nations Day, list France on the United Nations roster or even make a friendly statement commemorating the event for broadcast in Algiers. Any such gesture, he said, would be "premature."[35]

More symptomatic of the suspicion with which Roosevelt viewed the creation of the Committee was the statement he dispatched to Churchill. "I want to give you," he said, "the thought that North

Africa is in the last analysis under British-American military rule and that for this reason Eisenhower can be used on what you and I want." Quite explicitly, the President had returned to the conqueror's doctrine. But he had failed to take the measure of the Frenchman who, with contrary ideas, had just established himself in Algiers.[36]

De Gaulle Consolidates

June–September, 1943

D E GAULLE wasted no time in resuming his pursuit of power. Inside the Committee he was already dominant. Inverting Churchill's prediction of a two-to-five Gaullist minority, he had quickly consolidated a five-to-two majority in his favor. His chief argument before the Committee for deposing Giraud was that it was incompatible with French republican traditions for the same man to be co-president, the political leader, and commander in chief, the military leader. He sought to force Giraud into a position that would satisfy his yearning to command but would exclude him from any influence over policy.

Having been forsaken by Monnet, Giraud now turned back to Murphy for guidance. Roosevelt, Murphy's chief, was Giraud's principal hope for retaining power. Murphy assured Giraud that the President wanted him to give up nothing. Giraud thus adopted Roosevelt's argument and contended in reply to de Gaulle that since the Committee was not a government, his dual role violated no governmental tradition. He insisted further that the Committee, because it was without sovereign powers, had no authority to deprive him of leadership. He argued particularly that the Committee could not challenge his hegemony over the Army, which he claimed to hold by a principle akin to divine right. His divinity for this purpose was Roosevelt, who alone served as his guardian.

When on June 5th, the two generals agreed to double Committee membership to fourteen, Giraud had no reservoir of partisans from which to make his selections. He conceded a margin to de Gaulle by allowing him four of the selections, but even the three he chose himself were not, in any sense, Giraudists. More likely they shared a growing sympathy for de Gaulle and his objectives. De Gaulle knew that the enlarged committee would be both stronger and more responsive to his wishes.

While waiting for the new members to reach Algiers, de Gaulle executed a risky and curious maneuver. He wrote to each of his six colleagues that, because of the Committee's inadequacy, he was resigning both as co-president and member. Privately he said he contemplated going to Brazzaville to restore the independence of Free France. During the succeeding days, Giraud conducted the Committee's business. Washington, meanwhile, waited hopefully for confirmation of de Gaulle's departure. But Giraud proved himself incapable either of profiting from de Gaulle's strategem or of running the Committee in his absence. The Committee took no action to acknowledge the resignation. Six days later, when the full fourteen-member Committee met, de Gaulle left his self-imposed confinement. His gamble had emerged as a stunning display of strength. If his objective had been to intimidate wavering Committeemen, events proved that he had succeeded.[1]

As soon as Roosevelt learned how the power had become distributed inside the Committee, he ordered Hopkins to prepare a new directive for Eisenhower. It was dispatched on June 17th.

The President declared:

The position of this government is that during our military occupation of North Africa we will not tolerate the control of the French army by any agency which is not subject to the Allied commander's direction. . . . It must be absolutely clear that in North and West Africa we have a military occupation and therefore without your full approval no individual civil decision can be made.[2]

Churchill was filled with consternation when he read the directive. It left him in a desperate dilemma. On the one hand, he wrote to his Cabinet, "the whole course of the war depends on our cordial relations with the American government and President." But on the other, he knew that Roosevelt, for moral as well as practical reasons, could not enforce a military occupation of the colonies. To avert a collision between Roosevelt and de Gaulle, Churchill determined on a two-pronged attack of trying to reduce the General's provocations and attempting to humor the President into greater tolerance. He proposed that to clarify the area of Allied interest the British and American Governments set minimum conditions essential to the safety of their forces. Nonmilitary matters he suggested leaving exclusively to the French. Once again he predicted that the Committee would outvote de Gaulle rather than clash with the Allies, if the issue was clearly one of military need. But he warned Roosevelt not to contemplate crushing de Gaulle. The risk of constant trouble, he said, "will be better than sweeping away a Committee on which many hopes are founded among the United Nations as well as France."[3]

Eisenhower did not relish the assignment of telling de Gaulle that Roosevelt would tolerate no change in the command of the French Army. It was his responsibility to work with the French every day. He found he could do so successfully by treating them as friends. He had sought for months to persuade Roosevelt that to deal with them as a conquered people would be both unseemly and ineffective. Eisenhower, who was fastidiously proper in his contacts with the French, did not have much heart in his mission when he called the co-presidents of the French Committee to his villa on June 19th.

De Gaulle waited until all were seated before he opened the meeting with a polite but glacial declaration. "I am here in my capacity as President of the French government," he said. "I come only because it is customary that, in the course of operations, chiefs of state and government pay personal visits to the headquarters of the officer who commands the armies that they have imparted to him."

Eisenhower overlooked the intimation that he was de Gaulle's subordinate and proceeded to ask for assurances that the command structure of the Army would not be changed. According to de Gaulle's account, Eisenhower said that as spokesman for the British and American Governments he would not be able to continue shipments of equipment without such assurances.

De Gaulle seized upon the opening. "You have cited your responsibilities as commander-in-chief to the British and American governments," he said. "Do you know that I have a duty to France and, in view of this duty, cannot tolerate the intrusion of any foreign power in the exercise of French prerogatives? . . . You ask me for assurances that I will not give you. For the organization of the French command is a responsibility of the French government, not of yours."

Giraud suddenly broke his silence. "I, too, have my responsibilities," he said, "particularly to the army. That army is small. It can only live inside the framework of the alliance. That is true for its command and its organization, as well as for its operations."

When he had finished, de Gaulle abruptly stood up and asked Eisenhower to submit his requests to the French Committee in writing. He then excused himself and walked out. Giraud, somewhat startled, left several minutes later.

Eisenhower's message to the Committee was precisely the pretext de Gaulle had been seeking to strike his blow at Giraud. Though the note was gracious in tone, it did not compromise Roosevelt's demand that Giraud retain full military powers. The Committee, taking the cue from de Gaulle, notified Eisenhower that the contents were inadmissible and that the message, being in the form of an ultimatum, would not receive a reply. The Committee told Giraud that Eisenhower's demands demonstrated conclusively that the commander in chief would have to become its subordinate or surrender his position. Caught between friendly foreigners and antagonistic compatriots, Giraud retreated. He consented to put himself under the direction of a "military committee," of which de Gaulle would be chairman. The committee would be empowered to set military policy, which he as commander in chief would execute. But he would remain co-president and be a member of the "military committee." His subordination was thus only partial, since he still sat on policy-making bodies. De Gaulle, however, had established the principle he sought and was now free to continue his program of conquest.[4]

A few days after the Committee rejected Eisenhower's note, Roosevelt suffered a more dramatic defeat in Governor-general Pierre Boisson's abandonment of his rule at Dakar. The President had declared Boisson inviolable, out of gratitude for his rallying to the Allies without a fight. Roosevelt was determined that Gaullist influence be barred from the Atlantic coast. He even warned Eisenhower that he would send in naval and ground forces rather than let a Gaullist take over the Dakar fortress. Churchill, who bitterly recalled Boisson's role in the battle of Dakar in 1940, once again found himself forced to support Roosevelt. But Boisson, whom Giraud had already bargained away in the unity negotiations, gave up on his own. The French Committee hastily accepted his resignation and named Pierre Cournarie, a dedicated Gaullist, as his replacement. While Eisenhower waited apprehensively, Washington remained mystifyingly silent. Roosevelt accepted the transaction without even a protest.[5]

Eisenhower and his staff speculated on whether the President had resigned himself to Giraud's eclipse. But the events in Algiers and Dakar had actually spurred Roosevelt to promote Giraud's renaissance. The President decided that if he invited Giraud to Washington, the General would take on an irresistible glow. Officially, the invitation was extended to facilitate the solution of armament problems. In reality, Roosevelt wanted to dramatize his contention —widely criticized in the American press—that the French Army had returned to the war apart from France itself. The visit was arranged without the official knowledge of the French Committee. It was to be strictly military, without diplomatic connotations. Roosevelt was sure that a welcome at the White House would give Giraud the boost he needed to recoup in Algiers.

From the moment Giraud landed in Washington on July 7, 1943, he was dazzled with attention. The first day he took tea with the Roosevelt family and dinner with the highest officials. The next he lunched intimately with the President, talked freely at the Pentagon and dined sumptuously as the guest of honor in the White House. After dinner, Roosevelt took him aside and told him of his confidence that France's future was secure as long as the Army could be kept free of de Gaulle's control. The overwhelmed Giraud had never before been the object of such high echelon solicitude.

The succeeding days, busy with meetings and trips and courtesy calls, uniformly echoed a martial theme. Giraud discussed only military matters. He was constantly in the company of military men. In Detroit he saw tanks manufactured and in Fort Benning infantrymen trained. He held a press conference at which reporters were instructed to ask only military questions. By the time of his departure, Giraud had given some American officials serious reservations about his wisdom, but had won new rearmament commitments to bring back to Algiers. Roosevelt had succeeded in focusing attention on French military contributions and on Giraud's personal leadership.[6]

But while Giraud was away, de Gaulle took matters more firmly under his control. The French Committee, through his direction, began to assume the shape of a government. Each member was assigned what was, in effect, a ministry. His responsibility was not only to supervise normal administrative functions but to plan within his area for the government's return to France. De Gaulle did not hesitate to submit for discussion problems concerning the Empire, foreign relations and the Resistance. A veteran *New York Times* correspondent wrote that he found the Committee superior to any French cabinet of the previous generation. Without the distraction of the Giraud problem, the Committee functioned resolutely and efficiently.[7]

The French Committee gained further status in mid-July when Admiral Robert finally surrendered his control of Martinique and Guadeloupe. Before he did, Laval appealed to him to sink his ships and his gold. Roosevelt seriously contemplated establishing an American trusteeship. But Robert peacefully transferred his authority to the French Committee and quietly left the islands. De Gaulle named Henri Hoppenot, a member of his Washington mission, to succeed to the governorship. Roosevelt referred to the change as a "base on balls" for the Allies, by which he meant an advance for the war effort. But it was a retreat for his "local authorities" policy, under which the islands had been neutralized since 1940. It was de Gaulle, not Roosevelt, who brought the French Antilles back into the war.[8]

On Bastille Day, 1943, de Gaulle took his challenge to Roosevelt to the public platform. "Certain people," he told a large, spirited crowd in Algiers, "look upon the action of our armies independently of the will and the sentiment of the great mass of our people. They imagine that our soldiers, our sailors, our aviators, unlike all the other soldiers, sailors and aviators of the world, go into battle without caring about the reasons for which they risk death. These theoreticians, claiming to be realists, believe that for France and for Frenchmen alone a nation's war effort can exist apart from national policy and national morale. We declare to these realists that they know nothing of reality."[9]

As if he were answering de Gaulle directly, Roosevelt said in his own Bastille Day message that "the keystone of our democratic structure is the principle which places governmental authority in the people and in the people only. There can be one symbol only for Frenchmen—France herself. She transcends all parties, personalities and groups. . . . French sovereignty resides in the people of France." A translation of his message was incorporated into a propaganda leaflet, which was dropped by the million over France. Roosevelt took up de Gaulle's challenge as if the two were competing for votes in a national plebiscite.[10]

Roosevelt refused to attach significance to the growing reports of De Gaulle's popularity. Accounts in the Allied press said again and again that the people were with him. An experienced American observer, on a survey mission for Marshall, wrote that even the Army had become Gaullist. "While it is true," he stated further, "that the Gaullist organization was almost non-existent in North Africa on 8 November, it now includes a large proportion of the energetic and liberal Frenchmen of North Africa. A great majority of opinion among the active groups in North Africa is therefore sympathetic at the present time to the de Gaulle program." Roosevelt read these reports with skepticism. Hull and Leahy, among his closest advisers, remained convinced of the need for de Gaulle's elimination. Roosevelt rejected not only the claim that this surge of popularity established, in the absence of elections, de Gaulle's right to govern. He went further by denying that the reports were true.[11]

Roosevelt's efforts in Giraud's behalf turned out a grievous failure. De Gaulle was lying in wait for the commander in chief when he returned from abroad. The cheers were still ringing in Giraud's ears, not only from Washington but from New York, Ottawa and London, where he had called en route. But the Committee, far from being intimidated by his success, was more hostile than ever. Giraud had represented himself as the Army's commander, independent of its authority. Almost unanimously the Committee agreed that Giraud, having repudiated its supervision, must once more have his powers reduced. On July 31st, less than a week after his return, Giraud was excluded from effective political power. Under a new plan of organization, he retained the title of co-president, with its function of co-signing decrees, but he was deprived of any role in reaching decisions. His authority over military affairs was further curtailed by de Gaulle's assumption of increased ministerial responsibility. Without recognizing its meaning, Giraud also put his signature to a document by which the Committee appointed him commander in chief. What the Committee could bestow, it could take away. Roosevelt's grand effort to elevate Giraud thus became another step in his decline.[12]

The new decrees, whatever their injury to Giraud, succeeded in ending the absurdity of two separate and rival French armies. De Gaulle had refused to put Fighting French troops under a commander in chief whom the Committee could not supervise. The British, however, had turned over the provisioning of Fighting French units to Eisenhower, who refused to deal with more than one French headquarters. Left without choice, the Committee abolished the bicephalic military system by putting Fighting French units under

Giraud's direction. The two competing missions in Washington were at last merged. Eisenhower and the French could now get on with the serious work of rearmament.[13]

Eisenhower was impressed with the French Committee. He found it firmly established, friendly and efficient. He wanted to rely increasingly on it to administer French affairs. So that he could deal with it more easily, he recommended to Washington and London that they recognize it officially as the governing authority in North Africa. Murphy himself acknowledged that some degree of recognition would facilitate business between the United States Government and Algiers. But his orders from Roosevelt were to desist from discussing recognition with the French "until things are much clearer." Roosevelt would not hear of any gesture that might be interpreted as American approval of de Gaulle's regime.

Churchill, always disinclined to confront the President head-on, tried to persuade Roosevelt to change his mind about recognition with indirect arguments. The Committee, he said, actually exercised a restraining influence on de Gaulle. Failure to recognize it might cause its collapse, which would leave de Gaulle in command of the field. Moreover, he said, "what does recognition mean? One can recognize a man as an Emperor or as a grocer." He pointed out that Allied recognition could be limited to a specific formula. Finally, he appealed to a sense of comradeship among politicians. "I am under considerable pressure from the Foreign Office, from my Cabinet colleagues and also from the force of circumstances," he said. He pointed out rather timidly to Roosevelt that he might be pressured into independent recognition, which Russia would probably duplicate. "I fear," he wrote, "lest this be embarrassing to you."

Roosevelt, after a conference with Leahy and Hull, vetoed any departure from the policy of aloofness. On July 22nd, he notified Churchill that he would not modify his position until the Committee gave "further and more satisfactory evidence of complete and genuine unity." He refused to contemplate the word "recognition" for fear it would imply acknowledgment of the Committee's authority on the soil of France. But even *acceptance* of the Committee, he said, was contingent on eliminating "French political or factional controversies designed to promote either group antagonisms or individual aspirations." This was a verbose way of insisting on obedience from de Gaulle. Meanwhile, he told Churchill, he intended to deal only with Giraud on matters concerning the Army. Furthermore, he said, he would continue to pursue his policy of "local authorities" where it brought "military advantage to the Allied cause."

Churchill admitted that he found Roosevelt's position "rather chilling" and predicted that it "would not end the agitation there is for recognition in both our countries." In addition, he surely found Roosevelt's reversion to the "local authorities" doctrine peculiar, since Algiers now exercised its jurisdiction over all of France's colonies except Indochina, which was occupied by the Japanese. Only France itself remained outside the Committee's control, and Churchill could not believe that Roosevelt contemplated ever using the administrative machinery of Vichy. The Prime Minister told the President that he had instructed the Foreign Office "to suggest a certain modification in your formula designed to bring our two views into harmony." But despite his euphemisms he knew that they had reached a deadlock.[14]

Churchill's eagerness to win recognition for France proceeded from his anxiety about the postwar settlement. A strong France, carrying its share of responsibility for keeping the peace, was in his view essential. In July, 1943, the Foreign Office submitted an *aide-mémoire* to the State Department which argued that France had to play a prominent part in determining and executing policy in Europe after the defeat of the Axis. The French Committee, he believed, was the nucleus of that strong France. The memorandum proved premature, for the State Department had not begun to think about managing the peace. But the governments-in-exile of Poland, Belgium, Norway and Greece, which shared many of Britain's concerns about the postwar settlement, had already recognized the Committee. Only the United States stood in the way, not only of diplomatic recognition but of formal recognition that France was back in the war. Though Roosevelt saw no need to hurry, Churchill feared that time for peacemaking was growing short.[15]

At the Anglo-American Conference in Quebec in late August, 1943, Churchill forced the issue of French recognition. He and the President took up the matter personally after discussions broke down between the foreign ministers, Hull and Eden. After much talking, the Prime Minister convinced the President that something had to be said about French recognition. But despite Churchill's contention that the French Committee was the hope of liberals throughout the world, Roosevelt insisted he had a duty to protect France from a Gaullist dictatorship. Hull wrote in his *Memoirs* that Roosevelt believed he could have swung Churchill to his position had it not been for the presence of Eden, whom the Secretary of State thoroughly disliked. If this was Roosevelt's conviction, he was certainly deceived about the intensity of the Prime Minister's feelings. Churchill, who so rarely defied the President, refused categorically to subscribe to a statement that Roosevelt drew up. At last the two men agreed that they had no alternative but to make separate declarations. "I have pointed out in the plainest terms to the President," Churchill wired to the Cabinet in London, "that they [the divergent statements] will certainly have a bad press, but he says he would rather have a sheet anchor out against the machinations of de Gaulle."

The American statement, which apparently was drafted in the State Department, was mean and snide. The United States Government, it said, "welcomes the Committee's *expressed* determination to continue the common struggle," as if its *real* determination was in doubt. The chief affirmation in the declaration was that "the government of the United States recognizes the French Committee of National Liberation as administering those French *overseas* territories which acknowledge its authority." But the affirmation was followed by the disclaimer that "this statement does not constitute recognition of a government of France or of the French Empire." As a further limitation, relations with the Committee were made "subject to the military requirements of the Allied Commanders." The United States thus recognized nothing but that the French Committee performed the tasks of administering overseas France, under the supervision of an American general.

Roosevelt was unembarrassed by the contrast between the statements of the United States and its principal allies. Britain attempted to minimize differences by paralleling, where possible, the American wording. The statement was duly cautious but contained no condescending disclaimer. The declaration emerged as both more gracious and more generous. The Russian declaration, issued the same day, was totally free of innuendo. It stated simply that the Committee represented the "interests of state of the French Republic." Roosevelt had extended his hand to Algiers but in a manner so grudging that the good effect was virtually cancelled.[16]

Churchill, apprehensive of what de Gaulle's reaction might be, hastily wired his representative in Algiers to advise against any inflammatory assertions.

You should tell my friends on the Committee [he wrote] that I am sure the right course for them is to welcome the American declaration in most cordial terms and not to draw invidious distinction between any forms in which recognition is accorded. On the contrary, the more pleasure they show at the American declarations the more value it will have for them.[17]

De Gaulle heeded Churchill's admonition. Eisenhower's diarist, Captain Butcher, noted on August 27th that "limited recognition of the French Committee of National Liberation was tendered yesterday with misgivings as to acceptance, but lo and behold, the French received it with enthusiasm and gratification." After the declarations from the three major powers, the Committee was deluged with recognition from other governments. On September 3rd, the fourth anniversary of the war, de Gaulle asserted with obvious satisfaction that "the recognition by twenty-six states of the French Committee of National Liberation furnishes convincing proof of our solidarity for victory and for peace."[18]

De Gaulle, like Churchill, had long been thinking ahead to the victory and the peace. Since 1940 Free France had not aimed so much to win the war, since its military impact would necessarily be limited, as to be among the war's winners. This Roosevelt would not forgive. But neither would de Gaulle apologize. French divisions could gain victories on the battlefield without France rising from defeat. De Gaulle knew that his success would be measured not by how many battles he won but by whether France, from the rubble of battle, emerged a great nation again. As the war approached its final stages, his mind focused more and more on France at liberation.

Throughout the spring of 1943, the remarkable Moulin tightened his grip on the direction of the Resistance, which de Gaulle considered the key to his control of Metropolitan France. Coolly and skillfully Moulin shaped the Resistance into an army of Gaullism. Painstakingly he worked to channel its *mystique* toward de Gaulle's political aims. Gradually he was laying a foundation on which de Gaulle could build a government the moment he returned to France.

But in an instant it was all over. In June the Nazis captured, tortured and killed Moulin, at the same time as they seized and shot other Resistance leaders. De Gaulle's mechanism of control was shattered. The blow enfeebled him just as his rivals for power were moving into a position to threaten his plans.

To de Gaulle the United States represented one great rival. Every day he found more evidence that Roosevelt wanted to decide who would rule France at liberation. De Gaulle believed that the United States might conclude a bargain with Vichy to have Pétain or even Laval rule under the cover of American arms. The "local authorities" doctrine, with military expediency its only standard, endorsed such an arrangement. The North African experience, both during the Darlan period and after, provided the precedents. De Gaulle considered the American threat both real and frightening.

De Gaulle's other great rival was the Communist Party, the most energetic and most united element in the Resistance. De Gaulle did not doubt that the Party would turn its energy and unity to the seizure of control in France after the Nazis left. For the time being, he and the Communists cooperated within the framework of the Resistance. De Gaulle had the money and the matériel. The Communists had the men and the organization. Moulin had been successful in dominating the Communists, though they had been growing increasingly rebellious. But it was an open secret that the Gaullist-Communist relationship was a *mariage de convenance* that would likely tear asunder when the struggle for power replaced the struggle for freedom.

De Gaulle had counted heavily on Moulin's ability to take the play away from both the Americans and the Communists at the moment of liberation. A new phase in his relations with the Resistance necessarily began after Moulin's death. Moulin, in his dual capacity as president of the National Resistance Council and delegate of the French Committee, was never replaced. From within its own ranks the Council elected as president Georges Bidault, who was not a Communist nor a Gaullist but a Christian Democrat. Claude Serreules, a deputy of Moulin, was temporarily designated de Gaulle's delegate. Both lacked Moulin's tough constitution. Neither could be counted on to do de Gaulle's bidding. With astonishing rapidity, the Resistance recovered from the deadly Gestapo raids of June, 1943. But when it did, the power structure had been reversed. The Communists dominated the apparatus of leadership, and de Gaulle, though still the titular chief, was the challenger for control.[19]

De Gaulle's peculiar symbiosis with the French Communist Party in the middle years of the war made the Algiers Committee a favorite in Moscow. In 1943, the Soviet Union's goal was to divert Germans from the Russian front, not incite Communist revolution in France.

Stalin reasoned that by supporting de Gaulle he encouraged the French Resistance. Anti-Nazi ferment in the west relieved pressure in the east and hastened the moment of Allied landings on the Continent. Stalin, for reasons different from Churchill's, supported French recognition and the admission of France to postwar planning. It was unthinkable to him that Washington and London should be sapping de Gaulle's strength when Moscow considered it imperative to reinforce him.[20]

The first significant test of Allied willingness to admit France to postwar considerations occurred when Italy surrendered. On August 2nd, with the Fascists tottering, the French Committee sent identical notes to the British and American Governments claiming the right to participate not only in impending armistice negotiations but also in any enforcement machinery subsequently established. The British and the Russians raised no objections, but on August 29th, Washington and London asked the Committee to accept General Eisenhower, the chief Allied negotiator, as its representative. De Gaulle replied affirmatively, on the condition that France be permitted to examine the terms of the armistice prior to signature. At 5:30 P.M. on September 8th, however, Murphy and Macmillan notified the Committee that Italy had capitulated and that Eisenhower would make an announcement in an hour. They pointed out that the surrender had been negotiated in great confusion and that France, like Greece and Yugoslavia, had been excluded for reasons of security. The Committee, which had no quarrel with the text, protested mildly about the procedure. De Gaulle was not reassured about the intentions of the Allies by the circumstances of the episode.[21]

After the armistice, Roosevelt had no intention of letting the control of Italy slip out of American and British hands. He opposed giving a share to the Russians, who had signed the surrender. He surely had no sympathy with France's claim. Without ado, Washington and London established the Allied Control Commission under Eisenhower's direction to set policy for the Italian occupation. To make a place for the Russians and create the appearance of Allied unity, however, an Allied Advisory Council was established. Though it possessed no authority, Roosevelt still complained about seating France as an equal with the three major powers. Britain argued that the French, because they actually had forces fighting in Italy, had more right to membership than the Russians. Somewhat irritated,

Roosevelt conceded the point. It gave the French a share in the form, if not in the substance, of the military government in Italy.[22]

Britain tried to promote the French into more meaningful participation in Allied political planning at the foreign ministers' conference held in Moscow in August, 1943, where Eden urged the creation of a European Advisory Commission to discuss the organization of postwar Europe. Hull contended that "it would be unwise to attempt to solve postwar problems while hostilities were continuing," but with Russian support, the British position carried. Having once prevailed against the United States, Eden hesitated to make the Commission more unpalatable to Roosevelt by insisting on a seat for the French, which he had proposed earlier. American indifference already threatened the Commission's effectiveness. Effective or not, however, the European Advisory Commission was the only Allied body formally concerned with postwar planning. Exclusion gave de Gaulle further evidence that the Allies were conspiring to keep France out of the peacetime settlement.[23]

On September 9th, a few days after the Italians laid down their arms, the French Committee was submitted to its fiercest test in the liberation struggle. Resistance forces in Corsica had risen up. They seized control of Ajaccio, the capital, and other principal cities. The German garrison on the island, estimated at 20,000 men, was taking steps to crush the uprising. British and American forces could not be diverted from the fighting in Italy. The French had to act quickly and alone if they were to drive the Germans out and deliver the islanders from severe reprisals.

From an incongruous flotilla of merchantmen and fighting ships, Giraud landed a force of 15,000 French soldiers over a period of two weeks. The Nazis at first fought tenaciously, then, fearing entrapment, decided to withdraw. Though Giraud's units moved vigorously, the Germans succeeded in evacuating most of their personnel. The French, nonetheless, had won an important victory and liberated the first department of France. It had particular military significance in setting a pattern for cooperative effort between the Army and the Resistance.[24]

More significant, Corsica became the initial testing ground for de Gaulle's claim of dominion on French soil. The Resistance leadership, there as in Metropolitan France, was dominated by Communists, although the organization gave nominal allegiance to de Gaulle. As the

Germans fled, the Communists took control of municipal government throughout the island. On October 8th, four days after the fighting ended, de Gaulle arrived in Corsica to assert the sovereignty of the French Committee. He had the army to enforce his rule, but obviously it was against his interest to use it. On a tour of the island, de Gaulle was joyously acclaimed wherever he went. The Communist opposition, apparently irresolute, simply vanished beneath his insistence on reestablishing the French state. On quitting Corsica, de Gaulle left behind him a team of officials to direct his administration. The islanders proved perfectly willing to accept the rule he conveyed to them.[25]

The Corsican liberation contained the source of another bitter round in the continuing battle between de Gaulle and Giraud. The commander in chief, who won commendation from de Gaulle for his conduct of operations, had for months before the landings been secretly dealing with the Communist underground on the island. In his political innocence, Giraud failed utterly to realize that his unguarded cooperation might facilitate Communist seizure of power. When de Gaulle learned, after the Ajaccio uprising, that Giraud had conspired with the Communists, he determined to enforce subordination on the commander in chief once and for all. He could chance no repetition of the Corsican experience in Metropolitan France, where the Communists might not be so malleable.

On September 25th, de Gaulle proposed that the French Committee replace the system of the double presidency with a single, strong executive. Giraud protested that the proposal was a violation of the spirit in which the Committee was founded. He was outvoted by a large margin. At the same time, the Committee approved a further military reorganization that deprived the commander in chief of all but the most nominal powers over the Army. Appropriately Giraud, who took pride in his ignorance of politics, terminated his duties as co-president by committing political suicide. He cosigned de Gaulle's measures into law.

A month later, Giraud was no longer a member of the French Committee. De Gaulle, claiming a need to reshape the ministries, requested the resignation of all the Committee members. Giraud was astonished when de Gaulle announced that his was one of the four that had been accepted. De Gaulle had achieved at last his goal of getting the commander in chief out of the government. Five months after de

Gaulle's arrival in Algiers, Giraud—Roosevelt's man of destiny—was all but eliminated as a factor in French affairs.[26]

That same week, de Gaulle for the first time convoked in Algiers a body known as the Consultative Assembly. He had long contemplated its formation and had for many months been assembling its membership. The Assembly became one more effort to widen his regime's base of support. It was not a popular body in the conventional sense, since the means of electing members did not exist. It was drawn instead from what de Gaulle called "spiritual families." The Resistance, the left and center parties of the Republic and the original Free French movement were heavily represented. The Communist Party consented to accept several seats. To de Gaulle's disappointment, the Catholic hierarchy, citing its traditional abstention from politics, did not. The colonies sent delegates from both the French and native populations. Prominent parliamentarians who had voted against Pétain's authoritarianism were also invited. The Consultative Assembly was not meant to have governing powers. De Gaulle intended it rather as a source of ideas and a symbol of unity. His aim was not to dilute the French Committee's power but to bolster it by the support of the widest possible representation.[27]

Roosevelt contemplated events in North Africa with no pleasure. "I have very distinct feelings," he wrote to Marshall as Giraud faltered, "that we should not send further equipment or munitions to the French army in North Africa if our prima donna is to seize control of it from the old gentleman." After the "old gentleman" fell, he repeated his proposal. Marshall dissented from the President's view, on the grounds that Eisenhower needed the French divisions for forthcoming operations in the Mediterranean.[28]

De Gaulle had thwarted Roosevelt once again. He had swallowed Giraud, careful to heed Churchill's admonition to avoid a single conspicuous gulp. He was now the custodian of French military power, which had become an element in Allied strategic planning. He was still too weak to be certain of success. But he was, at last, too strong to destroy. As the battle approached the shores of France, de Gaulle's power to influence the course of the war continued to increase. He did not doubt that even Roosevelt would soon have to concede it.

TEN

Conquest or Liberation

October, 1943–June, 1944

I<small>T WAS NO SECRET</small> in the fall of 1943 that an invasion of the Continent was impending. The Germans waited apprehensively. The Russians pressed for it relentlessly. The French chafed with impatience. The invasion was to be the culmination of the Allied strategy to win the war in Europe.

In most of Europe, the invaders would arrive not as conquerors but as liberators. They would be fighting not among a hostile population but among friends. It was not their intention to replace one military occupation with another. But even among friends, they had to be certain of tranquillity behind the battle lines. The Allies had thus to determine how the liberated countries would be ruled.

In Belgium, Luxembourg, the Netherlands, Denmark and Norway, Roosevelt planned to rely heavily on the governments-in-exile to return to exercise power. Eisenhower's command was authorized to conclude agreements with each of them to assure orderly administrative transition from occupation to liberation.

But Roosevelt recognized no government-in-exile of France. The French Committee of National Liberation was stronger than any of the expatriated regimes. It was the only one that exercised effective authority over a significant segment of the national territory. It controlled a sizable army prepared to help drive the enemy from the national soil. By all reports, it was vigorously supported at home. But Roosevelt was convinced that its leader, once installed, would never

183

relinquish power. He was determined to prevent de Gaulle from getting a foothold in Metropolitan France. He made up his mind he would have nothing to do with the French Committee in administering liberated France.[1]

At one point, Roosevelt appeared on the verge of deciding to impose an Allied military government. He was in Cairo in November, 1943, consulting with Churchill and Chiang Kai-shek, when he became particularly incensed over what de Gaulle, farther down the African coast, was doing to consolidate his rule. "De Gaulle . . . now claims the right to speak for all of France," he wrote indignantly to Hull, "and talks openly of plans to set up his government in France as soon as the Allies get in. The thought that the occupation, when it comes, should be wholly military is one to which I am increasingly inclined."[2]

In more serene moments, however, Roosevelt recognized that the Allies could not govern France as if it were Germany or Italy. The actual management of civil affairs, as he saw it, had to remain in the hands of Frenchmen. But he determined that the Allies, not the French, would select these Frenchmen and establish how much autonomy they would have. Roosevelt would countenance no arrangement, whether or not military government was its name, that would leave the French independent of Allied supervision. He had resolved that the Supreme Commander must exercise ultimate authority.[3]

The Allied plan that emerged in the final months of 1943 provided for the designation of a French general to take charge of civil affairs. He would, on the one hand, be responsible to the Allied commander. But to lighten the onus of military occupation, he would, on the other, take his domestic authority from the French état de siège laws. He would function with as little interference as possible, although subject to an Allied veto. His mandate would run until the population was free to elect a government.

The plan assumed that the General's administration would be nonpolitical. It made the Allied commander responsible for enforcing Roosevelt's policy of "keeping the scales even" between competing political groups. But it provided explicitly that the Allies were to have no dealings with Vichy except to liquidate it. The French, presumably, would later conduct their own elections, under the supervision of Allied forces.

The flaw in the plan was that it needed a French general. The

Allies could conceivably have found another Giraud, but his claim to authority, as Torch had demonstrated, was not likely to evoke much support. All French generals of any significance were responsible to the French Committee in Algiers. De Gaulle, of course, would not hear of an arrangement that left to foreigners ultimate authority over his country.[4]

De Gaulle's counterproposal to Washington and London was not, in operating terms, profoundly different from the Allied conception. He offered to assign a general to direct a team of French liaison officers responsible for obtaining the cooperation of the civilian population. He had, in fact, already begun the recruitment and training of a *corps de liaison administrative*, whose members were to accompany the Allied armies in their march across France, reestablishing local government and attending to military needs. In the rear, his administration was to be independent, but geared to serving the liberators. At the front, the Allied command could exercise its jurisdiction directly. De Gaulle was willing to guarantee the Allies everything under his rule that they prepared to take by right of conquest under their own.

De Gaulle's proposal deviated most fundamentally from the Allied conception in its insistence on the establishment of a government in liberated France to make and execute policy, both for war and peace. This was precisely what Roosevelt did not want. The President believed that as long as fighting retained first priority France should be administered without being governed. De Gaulle, while recognizing the war's priority, denied that military demands would conflict with the restoration of French sovereignty. In fact, he believed a strong government was essential to maintain order and economic stability. De Gaulle pledged to the Allies the full resources of France. But he wanted it understood that they were transmitted by the grace of an independent state.[5]

In practice, the United States had already begun treating the French Committee like a government, whether it was admitted or not. In September, 1943, a few weeks after the announcement of Allied recognition, the French Committee acquired accreditation for a diplomatic mission in Washington. It superseded the military delegation that had hitherto conducted all French business. The argument that relations with the French were strictly military thus became difficult to sustain.

In Algiers, the change was more important. Robert Murphy, always antagonistic to de Gaulle, was at last transferred to another post. Reluctantly, Roosevelt gave his replacement, Edwin C. Wilson, the rank of ambassador, since the British planned to assign an ambassador to Algiers. Wilson, a partisan of the French cause, improved the tone of Washington's representation by comporting himself as the link between one friendly government and another.[6]

But by itself, increased American attention to the protocol of sovereignty did not satisfy de Gaulle. He insisted on its basic attributes as well, even at the risk of alienating his allies. He appeared, in fact, to go out of his way to provoke Washington and London. His aim was to demonstrate that the French Committee could exercise the powers of a sovereign state with impunity.

In December, 1943, de Gaulle arrested Marcel Peyrouton, Pierre Boisson and Pierre-Etienne Flandin, all major figures under Vichy who, at one time or another, had been useful to the Allied cause. He took his authority from the French Committee's decision to bring to justice Pétain and the principal architects of the Vichy regime. His haste was determined by a wish to assure the Resistance, for his own political purposes, that he would deal harshly with the Frenchmen who were its foes. But beyond immediate political aims, de Gaulle believed that the restoration of French self-esteem demanded the eradication of all vestiges of honor from Vichy. He rejected the claim that subsequent service to the Allies redeemed submission to the enemy. De Gaulle had resolved that the sins of Vichy would not be easily expiated.

Eisenhower, from the Italian front, sent a message of concern to Roosevelt when he learned of the arrests. He also dispatched to the French Committee in Algiers a warning that the action could have "the most serious consequences." Churchill, too, was disturbed. Though opposed to retribution, he was also embarrassed by the knowledge that the Allies owed an obligation to each of de Gaulle's three victims. He regarded their release as a matter of Allied honor. Churchill proposed to Roosevelt that they offer asylum to the three and admonish de Gaulle against further punitive action.

Spurred by the Prime Minister and the General, Roosevelt fired off a message to Eisenhower that summed up his most intense feelings against de Gaulle. "Please inform the French Committee as follows," he wrote. "In view of the assistance given the Allied armies during the campaign in Africa by Boisson, Peyrouton and Flandin, you are *directed* to take no action against these three individuals at the present time." On a copy of the note that he sent to Churchill he appended: "It seems to me this is the proper time to eliminate the Jeanne d'Arc complex and return to realism. I, too, am shocked by the high-handed arrests at this time."

Churchill, who was not feigning displeasure with de Gaulle, nonetheless was not prepared for a rupture. "To admit that a handful of émigrés are to have the power . . . to carry civil war into France is to lose the future of that unfortunate country," he wrote angrily to Roosevelt. But in an intimate meeting with de Gaulle at Marrakesh, where he had gone to convalesce from a touch of pneumonia, the Prime Minister did his best to restore friendly relations with the French. Roosevelt's menaces to the Algiers Committee were clearly more than Churchill had bargained for.

Eisenhower, who had begun the chain of protests, was also aghast at Roosevelt's instructions. Through his chief of staff, he gingerly suggested to Marshall that "you may see fit to inform the President" of the probable rejection of the proposed message. Such an eventuality, he said, would be "a direct slap at the President, which the United States could not accept and its only alternative would be to withdraw recognition of the Committee and to stop French rearmament. . . . Ambassador Wilson has recommended through the State Department that a more indirect method be used and I am hopeful that this recommendation will be accepted. . . . In the event of an abrupt break with the Committee which might upset our military plans, the onus would be borne by the United States."

While Eisenhower, with Marshall's approval, put off the showdown, Roosevelt reconsidered and drew up a milder note. The United States Government, it said simply, "views with alarm" the arrest of "these gentlemen" who aided the Allied war effort. Roosevelt by now seemed less concerned about the prisoners themselves than about his own posture in the dispute. He reduced his demand from "no action" to "no trials until after the liberation," which was nothing more than a face-saving condition. He instructed Eisenhower to negotiate his revised conditions, "if possible by informal discussion." Eisenhower's negotiating was apparently successful, for the three were not brought to justice during the war. Roosevelt, having been maneuvered once again into the uncomfortable position of defending Vichy, then withdrew from the encounter. The outcome was a standoff between Roosevelt and de Gaulle.[7]

De Gaulle defied the Allies a second time at the end of 1943 in a manner that was far less defensible. This time, his objective was to reassert his contention that the French Army was an instrument of policy of the French government. De Gaulle had become irritated by the Allied indifference to discussing with the French Committee its plans for using the Army during the liberation struggle. He was apprehensive that the Allies contemplated leaving French troops out of the fight. De Gaulle was not averse to shocking the Allies into considering his requirements. He had little right, even claiming the defense of French interests, to choose a method that did injury to Allied military operations.

The source of the episode, ironically, lay in the success of French units battling the Germans in the Apennines. The first two French divisions sent into Italy had proved so effective in combat that a call went out for more. Giraud promptly assigned the famous First Free French Division, which had made the great trek across the desert. But the Allied command asked for an alternate selection, on the grounds that the First Division's British equipment presented insoluble supply problems. Giraud named the Ninth Colonial, one of his own former divisions, but the next day the French Committee overruled him and restored the First Free French to the schedule, though it would take weeks to refit. De Gaulle further suspended all departures to Italy until agreement was reached on the place of the Army within the alliance. His action had no military justification whatever.

Eisenhower, angrier than he had ever been with the French, threatened to terminate the rearmament program then and there. He insisted that the French Committee give him assurances that it would henceforth cooperate with his military needs. De Gaulle answered that he was quite prepared to offer these assurances under reasonable conditions. He wanted, he said, nothing more than to discuss them with Eisenhower. His aim was to reopen the entire question of the relationship of the French Army to the Allied command, so that specific provision could be established for the consideration of French interests in strategic situations. Eisenhower, despite his outrage, acknowledged that de Gaulle's complaints had some merit and agreed to maintain arms deliveries while an attempt was made to deal with them.

De Gaulle failed to achieve a change in the principle, established by Roosevelt, that in return for arms the Allied command possessed the power to determine the destiny of the French Army. De Gaulle wanted this formula, which dated back to the Anfa agreement, replaced by the recognition that the French Committee, acting as the French government, had the final authority over its forces. He tried to bar direct communications between the Allied and French commands without prior agreement at the governmental level. But Eisenhower was powerless to modify the instructions that he deal with the French exclusively as a subordinate military agency. De Gaulle did not surrender the point. It simply remained as an area of difference that would become exceedingly troublesome later on.

De Gaulle pressed this grievance less vigorously than might have been expected because Eisenhower offered him important military satisfactions. The French Army, de Gaulle learned, had been assigned to invade France from the south and drive northward until it met the principal Allied thrust coming from the English Channel. The Army, functioning as an entity, would thus perform an important strategic mission inside Metropolitan France. This was precisely what de Gaulle wanted. He raised no objection to placing the French under overall Allied command after Eisenhower discreetly put the condition as a request instead of a demand.

De Gaulle also received a tentative commitment on his proposal to have Leclerc's Second Armored Division included in the cross-Channel landings. De Gaulle wanted Leclerc to liberate Paris. He found Eisenhower sympathetic to his sentimental and psychological arguments, but de Gaulle said nothing of his principal reason, which was to have faithful Free French troops on hand in Paris when the Germans departed. De Gaulle wanted neither a challenge from the Resistance nor a repetition of the 1871 Commune to upset his plans for government. His steadfastness persuaded Eisenhower to reconsider the shipping schedule to try to get Leclerc from Africa to England in time for the invasion.

Eisenhower and de Gaulle were thus on excellent terms when, on December 30, 1943, they bade each other farewell. The American was on his way to London to take command of the Supreme Headquarters Allied Expeditionary Force, the British-American directorate known to the world as SHAEF, which was preparing the greatest invasion in history. In what Captain Butcher, Eisenhower's diarist, described as a "love fest," the two acknowledged that they counted on each other heavily. Eisenhower was de Gaulle's best friend in the Allied camp. De Gaulle could assist Eisenhower in resolving the complex of problems attendant on liberating France from enemy forces.[8]

Eisenhower wanted nothing more than to conclude an agreement

with de Gaulle that would give the French Committee the responsibility for administering the liberated territory. He yearned to be free
of the burdens of civil affairs. A strong French authority could relieve him of such standard concerns of foreign armies as requisitioning
goods and labor, directing civilian police forces, handling money and
financial accounts, assuring public health and safety, supplying food
and fuel for the populace and providing for refugees and other dis-
placed persons. All were pedestrian problems compared to defeating
the enemy on the battlefield, but they nonetheless had to be solved.
Eisenhower wanted de Gaulle's Committee to assume some of the
responsibility for reconciling the French people to the necessity of
Allied bombing with its ensuing death and destruction. Not the least
important, he counted on the French Committee's authority to stand
behind the command of the Resistance. Eisenhower knew of no way
to handle civil affairs sensibly without the French Committee. His aim
was to negotiate an agreement that would guarantee his military requirements and leave de Gaulle free to do the rest.[9]

In mid-January, 1944, General Walter Bedell Smith, Eisenhower's
chief of staff, prepared a report for Washington that represented the
SHAEF viewpoint. He wrote:

De Gaulle is growing up, and is a much more sane and sensible individual than he appeared on his arrival in North Africa. . . . He has been
amenable to suggestions from both the British and American ambassadors,
as well as from the military, and such remnants as are left of the Joan
of Arc complex are pretty thoroughly submerged by his sober realization of the difficulties of his present political problems. . . . At its very
worst, the Committee, as now constituted, provides a recognized constituted group with which we can deal.[10]

But at the same time that Eisenhower reached his judgment on de
Gaulle's usefulness, President Roosevelt was confirming his own on
de Gaulle's unfitness. In a letter to Ambassador Wilson, he stated:

General de Gaulle and his associates have attempted to arrogate to
themselves the credit for resistance to Germany, ignoring or belittling
the efforts of other French and the enormous assistance rendered the
cause of France by the United States and the other allies. . . . We regard
it as *our duty to the French people,** for which we will be accountable to
history, to respect no other verdict than their own and to assist in bringing about conditions under which that verdict can be freely ascertained
at the earliest possible date.[11]

* Author's italics.

It is significant that Roosevelt should now cite such lofty principles as the basis of his French policy. When he dealt with Pétain, Weygand, Darlan and Giraud he never contemplated his duty to the French people. On the contrary, he justified his association with collaborationists and appeasers exclusively on military grounds. Now he disregarded the pleas of his military advisers to pursue a policy he defended on the grounds of ideology. Roosevelt had dressed up his resentment of de Gaulle in a noble precept. But if he succeeded in fooling himself, there were many around him who saw through the disguise.

Secretary of War Stimson, for one, recorded in his memoirs that he "was disappointed by the degree of personal feeling which seemed to enter into the thinking of Mr. Roosevelt." Pleading Eisenhower's cause, Stimson tried to persuade Roosevelt that the French Committee should be given at least some responsibility for the administration of liberated France. But, he noted wryly in his diary, "Mr. Roosevelt proved a tough customer."

During January and February, 1944, the military men put intensive pressure on the White House to have the President relent. Stimson tried unsuccessfully to work through Hull, "for whom," he wrote, "the very mention of de Gaulle was enough to produce an outburst of skillful Tennessee denunciation." John J. McCloy, the Assistant Secretary of War, called on Leahy. Eisenhower dispatched his civil affairs officer, Brigadier General Julius Holmes, to campaign in Washington. Wilson made several trips from Algiers for talks at the White House and the State Department. But the impact of the campaign was negligible.[12]

Roosevelt seemed to go out of his way to emphasize his contempt for the French Committee on February 12, 1944, when he turned over an American destroyer to the French war effort. The French mission in Washington had asked him to present the ship to the Committee, as governing body of the armed forces. Instead, Roosevelt told a large crowd assembled at the Washington shipyard that the United States presented the destroyer to the French Navy. He made no mention of the French Committee or de Gaulle. The press did not overlook the implication that the President thereby dismissed the French Committee as being of no account.[13]

In one instance, Roosevelt was forced to recognize the growing strength of the French Committee. Because French soldiers were fight-

ing so well in Italy, sentiment had increased to give France a seat on
the Allied Control Commission. "When you and I look back eleven
months," Roosevelt wrote angrily to Churchill, apparently referring
to their meeting in Casablanca at the beginning of 1943, "we realize
that de Gaulle and his committee have most decidedly moved forward by 'the process of infiltration'—in other words, here a little
there a little. For the life of me, I cannot see why France is entitled to
anybody on the Allied Control Commission for Italy." Then, betraying his real longing, he added: "I wish you and I could run this Italian
business. We would not need any help or advice." But despite his
irritation at the prospect of sharing the direction of Italy, the French
could not be contained. Because the Russians insisted on a seat, the
French, on the basis of their participation in the fighting, were entitled
to have one too. In mid-February, French and Russian delegates
joined the Commission, and, to Roosevelt's distaste, took a part of the
responsibility for setting Italian policy.[14]

Allied awareness of the growing potential of the French Resistance
also advanced the Committee's status. In February, 1944, the O.S.S.
estimated the strength of the Resistance "conservatively" at 200,000
and, though planners were uncertain how best to profit from it,
SHAEF maintained that the Resistance had to be brought within the
authority of the Allied command structure. Eisenhower, who opposed the proliferation of undisciplined partisan bands, insisted the
Resistance be centrally directed. He did not want a British or American officer, no matter how intimate his experience with the Resistance. He wanted as its commander a French general responsible to
Algiers.[15]

By spring, 1944, SHAEF headquarters was frantic that provision
still had not been made for ruling liberated France. D-Day was
scheduled for early June. From the Continent came a succession of
reports of support for de Gaulle's leadership. But, despite increasing
exhortations from both London and the Pentagon, Roosevelt would
not let Eisenhower talk to de Gaulle. Nonetheless, Eisenhower decided to proceed with planning. He assumed that because de Gaulle
was the only sensible answer to his problem, Roosevelt would ultimately be persuaded to relent.

On the contrary, however, on March 3, 1944, Eisenhower was instructed to discontinue any talks with the French, pending new
orders from the President. After two crucial weeks during which all

discussions were suspended, Eisenhower received a directive that resurrected nothing less than the old "local authorities" doctrine. Stimson, in his memoirs, represented it as a victory for those who favored "some freedom in treating with de Gaulle," but Eisenhower was shocked. He was authorized to "consult" with the French Committee and, when suitable, employ it to appoint administrative personnel. But he was forbidden to limit his dealings to the Committee. Most important, he was ordered to sign no agreements and to retain personally all the prerogatives of military government.[16]

"Already the French have the impression that the Allied armies will dominate the liberated areas," wrote William Phillips, SHAEF's chief political officer. "The President's proposal requires General Eisenhower to assume responsibility for the political situation in liberated France at a time when he will be required to give his whole attention to the battle against the Germans. This is asking a great deal." Phillips counseled Eisenhower to protest vigorously to Washington.[17]

Three weeks later, Ambassador Wilson reported to Eisenhower that the President had told him in a conversation at the White House that France did not need a strong central government.

It was his view [Wilson wrote], that in the period following the liberation and until such time as the shell-shocked people of France had recovered their balance and were ready to proceed with Constitutional questions, France would be governed by local authorities in the departments and communes, as in fact it had been mainly governed for the many years of the Third Republic. The President said that Eisenhower should have freedom of action to deal with groups other than the Committee because, for example, the Committee might appoint bad representatives in one region of France while another group might come forward with some worthy representatives who should be considered.

Wilson said he expressed to the President the opinion that the encouragement of competing groups would promote civil war. He persuaded the President, he said, that the best way to avert chaos was to deal with a single entity. Wilson declared that he closed the interview by asking permission to inform Eisenhower that SHAEF officers were free to work exclusively with the French Committee, as a practical matter, if it refrained from extremes, kept order and cooperated with the Allied armies. He reported that Roosevelt said: "That is all right. I have no objection to that. You may say that."[18]

But de Gaulle did not, by Roosevelt's standards, refrain from extremes. Early in April he struck the final blow at Giraud by relieving him of the cherished rank of commander in chief. The decision was the consequence of another acrimonious dispute. This time, it was over Giraud's secret contacts with an intelligence network in France that professed sympathy to Vichy. De Gaulle, aware of Giraud's value as a symbol of unity, proffered the former commander in chief the post of inspector-general, which was high in status and usefulness but without command functions. Allied officials in Algiers blandly tried to persuade Giraud to stay, arguing that the proposed assignment was most appropriate to a senior general who was without hope of obtaining a field command. But in reality Giraud's decision was to them a matter of indifference. They found him virtually impotent and barely competent. For action, they had long before become accustomed to going directly to de Gaulle. After much thought, Giraud stood on his honor and chose to resign. In Algiers, where a year before he possessed, at least in name, the power of an absolute monarch, his departure was unmourned. Not even Roosevelt sent him a word of condolence, but in the adjacent White House office, Leahy noted in his diary when he learned the news: "It is my opinion that we, the Americans, will have constant friction with General de Gaulle until he is eliminated from the problem of French participation in the war."[19]

But on April 9, 1944, Eisenhower was surprised and elated to learn that Hull had delivered a speech which appeared to break the deadlock on his treating with de Gaulle.

We have no purpose or wish to govern France [said the Secretary of State], or to administer any affairs save those which are necessary for military operations against the enemy. It is of the utmost importance that civil authority in France be exercised by Frenchmen. . . . The President and I are clear, therefore, as to the need, from the outset, of French civil administration—and democratic French administration—in France. We are disposed to see the French Committee of National Liberation exercise leadership to establish law and order under the supervision of the Allied commander-in-chief.

Eisenhower, without official notification, took Hull's speech to mean a change in policy. Encouraged by the British, he began cautiously to restore relations with de Gaulle's representatives in London. When weeks passed without confirmation of the new formula, Eisenhower became bewildered. The Foreign Office, in his behalf, sounded out Hull, who hinted that the President did not necessarily endorse the speech, although he had seen and approved it. Eisenhower continued to treat the speech as a policy guide, although he was now more confused than ever.[20]

While the Allied command floundered in uncertainty, de Gaulle acted with resolution. At a press conference on April 21, 1944, he said when questioned about Hull's declaration: "The French administration to be established in France naturally depends only on Frenchmen. You can be certain that Frenchmen will not accept in France any but a French administration. Consequently, the question is settled in advance. The only question that remains open is that of the cooperation between the French administration and the Allied command for the necessities of military operations." Preposterous as it seemed, de Gaulle was giving warning to the Allies that no matter what they decided, he and his Committee would be ruling the liberated territory.[21]

Throughout the winter and spring of 1944, the French Committee quite openly prepared elaborate machinery to assure its rule. In a series of ordinances, all published, the Committee provided for the transfer of power as the liberation progressed from liaison officers to national delegates to regional commissioners to the government itself. In most cases, it actually named the designees for each post, although the lists were kept secret to protect those who were in occupied France. General Pierre Koenig, hero of Bir Hacheim, was chosen as the Committee's representative at SHAEF, charged with directing the liaison teams and, when necessary, assuring the primacy of military requirements. De Gaulle's advocates in Washington pointed to the ordinance under which the Committee promised to relinquish power. His foes cited the one by which the Committee was to change its name on the eve of the invasion to the Provisional Government of the French Republic. But on the whole, though the United States' objective was to stop de Gaulle, Washington paid astonishingly little attention to these preparations.[22]

The French Army, meanwhile, figured with increasing prominence in military considerations. Juin's Expeditionary Corps in Italy, grown to nearly five divisions, in early May led the offensive to take Rome. The theater commander, General Harold Alexander, reported that French troops "drove like the wind" and exploited their successes "possibly quicker than United States or British troops." Clark, the senior American officer, was equally enthusiastic. Eisenhower declared that the French performance in the drive on Rome redeemed in "striking and spectacular manner" his judgment of the French as fighters and his decision to support French rearmament. Ironically, the possibility arose that the French might be penalized by their own success, for the Allied command in Italy clamored to retain those divisions. However flattering the tribute, the battlefield of France was the only one that counted for de Gaulle. Fortunately for the French, Eisenhower, despite severe pressure, refused to countenance any shift in strategy that would have taken de Gaulle's men away from the Riviera landings.[23]

In Algiers, the French had already joined the Americans in the feverish planning for the invasion. General Jean de Lattre de Tassigny, who broke with Pétain only in November, 1942, had been spirited from a Vichy prison to lead France's landing force. His American partner, General Alexander Patch, arrived from New Caledonia bearing the scars of his bitter struggle with d'Argenlieu. De Gaulle, happily, held no grudge against either. Both excellent commanders, they worked efficiently together. Their mutual esteem generated an atmosphere of harmony that was not surpassed between French and Americans during the entire war.[24]

In April, Leclerc's division arrived in England. Eisenhower's planners had shipped the men without their equipment, then had to find matériel with which to arm them. Though SHAEF had not made a commitment, Churchill ardently endorsed having Leclerc take Paris. Eisenhower was well disposed to the idea. Leclerc certainly had not come from Africa to be left in the rear. It was clearly understood that, operations permitting, his men would be the first into the capital.[25]

By early spring in France, the Resistance had begun its climactic drive against the Nazi occupants. So extensive was sabotage against the railroads that the Germans had to import 20,000 civilian workers from home, scarce as they were, to keep the trains running. SHAEF by now favored direct utilization of Resistance forces. General Koenig, for whom the Resistance was an additional responsibility, proposed a maximum of coordination between regular and partisan military action. As D-Day approached, SHAEF drew up plans for Resistance units to cut transportation and communication lines and to engage German forces in battle. In the final weeks, SHAEF organized dozens of inter-Allied radio teams and dropped them into France to facilitate communications. As de Gaulle had long before predicted, the Resistance had developed into a vital military factor.[26]

Still, Eisenhower had not settled the question of who would rule France. At the end of April, desperate for an understanding with the French Committee, he wired Washington for permission to sign an agreement on the basis of Hull's speech. Before he received an answer, he met with Koenig, who was no less anxious to reach an understanding. Koenig, more conciliatory and pragmatic than de Gaulle, himself suggested that they put aside the sovereignty question until some later time. He agreed to begin staff discussions at once on outstanding issues, including his own relation to SHAEF and command procedures for the Resistance. Obviously, both he and Eisenhower were exceeding the instructions handed down to them. But both were conscious of an acute need to resolve a multitude of problems in advance of an invasion that was only weeks away.

De Gaulle was the first to interrupt the talks, after the British, for security reasons, established an embargo on all communications emanating from the island. De Gaulle argued that the order, from which Americans and Russians were exempted, was not only an insult to an ally but a barrier to the private communications with Algiers necessary to conduct negotiations. The Allied command was in the process of working out a compromise that de Gaulle indicated would satisfy him. But suddenly, word came from Roosevelt ordering another break.

On May 11th, Eisenhower had dispatched a vigorous letter to Washington in an effort to provoke Roosevelt into reevaluating his thinking about the French Committee. Aware of the President's reflex on the political question, he phrased his plea exclusively in military terms.

The limitations under which we are operating in dealing with the French [he wrote] are becoming very embarrassing and we are producing a situation which is potentially dangerous. We began our military discussions with the French representatives here in the belief that, although we had no formal directive, we understood the policies of our governments well enough to be able to reach a working basis with any French body or organization that can effectively assist us in the fight against Germany. For the present there is no such body here except the French Committee of National Liberation. . . . From a military point of view, coordination with the French is of overriding importance. I request that this matter be treated as of the utmost urgency and that it be considered as far as possible on its military aspects.[27]

Roosevelt coldly notified Eisenhower two days later that he had received as much authority as he was going to get. The President refused categorically to let his commander make an agreement with the French Committee. Such an agreement, however limited, would force Eisenhower "to become involved with the Committee on a political level," the President declared. In his *Memoirs*, Hull wrote that Roosevelt remarked on May 20th, two weeks before D-Day, "that if anyone could give him a certificate proving that de Gaulle was a representative of the French people he would deal with him but that otherwise he had no idea of changing his mind."[28]

By contrast, de Gaulle a few days later wrote to his ambassador in London:

We are the French administration. . . . There is not the slightest chance that there will appear in liberated France any other effective administration, nor that such an administration can function independently of us. But let's recognize that we are asking for nothing. There is only us or chaos. . . . It is certain that for the battle, as well as in the country, the military command needs the cooperation of the French administration. . . . We will not accept any supervision or any intrusion on the exercise of our powers.[29]

Eisenhower, with a week to go before the troops began landing, still had not the remotest notion of how France would be ruled. He did not deceive himself into believing he could impose a military government, whether or not he had the means. He was equipped with the "local authorities" doctrine, which presumably meant that in the disorder of battle he would be free to select administrators from among the multitude who might be clamoring for power. He was expressly forbidden to rely on Vichy, but did that mean he could appoint administrators who for four years had served Vichy and the enemy? The Resistance would never stand for it. He himself was disgusted at the prospect of another Darlan deal or, worse still, a separate Darlan deal in each liberated region. De Gaulle had the organization that he needed. Eisenhower understood that he was being forced not only to spurn it but might very well have to contest with it for power.

Churchill was in a state of total exasperation. He found Roosevelt utterly unreasonable but was powerless to challenge him. The Russians, meanwhile, threatened to recognize the French Committee as the Provisional Government of France, as many smaller countries had already done. Churchill sent a hasty telegram to Moscow imploring restraint. Frantically, Churchill searched for a solution to a problem that he regarded as immensely dangerous and thoroughly absurd.

Churchill decided that he had to invite de Gaulle to London in the hope of reaching agreement. But Roosevelt set up an obstacle even to this proposal. The President refused to relax the security regulations to permit de Gaulle to communicate with Algiers and insisted further that, once in Britain, de Gaulle not be permitted to leave until after D-Day. Churchill knew de Gaulle well enough not to dare such a course. The only alternative was to invite him on the actual eve of the invasion. He took some small comfort in the likelihood that for at least a few days the Allied army would probably be confined to a small beachhead, with little liberated territory to administer. He believed the margin had to be put to good use.[30]

But while Churchill made his plans, Roosevelt went a step further to demonstrate that he had no interest in negotiations. When the President learned that de Gaulle would be in London before D-Day, he informed the Prime Minister that the United States would not send a representative to any discussions conducted with him. Furthermore, Roosevelt made his intention known to the press, so that de Gaulle understood it, too. When de Gaulle received the invitation to London, it was clear to him that the Allies wanted to add his prestige to the liberation effort without allowing him to participate in it. He accepted Churchill's bid for his own reasons. But, by leaving behind his diplomatic advisers, he demonstrated that he, too, was indifferent to negotiations.[31]

To de Gaulle, the most serious outrage planned by the Allies on the eve of the liberation was the issuance of military currency, designated "supplemental francs," for use in France. De Gaulle regarded no attribute of sovereignty as more firmly established than the exclusive jurisdiction of a government over its money. He considered the supplemental francs proof that France was simply substituting one occupying power for another. Both Eisenhower and Churchill had opposed using military money, but Washington insisted. By declaring that he would direct the French to treat the bills as counterfeit, de Gaulle made the currency dispute the principal focus of the battle for hegemony.[32]

Eisenhower and Koenig recorded the only achievement in the disintegrating relationship on June 2nd, when they reached agreement on the management of the Resistance. Eisenhower recognized the French General as the sole commander of the French Forces of the Interior (F.F.I.), official military designation given the Resistance. He, as Koenig's superior, would be empowered to determine the mission of the F.F.I. A special Allied headquarters was to be responsible for maintaining the delicate and complex communications network through which commands would be channeled. Eisenhower overrode the objections of Allied officers who wanted to maintain their own close association with the Resistance. He insisted firmly on the principle that the command of the Resistance be French.[33]

When de Gaulle arrived in Britain on the morning of June 4th, he was greeted by a friendly note from Churchill. But at lunch in Churchill's special railroad car near the invasion headquarters, the conversation quickly became caustic. In reply to the Prime Minister's suggestion that de Gaulle go to Washington to deal directly with Roosevelt, the General retorted sharply: "What makes you think I have to pose my candidacy for power in France to Roosevelt? The French government exists. I have nothing to ask in this domain either of the United States or Great Britain." Churchill, whatever his sympathies, explained to de Gaulle that in the event of open conflict, he would have to side with Roosevelt. He finally posed the question for which de Gaulle believed he had been summoned. Churchill asked de Gaulle to broadcast his endorsement of the invasion to the people of France. The request touched off a bitter denunciation of Allied intentions toward the French and an exchange of invective between the two men. The matter appeared further than ever from settlement.

After lunch, Churchill led the way to the command post, where Eisenhower gave de Gaulle a personal, twenty-minute briefing on the impending operations. The atmosphere was friendly until Eisenhower produced the proclamation he planned to deliver to Frenchmen. "In my capacity as Supreme Commander of the Allied Expeditionary Force," it said in French, "I have the duty and the responsibility to take all necessary measures for the conduct of the war. The immediate execution of the orders that I might have to give is essential." De Gaulle complained bitterly at the absence of any reference to a French authority and to the imperious tone it took. But when he asked for textual changes, Eisenhower answered that forty million copies had already been printed. De Gaulle was further outraged when Eisenhower confirmed that Allied soldiers had been issued supplemental francs. De Gaulle announced that he would not lend himself to the Allied designs and, furthermore, would not permit French liaison officers to accompany the invasion army.

Refusing Churchill's dinner invitation, de Gaulle returned to London that afternoon and put up in the Hotel Connaught, where he had first established quarters four years before. Because bad weather had delayed the landings by a day, he had an opportunity to reflect on the positions he had taken. It apparently made no difference. On the morning of June 6th, as Allied troops waded onto the shores of France, de Gaulle was silent. Eisenhower spoke. So did the King of Norway, the Queen of the Netherlands, the Grand Duchess of Luxembourg and the Prime Minister of Belgium. But de Gaulle insisted that had he spoken he would have given to the people of France the impression that he sanctioned Eisenhower's actions. De Gaulle emerged from his stillness that evening to step before the microphone of the B.B.C. It was only a few days until the fourth anniversary of his first and most famous B.B.C. address, when he told the people of France that they had not lost the war. After four years he could solemnly declare:

The supreme battle is underway. . . . It is, of course, the Battle of France and France's battle. For the sons of France, wherever they are, whatever they are, the simple and sacred duty is to fight the enemy, by every means at their disposal. . . . The instructions given by the French government and by the French leaders who have been authorized to give them must be exactly followed. . . . Behind the cloud so heavy with our blood and our tears there reappears the sun of our grandeur.

With uncharacteristic civility, de Gaulle had decided before the last ships sailed to let twenty of his liaison officers accompany the assault units. The gesture was the only *rapprochement* between the French Committee and the Allied command. In the midst of a great battle between powerful armies, there was now to be another contest to determine who, at last, would govern liberated France.[34]

ELEVEN

The Restoration Contest

June–October, 1944

W<small>HILE</small> B<small>RITISH</small> and American soldiers died on the beaches to liberate France, de Gaulle remained querulous and mean. He threatened and scolded. He complained to the press about supplemental francs and infringements of sovereignty. To the public, reacting to the news of the invasion with prayer and rejoicing, his behavior was utterly inappropriate. But de Gaulle had long before demonstrated his indifference to the censure of the crowd. His aim was to restore the French state, regardless of whom he thereby injured or offended.[1]

It was de Gaulle's good fortune that the SHAEF planners had put the administration of the Normandy beachhead under the direction of Britain's General Bernard Montgomery. As a subordinate to Eisenhower, Montgomery was theoretically subject to the same instructions on the conduct of civil affairs. But he had a Britisher's natural predilection for de Gaulle. He was less sensitive to Roosevelt's anti-Gaullist prejudices. Montgomery administered his patch of liberated territory without attention to the grave political issues that swirled about it.

On June 8th, Bayeux became the first major town liberated by the Allies. When Montgomery's troops entered, they found the subprefect, Pierre Rochat, still on the job. Rochat had received his mandate from Vichy, but he considered himself foremost a French civil servant, which meant he did his duty to the state without inquiring into its politics. Rochat's instructions were to prevent disorder and maintain a "correct" neutrality toward foreign armies. Beneath a portrait of Pétain, he told the British that he was quite prepared to carry out his responsibilities. The British disregarded the protest of the local Resistance leaders and accepted his offer. In the succeeding days, Rochat provided not only excellent administration but fresh vegetables, butter, eggs and cheese for the Army. Since he ruled in Pétain's name, for a week following D-Day Vichy reigned in liberated France.[2]

Nonetheless, Frenchmen understood that their government was no longer at Vichy. British intelligence officers reported that wherever they went they found the population talking of de Gaulle. "We are waiting for him. There is no other," they heard over and over again. They said it was certain the French would rally to de Gaulle and to the government he led.[3]

De Gaulle returned to France on June 14th. In his party when he stepped ashore was François Coulet, whom he had named Regional Commissioner of the Republic. De Gaulle dispatched Coulet to Bayeux as his first official act on French soil. He then called on Montgomery, who welcomed him graciously in the trailer that served as invasion headquarters. Casually de Gaulle mentioned that Coulet had been sent to relieve Rochat of his duties. Montgomery raised no objection. On the contrary, Rochat had become less important to him than the support of the local population and, particularly, the Resistance, who were irritated at the continued presence of Vichy. Montgomery was delighted to have de Gaulle make a try at running the liberated territory. With official acquiescence, de Gaulle thus took the first step in his master plan to achieve dominion over France.

From Montgomery's trailer, de Gaulle began a triumphal tour of the beachhead. His return to his native soil evoked the deepest expressions of emotion wherever he went. Emerging from the ruins of their homes and public buildings, the traditionally reserved Normans thronged excitedly around him to rejoice in his message of deliverance. "We will fight at the side of the Allies, with the Allies, as an ally," he told them. Even the most skeptical observer did not doubt the sincerity of his welcome or its meaning as a popular endorsement.

When de Gaulle reached the subprefecture in Bayeux late in the day, Pétain's picture was no longer hanging on the wall. Coulet had prepared his chief's reception. Rochat, without objection, had agreed to withdraw from office. The staff of the subprefecture willingly consented to accept de Gaulle as its new chief. The shift in loyalty, played out quietly and quickly, represented the assumption of authority by the Provisional Government of the French Republic. It was, to be sure, a *coup d' état*, but it was accepted as inevitable even by its victims. De Gaulle returned to England that night, his four-year-old claim to French leadership buttressed by power and, evidently, ratified by acclaim.[4]

The next day, Coulet posted on the walls of Bayeux a proclamation addressed to "The Liberated Population":

The Provisional Government of the French Republic [it declared] has given me the task of representing it and of exercising the rights of French sovereignty in the liberated territory of the Rouen region. . . . The war continues. . . . Frenchmen already liberated by the gigantic effort of the Allied armies have the duty to place all of their powers at the service of the fight for the liberation and the grandeur of France. To our British and American friends, fraternally united in the same battle for the same ideal, you must bring all the aid that you can. General de Gaulle told you that yesterday when he toured our liberated towns and villages. We will march together along the route that he has established for us.[5]

The British, having observed carefully what de Gaulle had done, chose not to interfere. They remained silent when Coulet appointed a local Resistance leader, Raymond Triboulet, to Rochat's position as subprefect. "The next days will show," said a report prepared by Montgomery's staff on June 19th, "whether Coulet and Triboulet can establish themselves and win the people's confidence and the *de facto* government. Meanwhile we are treating them as such. The high question of 'recognition' has left the stratosphere of diplomatic exchange and is being decided on the ground. . . . Paralysis . . . seemed likely so long as the identity of the French government remained in doubt. Its identity is no longer in doubt; its sovereignty remains to be established."[6]

Technically, Eisenhower had not violated the "local authorities" doctrine. Montgomery, his subordinate, had selected the French Committee to administer the territory thus far liberated. "It is impossible at this stage," said a SHAEF staff report shortly after the Bayeux incident, "to give a precise definition of the position of M. Coulet. Having been appointed by General de Gaulle, [he is] . . . under General Koenig, who is under General Eisenhower and for this reason the Supreme Commander is in fact in full control of the civil administration of the liberated territory. This anomalous situation must be accepted and made to work."

The analysis, which was made principally for Roosevelt's consumption, was more than a little casuistic. Koenig, it was true, exercised considerable authority over the French administration. Coulet, however, was not responsible to him but to Algiers. He took orders from de Gaulle's French government. He thus led a political regime, precisely the contrary of what the President had sanctioned.

Smith, Eisenhower's deputy, was discontented with the equivocation of the arrangement and the potentiality of collision when Roosevelt took stock of it. "Coulet is the de Gaulle-appointed Commissioner of the Republic for Normandy," he wrote candidly to Marshall's civil affairs adviser. "As such he represents the French Committee of National Liberation in liberated areas. He has general administrative responsibility and authority over prefectoral, subprefectoral and municipal authorities. . . . His relationship with Allied staffs has been generally satisfactory and cooperative." Smith wanted to end the fiction of Eisenhower's command over French civil administration. The French Committee, he believed, by its services to the Allied cause, had earned the right to exercise its authority over liberated France.[7]

Roosevelt, however, stood firm, despite the mounting evidence presented to him to support the French Committee's claims. Marshall, after a visit to the beachhead, wired the President that failure to resolve the French situation risked the loss of important help from the Resistance. Having undoubtedly been put up to it by Churchill, he warned Roosevelt that the British Cabinet might repudiate the Prime Minister's support of the American position and insist on a pact with the French.[8]

On the evening of June 14th, Stimson made one of his rare phone calls to the White House and pleaded with the President for more than an hour to modify his stand. "He believes that de Gaulle will crumble," Stimson wrote of the conversation, "and that the British supporters of de Gaulle will be confounded by the progress of events. This is contrary to everything I hear. . . . The President thinks that other parties will spring up as the liberation goes on and that de Gaulle will become a very little figure. He said that he already knew of some such parties." According to Stimson, Roosevelt had by now persuaded himself that to relax his stringent policy on de Gaulle would be a "departure from moral standards."[9]

In contrast to Roosevelt's inflexibility, de Gaulle became more conciliatory toward the Allies after he returned from Normandy. He seemed to be notifying them that, confident now of his ultimate success, he could be a generous friend. When he flew back to Algiers on June 16th, he left behind instructions to his subordinates to do their best to settle outstanding differences.

Koenig and Smith had no trouble reaching a military understanding on the status of French commanders fighting in SHAEF. Koenig's authority, they agreed, was "similar to that of any Allied commander serving directly under the Supreme Commander." This meant that French officers, like others within the alliance, could appeal to their government if they considered a military order in serious conflict with the national interest. De Gaulle had sought this concession because the French were not represented either at SHAEF or in the Combined Chiefs of Staff, where the important decisions were made. Foreseeing the need to challenge orders from time to time, he considered it important that a procedure be established. The visible and inexcusable flaw in this procedure, however, was in Roosevelt's refusal to recognize de Gaulle's claim to represent the interests of France or even to set policy for the French Army. The procedure established the means for putting vital military questions on the diplomatic table. But since Roosevelt refused to sit at that table with de Gaulle, he denied the French the means of having their national interests considered. Roosevelt thus left open the possibility of an enormous dispute between friendly armies on the battlefield.[10]

But Koenig was satisfied with the good faith he found at SHAEF. After his talk with Smith, he revoked de Gaulle's limitation on the assignment of French liaison officers to the Allied armies. He arranged to send tactical experts to all major military headquarters and administrative specialists to the liberated communities. A few weeks later, Eisenhower reported to Washington that French liaison officers were working closely and effectively with the Americans and British in all instances.[11]

In the beginning of July, Koenig also ended the controversy over the supplemental francs. In the field, the problem had actually proved of small dimension. Relatively little of the currency went into circulation. The population, despite de Gaulle's admonitions, accepted it without thinking of its political implications. One intelligence report noted, in fact, that the bills were "worn in the lapel like a favour, with the tricolor showing." Coulet came near to precipitating a crisis when he announced that he would declare the supplemental francs invalid for the payment of taxes. But Koenig overruled him. He assured SHAEF that, since the matter was being negotiated by the French mission in Washington, the supplemental francs would continue to circulate without interference.[12]

The stability of the French Committee's administration and its excellent relations with the Allied command persuaded the British that de Gaulle had to go to Washington to resolve the persistent uncertainty about French affairs. SHAEF was building up to a major offensive to break through the Nazi perimeter that confined its armies to Normandy. Smith pleaded with de Gaulle to get Roosevelt's consent to extend the French Committee's rule into the heart of the country. The British thought they discerned a change of attitude in Washington. They convinced both Roosevelt and de Gaulle of the wisdom of a meeting. At the last minute, arrangements snagged on the inane question of whether the public announcement would say the visit was at the invitation of the President, which de Gaulle wanted, or at the request of de Gaulle, which Roosevelt wanted. Eden finally cleared away the obstacles, with the terms of the voyage left undefined. The British understood that the visit would at last seal the French Committee's authority to govern France.[13]

De Gaulle was greeted by a seventeen-gun salute when he landed at Washington's National Airport on the sultry afternoon of July 6, 1944. His first speech in the United States, given in English as a gesture of amity, dwelt on the community of interests between France and the United States. From the airport, he went directly to the White House, where the President welcomed him effusively in French, which also was meant as a friendly offering. Inside the White House, the President's cabinet and his family were waiting. After a round of introductions, Roosevelt led de Gaulle and his guests to the south veranda, where Mrs. Roosevelt served tea. The pleasant tone was a remarkable improvement over that of their previous encounter at Casablanca.

Leahy, who seemed to be hoping for the worst, wrote in his diary, "I found General de Gaulle in my first meeting with him less forbidding in manner and appearance than I expected." Hull, whose attitude had scarcely changed since Saint-Pierre and Miquelon, conceded that the General "went out of his way to be agreeable."

De Gaulle remained affable and outgoing through four days of dinners, lunches, sight-seeing, receptions and ceremonies at national shrines. Though he seemed suspicious at first of the crowds that assembled at Blair House, he responded warmly as soon as he learned they were friendly. He shook the hands of hundreds of diplomats, military officers and government officials at a party he gave near the end of the visit. It evoked from the Washington *Post* the comment that "de Gaulle produces a fresh smile for each visitor, giving an impression of elasticity." The press, which reported voluminously on his activities, conveyed to the American people the picture of a sympathetic and attractive figure. Roosevelt himself commented that "the visit has gone very well." De Gaulle, renouncing the scowl for the smile, registered in Washington an important personal success.

His cultivation of the President was less successful, however. Over the course of the stay, Roosevelt received de Gaulle three times in the White House for private, unhurried conversations. Their subject was not civil affairs, supplemental currency or national sovereignty but the world and its future. As at Casablanca a year and a half before, Roosevelt talked at great length and listened little. In broad strokes, he painted his plans for postwar harmony, based on the dream that the great states would no longer be motivated by a thirst for power but would live in mutual trust. He did not foresee a major place for France among the nations responsible for assuring world peace. The President, de Gaulle found, was acutely conscious of the chaos of the 1930's and the collapse of the 1940's, and had little confidence in France's regeneration. Roosevelt's monologue was gracious, even benevolent, but it afforded de Gaulle little satisfaction, either for his immediate needs or his long-term aspirations. However friendly, the talks served only to affirm the political and personal irreconcilability of the two men.[14]

American officials, unaware of the emptiness of these encounters, were elated at their superficial cordiality. The top officials in the State, Treasury and War Departments who had been trying vainly to resolve problems with the French were convinced now that the obstacles had been swept away. General Holmes, whom Eisenhower had sent to Washington to lobby for a settlement, wrote to Smith: "I was greatly surprised at the smoothness with which the French visit went off and at the friendly atmosphere that rapidly developed. . . . We propose to strike while the iron is hot and get the basic agreement on civil affairs concluded."

On July 8th, the day before de Gaulle left for home, Hull, McCloy and Treasury Secretary Henry Morgenthau presented to Roosevelt a new proposal for an accord with the French. "We would like to suggest to you a fresh approach to the French situation," their memorandum said gingerly. It continued:

This new approach would be to deal with the French Committee as the "civil authority," "administrative authority," "de facto authority" or "French authority" and to reach agreement on civil affairs administration along the lines of those reached with Belgium, the Netherlands and Norway. These agreements, reconciled in the Combined Chiefs of Staff, were signed on behalf of the United States by General Eisenhower as U. S. Theater Commander and on behalf of Great Britain by the British Foreign Secretary.

The memorandum pointed out that a settlement on these terms would be practical, without being prejudicial to the right of the French people to elect a government in the future.

Roosevelt consented at once to the principles submitted to him in the proposal. He specifically approved the expression "de facto authority." He also gave his agreement to resolving the currency dispute by designating the French Committee as the issuing authority for the supplemental francs. In initialing the memorandum, Roosevelt stipulated only that he had to see and assent to the final text.

After he made this decision, Roosevelt notified Churchill that he was prepared "to accept the Committee as de facto authority for civil administration provided two things are made clear: 1. Complete authority to be reserved to Eisenhower to do what he feels necessary to conduct effective military operations, 2. That French people be given opportunity to make free choice of their government." He added further the admonition that "no publicity be given these arrangements until they are finally cleared." But Roosevelt himself could not keep the secret. The following day he announced to the press that the United States Government had decided to deal with the French Committee of National Liberation as the dominant political authority in France.[15]

On the same day that Roosevelt assented to the resolution of the civil affairs conflict, de Gaulle gave public notice of the next challenge in his grand scheme. "France is once more on her feet," he told the Parliament in Ottawa, where he was completing his tour. "She now appears as a very important element in the work of organizing the world which must come forth from this terrible war. . . . France, emerging little by little from her temporary misfortune . . . declares herself ready to assume in this universal effort the full share of which she is capable."[16] For a country that was still largely occupied by an enemy, his words revealed a mighty ambition. De Gaulle was telling Roosevelt that he must not count France out as a factor in determining the fate of the postwar world.

Shortly after de Gaulle's return from America, the enemy's withdrawal from France was settled by Allied arms. On July 25th, the United States First Army cracked through the Nazi line at Saint-Lô. The Germans, rather than retreat in good order to a new line, chose to stand their ground. For three weeks they fought tenaciously while British and American armies, powerfully assisted by the F.F.I., drove to surround them. In the end, the Nazi army defending northern France was all but destroyed on the battlefield around Falaise. By mid-August, the Germans no longer had the capacity to conduct more than rearguard action against the Allied offensive. The road to Paris was open and the liberation of France assured.

Among the leading echelons of the Allied columns that swept across the French plains after Saint-Lô were the bearers of Gaullist power, intent on supplanting Berlin's authority with their own. The French liaison officers attached to Allied combat units were normally the first to plant the Gaullist standard. They were followed by a bizarre, gypsy-like caravan that made its way from town to town, bumping along between tanks and supply trucks, carrying a team of functionaries responsible to the French Committee in Algiers. The mission of this vanguard of Gaullism was to prevent a vacuum of authority from forming between the old government and the new.

De Gaulle regarded a vacuum of authority as the greatest threat to his efforts to rule France. His basic strategy was to rush Gaullism into the positions of power before any rival could reach them. As long as the Allied armies followed hard on the German heels, his men could be first to take hold of the apparatus of government. But where the Germans abdicated, the Resistance could step in. The cunning game he played with the Communists required him, on the one hand, to encourage popular activity against the Germans but, on the other, to avert the kind of general disorder which could destroy all authority and facilitate Communist seizure of control. While paying homage to "national insurrection," the goal of the Resistance, he opposed any mass uprising of the French people. As for the F.F.I., de Gaulle gave

Koenig strict orders to keep its members busy with military missions to divert their attention from politics. De Gaulle was certain that whoever first took over the power of the state was the most favored to retain it.

Typically, de Gaulle's caravan, under the leadership of Colonel Pierre de Chevigné, rolled into a town within hours after the German departure. Stopping in the central square, Chevigné's men raced out and posted their proclamations, in the name of General de Gaulle, on the walls of the city hall, the prefecture or the subprefecture. Then Chevigné himself stood up before the crowd that had by now assembled and read from a list he carried with him the names of the new local officials, invested by Algiers. Normally, they were Resistants of assured loyalty to de Gaulle. Most had already been notified of their appointment through underground channels or by a liaison officer. Chevigné frequently assigned members of his caravan to remain with them, to supervise the police, the administration of justice or the local branch of the Bank of France. When he was convinced that all was in order, he directed the caravan to proceed to the next town.

In a few instances, de Gaulle's men were late in arriving. In Rennes, for example, three collaborators were shot by order of a kangaroo court in the hours between the German departure and the Allied entry into the city. But in each case French Committee agents restored order as soon as they reached the scene. They knew exactly what they wanted and how to achieve it. Nowhere that the armies went did they encounter serious challenge to their authority.[17]

De Gaulle, however, had to prevail in Paris before he could claim his victory. It was only from there that France could be mastered. Paris, the great stronghold of the underground, seat of the National Resistance Council, represented the supreme test. It was here his gigantic effort could be defeated.

As the armies of the liberation approached, the population of Paris, stirred up by hunger and excitement, became difficult to contain. In mid-August the Paris police abandoned their docility and began harassing the occupants. Strikes broke out, interrupting municipal services. Armed partisans openly roamed the streets. In the tradition of 1792 and 1870, barricades were erected in the working-class quarters. It appeared possible that a mass uprising might break out at any moment. De Gaulle's principal representative in Paris, Alexandre Parodi, seemed helpless to stop it. On August 19th, the order to begin the insurrection was actually issued by Parodi and the Resistance Council.

It was de Gaulle's good luck that the German commander, General Dietrich von Choltitz, had no desire for a fight against the fired-up populace. On August 20th, Jacques Chaban-Delmas, a Gaullist agent who a few days earlier had slipped into the city, persuaded the Resistance Council to accept a truce with von Choltitz. Under its terms, the 20,000-man Nazi garrison withdrew to a few strongpoints, leaving most of Paris in the hands of the partisans. But the mood of the Parisians was volatile. De Gaulle wanted the capital taken before violence and disorder replaced the uneasy cease-fire.

De Gaulle returned to France on August 20th. Eisenhower, anticipating his intention, had for days sought approval to receive him. Only when de Gaulle declared that his coming did not depend on the Allies did Washington relent. Fearful of de Gaulle's safety, Eisenhower offered him an American Flying Fortress. But suspicious of an American plot, de Gaulle chose to take his own plane, though it was unarmed. Only with difficulty was he persuaded to follow prescribed air corridors to avoid hostile gunfire. De Gaulle landed at a tiny airport in Normandy, prepared to remain in France until his government was safely installed.[18]

De Gaulle was still convinced the Americans were plotting to make a deal with Vichy. He saw every obstacle placed in his way as evidence of a conspiracy. Though Eisenhower's orders to disregard Vichy were unequivocal, ugly rumors of American dealings persisted throughout the country. The indefatigable Laval was scheming to restore the Republic in a desperate effort to retain his own power. Until his intrigues collapsed, de Gaulle was certain that American secret agents in Geneva were encouraging him. By August 20th, Laval and the pathetic Pétain, who had vainly tried in his last moments in office to confirm Vichy's legitimacy by passing it on to de Gaulle, were on their way to Germany in the custody of the Gestapo. The final remnant of the collaborationist state thus disappeared. De Gaulle was freed of the apprehension that the Vichy regime, with American aid, could deprive him of his triumph.[19]

But de Gaulle remained apprehensive of defeat in the capital. On August 21st, he dispatched a letter to Eisenhower from Rennes warning that "if disorder breaks out in Paris now, it would be difficult to master it without serious incidents which might even interfere with later military operations." Eisenhower had delayed a decision on taking Paris. He had hoped he might bypass it to avoid the burden its provisioning would put on his supply lines. Unsure of German intentions, he did not want to fight a battle inside the city. But de Gaulle was willing to risk warfare and even some damage. He pleaded with Eisenhower to send forces to take the capital at once.[20]

Leclerc had for some time been standing by, waiting for the order to move. Since the Falaise battle, he had repeatedly asked higher headquarters for permission to deploy his forces to strike at Paris. On August 21st, aware of his political responsibilities to de Gaulle, he sent a patrol to probe the city's defenses in clear violation of military discipline. The next morning his commander, General Leonard Gerow, ordered the patrol recalled. But that same afternoon Eisenhower was deliberating on de Gaulle's plea. The city's capture would give him an important communications center and pay off a debt he felt he owed to the Resistance. On the top of de Gaulle's letter, he scribbled the following note to his chief of staff: "I talked verbally to Koenig on this. It looks now as if we'd be compelled to go into Paris. Bradley and his G-2 think we can and *must* walk in." Later that day, Leclerc received the order to march.[21]

Leclerc, anxious to find the fastest route into the city, by bad luck stumbled into a major German strongpoint on the outskirts of Paris. While his American superiors fumed, certain his troops were delayed by wine and kisses, Leclerc was engaged in a full-scale battle. Gerow, to restore momentum, sent in the American Fourth Division as reinforcement. But by midnight on the twenty-fourth, Leclerc had infiltrated one of his columns through the German lines. It kept moving until it reached the Hôtel de Ville. During the night, German resistance around the city disintegrated. By noon on the twenty-fifth, Paris, delirious with joy, was free.

That afternoon a squadron of Leclerc's tanks rumbled up to the Hôtel Meurice, the German Army's headquarters. His tankers pitched several smoke grenades through the windows and, without a struggle, made prisoners of all the officers inside. Von Choltitz was escorted not to Allied headquarters, where Gerow stood by as senior officer of the command, but to the Prefecture of Police, where Leclerc waited with a group of Resistance leaders. There von Choltitz signed the surrender document. In the presence of the Resistance chiefs, Leclerc accepted it, not for the Supreme Allied Commander, whose subordinate he was, but in the name of the Provisional Government of the French Republic.[22]

De Gaulle, having spent the night in the Presidential château at Rambouillet, entered the jubilant city in midafternoon of the day of liberation. His objectives were clear. His program had been thought out with care. The National Resistance Council was waiting for him at the Hôtel de Ville, symbol of insurrectionary Paris. But de Gaulle went first to the Montparnasse Station, where he congratulated Leclerc on his victory, then reprimanded him for sharing the surrender with the Resistance chiefs. He went next to the Ministry of War, which he and Paul Reynaud had abandoned on June 10, 1940, and which to him stood for the authority of the state. There he received the group of men he had organized in Algiers to commandeer the machinery of government. When he was satisfied that they were safely installed in the ministries, police headquarters and the principal municipal offices, he left to review the Paris police force, whose uprising had sparked the liberation and whose support he needed if his regime were to survive. Finally, making his way on foot through the ecstatic crowds, he reached the Hôtel de Ville, where the great leaders of the Resistance welcomed him to their midst.

"There are moments," said de Gaulle, the first and most eminent of the rebels, "which surpass each one of our poor lives." The General then embraced each of the Resistance heroes. But even in the rapture of this long-awaited meeting, de Gaulle remained the master of the situation. Georges Bidault, successor of the martyred Moulin, called on him to go to the balcony and announce to the tumultuous crowd the restoration of the Republic. Softly de Gaulle refused. "The Republic has never ceased to be," he said. "Free France, Fighting France, the French Committee of Liberation, each in its turn has embodied it. Vichy was always and remains null and void. I am the President of the Government of the Republic. Why should I go out and proclaim it?" De Gaulle then stepped to the balcony to acknowledge the acclamation from below.

Thus de Gaulle informed the Resistance Council that his regime alone governed France. His swift, ruthless seizure of power had left its members stunned. They, too, had dreamed of remaking the French nation. But in contrast to his cold resolution, their vision was cloudy, their leadership disunited and their intentions uncertain. The Communists, who occupied the positions of dominance, received vacillating direction from Moscow. The non-Communists looked on regeneration more in spiritual than in political terms. De Gaulle's esteem for the Resistance was great. But it did not diminish his determination to acknowledge to no one a share in the prerogatives of the state.

On the day after the liberation, millions of Parisians turned out to watch de Gaulle lead a parade of heroes down the Champs Elysées. Behind de Gaulle was Leclerc, heading the division that had made the long journey from Chad. At his side were Juin, Koenig and d'Argenlieu, who returned with him from exile. Bidault and the Resistants also marched, but by invitation, not in an official capacity. The parade was a tonic that Paris, enfeebled by four years of occupation, badly needed. It was an explosion of rejoicing and national fervor. It represented the redemption of de Gaulle. It was his moment of popular triumph.

Later that day, shots rang out as de Gaulle entered the great church of Notre-Dame. Though the crowd panicked and jostled him against a pillar, he continued inside, ostensibly unperturbed. But from the rafters of the church more shots sounded. In an exhibition of cool courage, de Gaulle paid no attention to them. He remained seated in his pew until the service of thanksgiving, somewhat abbreviated, was concluded.

There was firing throughout Paris that day. It had no discernible pattern, but several persons were wounded. De Gaulle, in his *Memoirs*, maintained that this was the final attempt by extremist leaders, presumably Communists, to trigger an insurrection. The charge has not been proved. But even if the source was innocent it was clear that in disorder de Gaulle's designs could perish. De Gaulle determined to disband the partisan armies as fast as possible.

Two days later, the general summoned the Resistance Council and the principal underground commanders to notify them that they had served France loyally and well but that their usefulness had come to an end. Individual Resistance leaders, he said, would be invited to join his cabinet. Others would be given seats in the Consultative Assembly when it moved to Paris. The bulk of the Resistance forces, he said, would be incorporated into the Regular Army. The rest would be disarmed.

The Resistance leaders grumbled, lamenting that de Gaulle had snatched their dreams away from them. But in Paris, the private armies quickly vanished. The National Council lived on passively for a few more months before its members dissolved it. As an organized political force claiming authority throughout the nation the Resistance was dead.[23]

To de Gaulle, the United States now represented the chief threat to his rule. The Americans, he believed, still sought a pretext to overthrow him. General Gerow, the highest-ranking American in the city, conducted his French relations with remarkable insensitivity. It was his bad luck that the pronunciation of his name persuaded many Parisians that the Americans had brought back Giraud to harass them. Gerow had forbidden Leclerc to participate in the liberation parade, which an angry de Gaulle regarded as absurd. Later he notified Koenig that the United States Army was transferring the administration of the city to French hands. De Gaulle was furious. Not only had the French never acknowledged American jurisdiction over civil administration, but never, in fact, had Americans exercised any control over Paris. De Gaulle, hypersensitive about American motivations, was persuaded that Gerow could not have been so consistently insulting without orders from a higher authority.[24]

Eisenhower, in some measure, offset Gerow's imprudence by paying a formal call on de Gaulle shortly after Paris was freed. He personally was anxious, for military if not political reasons, to fortify the Gaullist regime. When he learned of the apprehension created by the Resistance bands, he agreed to turn Leclerc's division over to de Gaulle for the remainder of the month. He consented to deliver to de Gaulle as many uniforms as he could spare to speed the incorporation of the F.F.I. into the French Army. Finally, he directed the 28th American Division to parade through Paris and pass in review before de Gaulle. Many years later he and de Gaulle argued about who had proposed the parade, but whoever it was, it served as a show of strength in the regime's behalf. The parade seemed to say that the full force of the Allied army was behind the government de Gaulle had established.[25]

Yet it was only after the liberation of Paris that the United States sealed the agreement that acknowledged de Gaulle's administration of civil affairs. And even then, the American Government was unable to perform its part with elegance or grace.

Eisenhower had been instructed to sign the accord with Koenig in mid-August, several weeks after the terms had been settled. The

French protested against the American decision to treat it as a battle-field agreement, since the British regarded it as an intergovernmental treaty. But they withdrew their protest, only to have Eisenhower object to Washington that it was inappropriate for him to sign with Koenig, an officer of inferior rank. The Pentagon pondered Eisenhower's objection for a few days. On August 16th, General John F. Hilldring, Marshall's chief civil affairs adviser, phoned SHAEF with the answer. According to the transcript of the conversation, Hilldring said: "The French are going to squeal and squawk and raise hell again if somebody other than General Eisenhower appears with a pen in his hand." So Eisenhower consented and set the ceremony for August 22nd.

But two days before the scheduled rite, the Supreme Commander received a telegram from Washington notifying him that plans again had been changed. The next day, he was directed to suspend all arrangements. The personal instructions from Roosevelt which followed told him that he was not to sign anything at all. Instead, he was to exchange with Koenig letters of ratification.

The text that Roosevelt furnished Eisenhower retained the quality of pettiness that characterized the American approach to the entire matter. After recognizing the French Committee as the "de facto authority," the letter stated: "My dealing with the Committee . . . is based upon the support which the Committee continues to receive from the majority of Frenchmen who are fighting for the defeat of Germany and the liberation of France." It was dated August 25th, the day Leclerc reached Paris. Koenig received it when Eisenhower arrived in the city the next day. The letter was Roosevelt's grudging and tardy acknowledgment of the reality of events, though events had passed the agreement by long before it took effect.[26]

At the beginning of September, Eisenhower began to press Washington for diplomatic recognition of the de Gaulle government. Samuel Reber, SHAEF's political adviser, notified his superiors at the State Department on September 13th that recognition might "insure the stability the French require not only for the future prosecution of the war but for the difficult early period of reconstruction." He said the French people would fail to understand any prolonged delay. Sooner or later, he asserted, recognition had to be extended and "it would seem desirable to have this come at a time when Allied popularity is high." But Reber, as well as Eisenhower, was wasting his energy. The tone Roosevelt had set in Washington made any consideration of diplomatic recognition impossible.[27]

Meanwhile de Gaulle, who had consolidated his regime in Paris and the north, still had to assure his dominion throughout the remainder of the country. On August 15th, Patch and de Lattre began the liberation of southern France. Within a few days of landing, their armies had taken Marseilles and the other major coastal cities, then pushed forward into the Rhône valley. Their objective was to unite with Eisenhower's columns in northeastern France, leaving substantial enemy forces trapped behind them in the southwest. Wherever they went, Gaullist agents followed, imposing their authority much as they had from Normandy to Paris. But they did not go into the great southwestern region. From there the Germans fled at top speed, leaving in their wake the vacuum of authority that de Gaulle had dreaded. Into the vacuum spilled armed partisans. The wide quadrilateral roughly bounded by the Pyrenees, the Loire, the Atlantic and the Rhône thus fell under Resistance rule.

The Communists dominated most of the region. They controlled four large cities—Bordeaux, Montpellier, Toulouse and Limoges. Their chiefs or their committees sat in the public buildings from which *arrondissements* and departments were ruled. They functioned in virtual isolation, for communications and transportation with Paris had been cut by the fighting. But they were not alone, for non-Communist rivals and a variety of opportunists were in their midst, seeking a share of the spoils of power. In the administrative confusion, effective government began to disintegrate. Municipal services collapsed. Hundreds were summarily executed on real or fabricated charges of collaboration. By late August, southwestern France had fallen into a state of disorder. The country appeared to be on the brink of chaos or civil war.[28]

In mid-September, 1944, de Gaulle initiated a campaign to extend his authority into the southwest. He tried to acquire military backing, but Eisenhower objected to the diversion of French troops from the front lines. He was more successful in siphoning off military opposition by incorporating F.F.I. bands into de Lattre's army. Within a month after landing, de Lattre had absorbed 40,000 partisans and was taking on more at the rate of several thousand a week. Those who went to the front were usually the best disciplined and most patriotic, leaving behind those whose motives were pillage and power. Nonetheless, the drain of manpower toward the front, by removing from temptation armed and idle men, weakened the capacity of those who remained behind to organize an effective challenge to the state.[29]

On September 14th, de Gaulle began a personal tour to make his own presence and that of the central government felt in the affected regions. On the sixteenth, he visited Toulouse and on the seventeenth Bordeaux, the most defiant of the rebel bastions. His practice was to review the partisan forces, flatter them with praise and gratitude and admonish them sternly to leave the responsibility of government to the authorities in Paris. Wherever he went, he mingled freely with ecstatic crowds, in disregard of his personal safety. In every city, he was welcomed with unreserved enthusiasm. De Gaulle saw perhaps ten million Frenchmen during September and October. His personal impact unquestionably contributed to the restoration of the authority of the central government.

But the most important reason, almost certainly, for France's averting civil war was that no one gave the order to begin it. The Communist Party, paralyzed with indecision, simply could not settle on a plan for acquiring power. The Resistance leadership, on the whole, wanted to fight. But the top party chiefs, most of whom had spent the war in Moscow, did not. They knew that the F.F.I., though dominated by Communists, was not monolithic and, as a consequence, not reliable for a civil war. The French Army, with the Allied armies behind it, was a powerful deterrent. But most decisive was Moscow's unwillingness to provoke any action that could disrupt Western unity. Stalin did not want a civil war in the fall of 1944, before Germany was defeated. In contrast to the armed militants in the countryside, the top leaders of the Communist Party declared their allegiance to de Gaulle, joined his cabinet and accepted seats in the Consultative Assembly. De Gaulle himself cultivated good relations with the Soviet Union, which culminated in a disarming trip to Moscow at the end of November. Thus the weeks passed without the expected military confrontation. As the Government pushed its authority deeper and deeper into the provinces, the threat of civil war steadily receded.[30]

Eisenhower could never be sure, however, that fighting in his rear would not begin at any moment. "From the military point of view," he wrote to Marshall on October 20th, "the existence of a strong central authority in France is essential, particularly in view of the difficult economic and supply situation which faces us this winter. The only French authority with whom we can deal is the present Council of Ministers and we urge that every support be given to it, including formal recognition as the provisional government of France." At this stage of the conflict, the last thing Eisenhower wanted was a disruption of the harmonious relations that had been established between SHAEF and the French.[31]

Roosevelt was not impressed by the argument that the United States ought to help de Gaulle when he needed help. On the contrary, he seemed to derive a sense of vindication from de Gaulle's internal difficulties. When Churchill informed him of de Gaulle's plan to enlarge the Consultative Assembly, Roosevelt seized the issue—which was intrinsically meaningless—and said he would not contemplate recognition until the move was actually made. "I would not be satisfied," he said testily, "with de Gaulle merely saying he was going to do it." Irritated that the State Department favored recognition, Roosevelt said further to Churchill: "I am anxious to handle this matter for the moment directly between you and me and would prefer, for the moment, that the *modus operandi* should not become a matter of discussion between the State Department and your Foreign Office."

In fact, Roosevelt suddenly chose the *modus operandi* on his own, without consulting Churchill, much less the State Department and the Foreign Office. He had become irritated with the Prime Minister for taking the position that Britain could not resume diplomatic relations with the Italians, former enemies, while recognition was denied the French. On October 23rd, three days after rejecting Churchill's latest proposal on France, Roosevelt notified the Prime Minister that he planned to recognize de Gaulle's government at once. Churchill, who was in Moscow at the time, was angry at the abruptness of the President's decision. But, he replied, "we shall of course take similar and simultaneous action." Roosevelt also irked the Russians, who had long delayed a similar move in deference to United States wishes. Churchill thus decided to bring them in, too.

At 5 P.M. on October 23rd, the representatives of the United States, the Soviet Union and Great Britain called on Foreign Minister Georges Bidault at the Quai d'Orsay in Paris. Together they announced the diplomatic recognition by their countries of the Provisional Government of the French Republic.

Three days later, the United States recognized the government in Rome.

In his *Memoirs*, Churchill took sentimental note of the gesture toward de Gaulle. The establishment of de Gaulle's government in Paris was, after all, the grand fulfillment of Churchill's decision to support the rebel general in his rejection of the Pétain regime and in his refusal to accept defeat. "Thus," he wrote, "we completed the processes begun in the dark and far-off days of 1940."[32]

De Gaulle's feelings toward the Allies were not nearly as tender. He took no official notice of the action of the three countries, much less thank them for it. When questioned on his reaction at a press conference on October 25th, he had a bitter answer ready. "I can tell you," he said, "that the government is satisfied that they are willing to call it by its name."[33]

The long struggle over who would rule France was officially over. Roosevelt, who had insisted he would not give de Gaulle the "title deeds," had lost. "The formal recognition of de Gaulle," said Leahy in unaccustomed understatement, "must have been a difficult decision for Roosevelt."[34]

Roosevelt's decision was too late to have any meaning for France. Made out of animosity, it did not even serve as a balm to heal the raw relations between Washington and Paris. By so long begrudging France its government, the United States was deprived of much of the credit it had earned by the shedding of its blood for France's independence. The French press, while generous in its gratitude for the liberation, reflected a deep resentment of American diplomacy. As the war drew to a close, France and the United States, united in victory, should have been the most intimate friends. But all the world knew that Roosevelt and de Gaulle were hostile allies. Their mutual distrust was a hardship on the alliance. It was a heavy cross both nations had to bear.

Bitterness in Triumph

October, 1944–September, 1945

By THE FALL of 1944, France was liberated. The Germans clung tenaciously to a mountain salient in Alsace and to a series of fortress cities on the Atlantic coast. Thrust back upon itself, Germany was still far from beaten. But its ability to wage sustained offensive warfare had been destroyed. France could concentrate on the problems of political and economic reconstruction without fear of the enemy's return. De Gaulle could intensify his campaign to restore France's rank as a major power.

It was inconceivable to de Gaulle that Roosevelt contemplated a postwar Europe without a strong France helping to shape its destiny. Though he recognized that France had been discredited in 1940, he rejected Roosevelt's contention that his country had thereby forfeited its influence in Europe. On the contrary, he felt the very countries that now sought to impose their will on Europe had abandoned France between the wars to face Germany alone. The United States and England, he pointed out, had abdicated their international responsibilities after Versailles, while Russia had actually abetted Nazism until Hitler sprang at its throat. De Gaulle did not deny the debt France owed for its salvation. But he affirmed that French blood provided much of the respite that England, Russia and the United States needed to forge their anti-Axis alliance. He warned that France, constantly vulnerable to German energy and ambition, would not consent to put its fate in the hands of these countries. De Gaulle did not intend to submit to a European system devised by non-European states which might abdicate their responsibilties again.

Roosevelt found de Gaulle's claims to a voice in European affairs irrelevant. He believed the postwar world would be a new world, in which the old rules for keeping the peace in Europe would no longer apply. The argument that France had an interest in Europe did not impress him. On the contrary, disinterestedness was his standard. "The President," wrote Hull in his *Memoirs*, "favored a four-power establishment that would police the world with the forces of the United States, Britain, Russia and China. All other nations, including France, were to be disarmed. . . . He believed in the efficacy of direct personal contact between Churchill, Stalin, Chiang Kai-shek and himself and he thought that this direct relationship among the chiefs of the four nations would result in efficient future management of the world."[1] It was characteristic of Roosevelt, who had become more and more paternalistic about his global responsibilities and prerogatives, to think in terms of managing the world. He conceived of international order as being enforced by the wise and the mighty, acting as great impartial judges. He, of course, thought of the United States and of himself as the wisest, the mightiest and most impartial. He saw no place for France in his global magistracy.

As the war drew to a close, Churchill more than ever became de Gaulle's chief backer. Churchill regarded as absurd the belief that the nations of the world would submit to having justice imposed on them by four self-appointed pontiffs, even if the pontiffs could agree on justice among themselves. Churchill understood relations between nations in terms of power and self-interest. By these standards, France had to be a force in post-war Europe. France alone, he affirmed, could serve as the anchor of postwar stability. Churchill foresaw that insular Britain would rely on France as its first line of defense against a renascent Germany and, almost certainly, a bellicose Russia. He thoroughly shared de Gaulle's view that the future of Germany and the European continent could not be settled without French participation.

Churchill and de Gaulle made a dramatic display of their mutual interest and esteem on Armistice Day, 1944, when to the cheers of hundreds of thousands of Parisians they marched together down the Champs Elysées. Roosevelt had declined an invitation to join them in the celebration. He left Churchill alone to accept the public gratitude for France's salvation. The visit symbolized France's return to equal partnership with England, a partnership sentimentally linked with the past but pragmatically turned toward the future.

Churchill and de Gaulle remained together for three days, the last of them spent inspecting French troops in Alsace on the eve of an offensive. They had many occasions to talk, sometimes intimately when they were alone, sometimes formally in the company of ministers. De Gaulle found that with Churchill, unlike Roosevelt, he could probe the most fundamental and most sensitive areas of their relationship and expect candid answers. He learned that despite the many wretched moments of their long association their views were never more in harmony. Churchill and de Gaulle, at their Armistice Day conference, established a united front against Roosevelt's postwar designs.

At the Armistice Day meeting Churchill told de Gaulle that the United States had withdrawn its blackball of French membership in the European Advisory Council. Though Roosevelt's preference for private decisions had enfeebled the Council, de Gaulle regarded it as the only available forum for setting forth France's proposals for a postwar settlement. Once again, an inevitable concession, unimportant as it was, had to be wrested painfully from Roosevelt. He gave his approval just in time for Churchill to receive credit for it in Paris, while the United States suffered reproach.[2]

A much more important objective to de Gaulle was the enlargement of the French Army. De Gaulle wanted the Army to take a bigger part in the last stage of the war, so that France could be a real conqueror. He believed it vital that the French secure the feeling of having beaten Germany and the Germans of having lost to France. Politically, his aim was to obtain an occupation zone of Germany and participation in the military government. He was convinced that the Army was the instrument to achieve that aim. De Gaulle thus considered the success of his political program to be, in large measure, contingent on strengthening France's armed forces.

When Churchill returned to London after his visit with de Gaulle, he dispatched his plea to Roosevelt. He was determined to be candid but anxious not to offend raw sensibilities. "I hope that you will not consider that I am putting on French clothes," he said, apologetically. He assured Roosevelt, rather meekly, that the "tendentious statements being put out in the press" about his commitments to de Gaulle were false. But he was nonetheless firm in presenting his case.

I sympathize with the French wish to take over more of the line [he wrote], to have the best share they can in the fighting or what is left of it—and there may be plenty—and not to have to go into Germany as a so-called conqueror who has not fought. . . . The important thing for France was to have an army prepared . . . to assist in the holding down of parts of Germany later on. . . . The French pressed very strongly to have a share in the occupation of Germany, not merely as sub-participation under British or American command, but as a French command. I expressed my sympathy with this, knowing well that there will be a time not many years distant when the American armies will go home and when the British will have great difficulty in maintaining large forces overseas, so contrary to our mode of life and disproportionate to our resources.

Roosevelt's answer sounded preposterous to the Prime Minister. He said that, on the one hand, he had no authority to provide arms for a postwar French army, however much he wanted "to help her meet postwar responsibilities." On the other, he added: "You know, of course, that after Germany's collapse I must bring American troops home as rapidly as transportation problems will permit."

The dumbfounded Churchill proceeded to ask:

If the French are to have no equipped postwar army or time to make one, or to give it battle experience, how will it be possible to hold down Western Germany beyond the present Russian occupied line? We certainly could not undertake the task without your aid and that of the French. All would therefore rapidly disintegrate as it did last time.

The President, in reply, could only mutter the weak suggestion that the French be armed with captured German equipment. It brought the Prime Minister small comfort.[3]

Churchill and de Gaulle also joined forces against the President on the question of empire. As the war pressed to a conclusion, Roosevelt looked on himself more and more as the savior of exploited peoples. Though it was clear he coveted at least military rights over some French Pacific possessions and intended to retain the concessions in the Caribbean he had acquired from the British in 1940, Roosevelt had determined that colonialism must die. A new period of the world's history had opened, he believed, to which the imperial powers had to adjust.

Churchill had become alarmed at the President's attitude as early as December, 1941, when Roosevelt sought to give him advice about handling unrest in India. "States which have no overseas colonies or possessions are capable of rising to moods of great elevation and detachment about the affairs of those who have," Churchill remarked tartly in his *Memoirs*. The Prime Minister had little further trouble with Roosevelt on the question in the early war years. But in November, 1942, Churchill made the statement, as a warning to America, that has since become the classic expression of his colonial philosophy:

We have not entered the war for profit or expansion, but only for honour and to do our duty in defending the right. Let me, however, make clear, in case there should be any mistake about it in any quarters. We mean to hold our own. I have not become the King's first minister in order to preside over the liquidation of the British empire.

Halifax, the British Ambassador, tells the following story about a meeting with Roosevelt late in the war:

One day we had been chatting away about something or other when the President suddenly said that he thought after the war we ought to do this or that about some French colony. What did I think of his idea? I said that I scarcely saw how he could reconcile it with various pledges he had given to General Giraud and General de Gaulle. That he thought was all right. Had I any other objections? I said that I still did not like it for there was nothing to prevent him from waking up one morning and having a similar brainwave about a British colony, and we shouldn't like that at all. At that the President laughed and said that our case was quite different.

Roosevelt's particular target was Indochina. In early 1944, Hull asked the President for a clarification of policy. The United States was committed to the restoration of the French Empire but Roosevelt had been heard to say that he favored putting Indochina under international trusteeship. Roosevelt acknowledged that he opposed Indochina's return to France. "As a matter of interest," he added, "I am wholeheartedly supported in this view by Generalissimo Chiang Kai-shek and by Marshal Stalin. I see no reason to play in with the British Foreign Office in this matter. The only reason they seem to oppose it is that they fear the effect it would have on their own possessions. . . . Each case must, of course, stand on its own feet, but the case of Indo-China is perfectly clear. France has milked it for one hundred years. The people of Indo-China are entitled to something better than that."[14]

As early as March, 1943, the French were petitioning for a role in the Pacific war, particularly as it affected Indochina. Giraud talked about it during his trip to Washington. Later, de Gaulle's delegation asked sanction to build a task force of two divisions to send to the Far East. In the spring of 1944, de Gaulle actually dispatched a general to New Delhi to establish a staging area for rushing French troops into Indochina. But at no point did the French receive encouragement or cooperation from the United States and the effort had no results.[5]

After the Armistice Day conference, Churchill concluded that the enormous gap between the positions held by the United States, on the one hand, and France and Britain, on the other, could be narrowed only by a meeting between Roosevelt and de Gaulle, at which he could act as broker. He made such a proposal at once to Roosevelt, suggesting as an afterthought that they might also invite Stalin in order to enlarge the scope of the discussions. Late in November, 1944, Stalin agreed to attend a four-power meeting. But Roosevelt suddenly interjected a veto of de Gaulle, which defeated Churchill's original purpose. "Any attempt to include de Gaulle in the meeting of the three of us," he told Churchill on December 16th, "would merely introduce a complicating and undesirable factor." Churchill dutifully accepted the decision and the meeting was set for February at Yalta. But he remained disgruntled and hoped to change Roosevelt's mind later. He told Stalin he thought de Gaulle should, as a minimum, be invited to participate in the discussions that affected France.[6]

Before the Yalta conference began, however, the Battle of the Bulge intervened to generate another serious crisis between Roosevelt and de Gaulle. The German Army, in its great Ardennes counteroffensive in mid-December, 1944, threatened to retake the Alsatian capital of Strasbourg, which had recently been liberated by French forces. Eisenhower, anxious to shorten his lines in order to create a mobile reserve, decided to give up the city. To abandon Strasbourg, at the tip of the Allied salient in Alsace, made good strategic sense. But when de Gaulle learned of Eisenhower's intention, he ordered de Lattre to make provision for Strasbourg's defense, no matter what were his instructions from higher headquarters.

To de Gaulle, the defense of Strasbourg was a situation where national interest overruled conventional strategy. Strasbourg, a prize disputed by France and Germany for centuries, was a great patriotic symbol. Incorporated by Hitler into the Reich, its liberation was second only to Paris as a source of national gratification. Its military governor warned that returning Nazis might conduct a wholesale massacre of civilians who had demonstrated their allegiance to France. De Gaulle realized that the loss of Strasbourg would put an enormous strain on his regime. He believed that, whatever the price, Frenchmen could not relinquish the city without a fight.

Eisenhower, who sympathized with the French viewpoint, was nonetheless unable to reconcile it with his military responsibilities. He reaffirmed the order to abandon the city and threatened to cut off the French Army from ammunition, supplies and food unless it obeyed. De Lattre pleaded first with de Gaulle to rescue him from the dilemma and then with Patch to cover his left flank while he moved his already overextended forces into position around the city. On January 2nd, de Gaulle fired off a telegram to Roosevelt, asking him to authorize Eisenhower to take into account French national needs. On the same day he wired Churchill an entreaty "to support me in this grave affair."

Roosevelt refused categorically to act. He declared that the matter was purely military and concerned only Eisenhower. Churchill, however, flew to SHAEF headquarters the next morning. He attended meetings with Eisenhower, Smith, de Gaulle and Juin. By midday, Eisenhower began to see some military virtue in the French position. The loss of Strasbourg, by weakening the French government, would endanger the Allied rear. It might force the French to break away from the alliance. Some estimated it would send 100,000 refugees from the city scurrying for safety behind the Allied positions, blocking roads, impeding operations, requiring food and shelter. Late in the day Eisenhower ordered changes in the disposition of American forces to protect the Alsatian capital. But by this time the German offensive had exhausted itself and the enemy lacked the strength to push onward. Strasbourg was saved. But what mattered was that Churchill had once again demonstrated that, in contrast to Roosevelt, he could be counted on the side of France.[7]

By the time the Strasbourg incident was happily settled, the Allies were on the offensive again, pushing the depleted Germans closer and closer to defeat. De Lattre's army, reinforced by the American XXI Corps, drove the Germans from Alsace by early February. But the question from which the Strasbourg episode grew was not resolved. The French still had no voice in making decisions at SHAEF, even when their own forces were involved. They had no liaison to the Combined Chiefs of Staff, where overall strategy was determined.

Roosevelt, of course, had no contact with de Gaulle on military policy. The French were thus deprived of any influence over the course of action, including that action which affected the French national interest. Indifference to the lesson of the Strasbourg incident presaged another clash between partners in the coalition.[8]

The Battle of the Bulge produced, however, one unanticipated benefit for the French. It persuaded Eisenhower that substantial forces would still be needed to beat the Germans. On December 28th, he recommended to the Combined Chiefs of Staff that eight more French divisions be rearmed, along with substantial service and air units. Within twenty-four hours, the entire proposal was approved. The German counteroffensive thus propelled the French a little closer to their objective of an expanded army to share in the final conquest.[9]

De Gaulle might have had cause for further rejoicing at the end of 1944 when Cordell Hull, his bitter foe, retired as Secretary of State. But Hull had long before ceased to be a decisive factor in the determination of policy toward France. His virulence against de Gaulle, once greater than anyone's, was now surpassed by Roosevelt's. By contrast, the State Department, in the final months of Hull's term, sought to be a moderating influence on the President. Hull's retirement was bound to make the State Department more pro-French. But toward de Gaulle, Roosevelt had developed such an obsession that he alone issued the decrees on the American stand.

Edward R. Stettinius, Jr., Hull's replacement, was an open Francophile. Early in January he notified the President that France had submitted a memorandum to the European Advisory Council formally proposing French participation in the surrender, occupation and control of Germany. Stettinius recommended approval of the proposals.

> It can be justifiably argued [he wrote to Roosevelt] that the French requests are out of all proportion to France's power today. But in the long run this government will undoubtedly gain more by making concessions to French prestige and by treating France on the basis of her potential power and influence than we will by treating her on the basis of her actual strength.

Stettinius pointed out that the United States gave the appearance of being the only obstacle to French restoration. Acceptance of the French, he said, would reassure the smaller European states that the peace would not be imposed on them by non-Europeans. But Roosevelt, who believed the smaller European states trusted him more than they trusted France, could not bring himself to accept Stettinius' advice to act now "rather than to wait until it is made to appear that the concessions are won from us grudgingly."[10]

When de Gaulle learned from the press in the middle of January that a major Allied conference was impending, he vigorously protested against his exclusion to Roosevelt, as well as to Churchill and Stalin. In identical notes, he reminded them that all military operations on the Western front were based on French soil, that France had committed its entire military capacity to the war and that French port and transit facilities, completely at the disposition of the Allies, were vital to achieving victory. His tone was not unfriendly, but he left the Big Three with an unmistakable warning. "The Provisional Government of the French Republic," he said, "obviously cannot consider itself bound by any of the decisions taken without it."[11]

Though Roosevelt was not intimidated, he was persuaded by Harry Hopkins, who was sympathetic to the French, that it would be useful to try to mollify de Gaulle. The President agreed to let Hopkins stop in Paris on the way to Yalta. On January 27, 1945, Hopkins, after a cordial session with Foreign Minister Bidault, met de Gaulle. The result was not auspicious. Hopkins candidly acknowledged to de Gaulle that the President had little confidence in the French, which he attributed to France's disintegration in 1940. De Gaulle, conceding France's haplessness during that period, maintained that the French were earning back their rank as a great people. The two men parted amicably, pledged to the objective of improving relations but uncommitted on resolving any of their differences. Hopkins was himself discouraged by the outcome. He pinned his hopes for bridging disagreements on a meeting between Roosevelt and de Gaulle after the Big Three conference.[12]

During Roosevelt's first conversation with Stalin at Yalta, he asked the Russian leader for his impressions of de Gaulle, based on their meeting in Moscow two months before. According to the official record, "Marshal Stalin replied that he had not found de Gaulle a very complicated person but he felt he was unrealistic in the sense that France had not done very much fighting in this war and de Gaulle demanded full rights with the Americans, British and Russians who had done the burden of the fighting." Always alert for a sympathetic listener, Roosevelt proceeded to relate one of his favorite stories. "The President," said the record, "then described his conversation with de Gaulle in Casablanca two years ago when de Gaulle compared himself with Joan of Arc as the spiritual leader of France and with Clemenceau as the political leader."[13] Roosevelt thus wasted no time in establishing a community of interests with Stalin, who seemed to share his reservations about de Gaulle and the French.

Stalin's attitude toward the French had clearly taken a strange shift at Yalta. The Soviet leader was, in contrast to his earlier friendliness, exceedingly hostile. He quite obviously believed that the French, besides refusing to endorse Soviet peacetime aims, had little to contribute to the remainder of the war. But his hostility appeared to go deeper than that. De Gaulle, it was apparent, had offended him in Moscow by refusing to subscribe to many of his proposals, especially those having to do with the installation of a Communist government in Poland. It was also likely that Stalin now looked beyond the battle to the postwar period, when Communist revolutions would be more important to him than Allied unity. A Communist France would be a surer European partner than a Gaullist France. Whatever his motives, Stalin at Yalta proved to be the hardest member of the Big Three toward France's interests.

Churchill, backed by Anthony Eden, felt compelled personally to fill the gap created by de Gaulle's absence. Convinced that French and British interests were identical, "Winston and Anthony," Hopkins noted, "fought like tigers for France." Their mission brought them into constant, sometimes angry conflict with Roosevelt and Stalin. Roosevelt more than ever showing the strain of the many difficult years of responsibility, was the first to give way. Under discreet but telling pressure from Hopkins, he yielded to Churchill's proposals one by one. More than anything, he seemed motivated at Yalta by a desire for harmony. Stalin, preoccupied by Russia's more immediate interests, did not persist in objecting to concessions to France. As a consequence, Churchill and Eden emerged with most of what they wanted for the French.

The Big Three at Yalta conceded to France an occupation zone of Germany, though they did not yet delineate its borders. Since Stalin refused to surrender any of his occupational rights, it could only be carved out of the contemplated British and American zones. The

French were also granted a seat on the Allied Control Commission for Germany, after the British argued that it would be absurd for the French to accept a zone without a share in its rule. Finally, France was to be invited to serve as a sponsoring power for the San Francisco Conference, at which a charter of the United Nations Organization was to be adopted. France was blocked, at Stalin's insistence, only from membership in the proposed Commissions on Reparations and Dismemberment, both relatively minor. Had de Gaulle himself attended the deliberations, France would not have done much better.[14]

De Gaulle admitted that the outcome of the conference was "in no way prejudicial" to France. He pronounced himself satisfied with the communiqué published by the three powers at the termination of the meeting. He indicated he had no serious dispute with any of the other announced decisions. But he made clear that the outcome of the conference did not mean that France's exclusion from it was any less intolerable.

De Gaulle was thus ill disposed to a display of amity when he received an invitation from Roosevelt, two days after the conference ended, to a private meeting in Algiers. The President, convinced the Big Three had been generous to France, saw an opportunity to repair his relations with the French. De Gaulle, looking from another perspective, saw nothing but the prospect of a new humiliation to France. It was grimly appropriate that the relationship between these two men should finish in an incident that was both tragic and absurd, yet the inevitable consequence of a mutual incomprehension that neither sought to overcome.

A misunderstanding of facts apparently started the episode. When he was in Paris on January 27th, Hopkins had proposed that Roosevelt and de Gaulle get together after Yalta. He suggested at the same time that de Gaulle might attend the concluding sessions of the conference. According to Hopkins, Bidault was receptive to these proposals and promised to take them up with his chief. De Gaulle, in his *Memoirs*, wrote that Bidault later advised Hopkins not to extend the invitation to meet Roosevelt, the implication being that the General would decline. But somewhere the lines of communication broke down. Hopkins' biographer wrote that Bidault told the American Embassy in Paris that de Gaulle would not go all the way to the Crimea but that he "had stated that he would be delighted to meet Roosevelt on his trip home from Yalta at any place and at any time that the President designated." Though such an offer was uncharacteristic of de Gaulle, Hopkins took it at face value and persuaded the President to send the invitation.[15]

De Gaulle's bitter, suspicious reaction was totally unrelated to the innocent spirit of the bid. He saw a call on Roosevelt as implying sanction of a conference of which he disapproved. He detected a device to win his support for whatever decisions he opposed. He resented the indignity of being summoned to the President's side in much the same fashion as the heads of the Middle Eastern states whom Roosevelt had received, two of whom served under French mandate. Most of all, he was infuriated by the presumptuousness of a foreign leader inviting him to a meeting on French soil. Roosevelt, though guilty of a breach of protocol and of indifference to de Gaulle's sensibilities, intended none of the aims the General attributed to him. But de Gaulle insisted that the incident was an affront to France.

De Gaulle declined the invitation in an insolent letter that was unimpeachably phrased. On the one hand, he regretted that he could not go to Algiers "so unexpectedly" and, on the other, he renewed the invitation that Roosevelt come to Paris. But the pith was in an impeccable diplomatic insult. "So that everything may be prepared according to the President's desires," he said, Roosevelt must notify the French government of his intentions before stopping in Algiers. The President of the United States was not accustomed to being told that his host had to approve before he could call.[16]

Roosevelt was not only angry but deeply hurt by this response. De Gaulle's attitude, as it had in Casablanca, injured his pride as President. But he was wounded more seriously by de Gaulle's challenge of the motives he regarded as so irreproachable. His reaction, in turn, became excessive.

"The poor dear man," Roosevelt said to a press conference shortly after his return, "I am inclined to think he has no knowledge of what to do. It was a very bad break for him. Not for my part but for his. He was all tied up in engagements." A week later, he made another unmistakable reference to de Gaulle when he improvised in a speech to Congress a complaint about "a great many prima donnas in the world who want to be heard."[17]

The animosity between the two men had never been more intense than on April 12, 1945, when Roosevelt died.

De Gaulle was gracious in tragedy. His message of condolence observed that Roosevelt was, "from his first to his last day, the friend of France. France admired him and loved him." But the death in no way modified his resolve to persevere in his aims.[18]

After Yalta the weeks had passed without France hearing more about its contribution to the conquest and occupation of Germany. The fortunes of battle had maneuvered de Lattre's army into a position on the Rhine directly across from the Black Forest, making penetration into the enemy heartland virtually impossible. Eisenhower's principal assault was directed against the Ruhr, far to the north of the French dispositions. De Gaulle was apprehensive that the French Army, through American indifference, might remain immobilized and thus deprived of a share in the victory.

On March 29th he wrote to de Lattre: "You must cross the Rhine, even if the Americans do not consent to it and you have to cross on boats. This is a question of the highest national interest. Karlsruhe and Stuttgart are waiting for you, even if they do not want you."

But fortunately for de Lattre, the battle situation was fluid and he was ordered to move his army north, away from the impenetrable forest wall. On March 31st, de Lattre was directed by the Allied command to press on into Germany. Once on the move, he began a race with Patch to the Pforzheim Gap, the natural invasion route through the mountains and forests of Bavaria. On April 4th, Karlsruhe was in French hands, and de Lattre, a step ahead of the Americans, was headed for Stuttgart.[19]

Stuttgart, which fell on April 20th, was France's greatest prize of the war. De Gaulle intended to retain it. Many months before, he had received Eisenhower's approval to a proposal that the French establish military government over any territory they captured. Only a week earlier, Juin had reminded SHAEF that "it is, of course, understood that . . . the First French Army . . . will undertake the occupation of such German territory as it may conquer with its own resources." De Gaulle was thus astonished to learn on April 22nd that the American command, in order to simplify its supply problems, had taken Stuttgart out of the French sector and assigned its administration to an American general. When American soldiers arrived to claim it, General de Lattre invited them to make full use of its facilities but refused to surrender control. Denying any violation of discipline, he argued that since Stuttgart was no longer in a combat area, its fate was a political matter under the jurisdiction of Paris. He said he had instructions from de Gaulle "to hold and administer . . . until the French zone of occupation is fixed between the interested governments."

Eisenhower, aware that another Strasbourg crisis was gestating, notified de Gaulle a few days later that he would accede to the French action in order to avert a struggle "which could result only in weakening bonds of national friendship." But he protested vigorously against it. "I believe," he told de Gaulle, "that the issuance direct to the First French Army of orders based on political grounds which run counter to the operational instructions given through military chains of command violated the understanding with the U.S. government under which the French divisions armed and equipped by the United States were to be placed under the Combined Chiefs of Staff whose orders I am carrying out."

It was odd that Eisenhower, in his note, should have resurrected the Anfa doctrine, under which Giraud had agreed to turn over the French Army to the United States in return for arms. De Gaulle had long before repudiated that doctrine. Eisenhower had himself acknowledged its invalidity. On several occasions, he conceded the prerogative of de Gaulle's government to determine the use of the French Army on the basis of the national interest of France. Yet, after the Stuttgart incident, he said he could not recommend further French rearmament because he "could no longer count with certainty upon the operational use of any French forces." Eisenhower's note was a step backward from the treatment of France as a full ally.

A few days later, de Gaulle received a letter from President Harry S. Truman which suggested strongly that Eisenhower had written under instructions from his new commander in chief. Truman appeared more astonished than Roosevelt had been by the contention that the French Army was an instrument of national policy. "If the time has come, in your opinion," Truman wrote, "when the French Army is to be considered as engaged in carrying out the political desires of the French Government, then an entire rearrangement of command will have to be made." Truman's note did not presage an improvement in relations between de Gaulle and the White House. Though free of Roosevelt's personal bitterness, he was even more bewildered by de Gaulle's French mentality, which was so different from his own. The new President was more amenable to reason on the subject of de Gaulle but less given to self-restraint.

De Gaulle replied to Truman's note politely but without concession. "In answer to the frankness that you have chosen to employ in my case," he wrote, "I would like to express the hope that such nasty incidents can be avoided. All that is necessary is for France's allies to recognize that questions which affect it as closely as the occupation of German territory must be discussed and decided with France. As you know, that has unfortunately not been the case until now, in spite of my repeated requests."

De Gaulle was not deeply distressed when Truman, making good on Eisenhower's threat, terminated the French rearmament program. It had, in reality, never been resumed after the grandiose pledges uttered during the Battle of the Bulge. Once the Germans began retreating, the United States, in sharp contrast to the British, again lost interest in shipping equipment to the French. The British, in the last months of the war, rearmed three new divisions. The United States rearmed none. France finished the war, with some exceptions, using the American equipment that had been furnished to the divisions rearmed long before in Africa.[20]

Two weeks after the capture of Stuttgart, the war in Europe was over. The First French Army had penetrated to the Danube at Ulm and deep into the Austrian Tyrol. A German general, who found it less humiliating to give up to the Americans, had cheated de Lattre of the field surrender of an enemy army. But when the Third Reich capitulated in a little schoolhouse in Rheims on May 7, 1945, France was represented.

De Lattre himself attended the ceremonial surrender in Berlin the following day. Its solemn dignity verged on burlesque while Allied dignitaries debated who would sign on what line, while secretaries and translators labored to make identical texts in three languages and while the absence of a French flag was rectified by some last-minute stitching. The arrangements took from 4 P.M. to midnight. "I wanted to insist on the rights of the French language," quipped de Lattre in his memoirs, "but I had the impression that then the war would never end." The Germans signed the document of surrender during the first minutes of May 9th. De Lattre wrote that German Field Marshal Keitel was overheard grumbling as he walked out: "Ach, the French are here, too. That's the last straw." After the ceremonies, the delegates of the four powers withdrew to a gala banquet. There the band played the "Marseillaise" in the medley of anthems and among the toasts to the war's victors, glasses were raised to France.[21]

But even surrender did not end the bitter difference over the right of the Allied command to require the French Army to disregard the national interest. On the contrary, the dispute was aggravated by de Gaulle's contention that the Allies no longer had command prerogatives. Shortly after the surrender, de Gaulle refused to order the evacuation of a small area in the Italian Alps which French troops had occupied during the final offensive in Italy. Though the Rome government was apprehensive, de Gaulle denied any designs on Italian territory beyond a few French-speaking towns on the western slope of the mountains which had been in dispute since 1860. The Italians were sure he coveted more. The Allied command in Italy wanted to extend the jurisdiction of its own military government into the area that the French held.

"We do not have to accept the intrusion of the Allies in this case," de Gaulle wrote sullenly to one of his ministers. "Besides, we do not have any commitment to them on this matter, since they signed the Italian armistice without us. The question of the future delineation of the French-Italian frontier is an affair which concerns France and Italy."

The dispute might have been resolved with civility had not the French Alpine commander, General Paul Doyen, become unnecessarily provocative. "General de Gaulle," he wrote in early June, in response to an Allied notice to evacuate, "has instructed me to make as clear as possible to the Allied command that I have received the order to prevent the setting up of Allied Military Government in the territories occupied by our troops and administered by us, with all necessary means *without exception*."* The note could have been interpreted only as an inadmissible threat.

General Alexander, who commanded the Italian theater, was ready to accept the challenge. On June 5th, he wired the Combined Chiefs of Staff the recommendation "that I be directed by you to complete the occupation of Northwest Italy and to establish Allied Military Government, *using force if necessary*."* Though he cautioned his troops not to risk actual hostilities, he ordered them to take positions in direct confrontation of the French.

The next day, Bidault received a note from the State Department protesting Doyen's "highly inflammable" actions. The American

* Author's italics.

Government promised no prejudice to subsequent territorial claims but insisted unequivocally that the French get out.

On the seventh, Truman expressed to de Gaulle his outrage at "the almost unbelievable threat that French soldiers, bearing American arms, will combat American and Allied soldiers whose efforts and sacrifices have so recently and successfully contributed to the liberation of France itself." The American people, he said, "would be profoundly shocked if they were made aware of the nature of the action which your military officers, presumably with your personal approval, have threatened to take." Truman then announced that he was cutting off all military deliveries to the French until the matter was settled.

De Gaulle beat a judicious retreat. He replied immediately to Truman that "it had obviously never been the intention nor the order of the French government, nor of General Doyen, commander of the Alpine detachment, to oppose by force the presence of American troops in the little zones occupied by us." Within a few days, the French troops began evacuating. No publicity was given the incident, which the Allied command described as "normal military relief." But the episode proved to be the final blow to the alliance.

Truman did not lift the ban against military deliveries. He made an exception for units designated to fight in the Pacific, but when the Japanese surrendered a few weeks later, that program was also terminated. Apart from gasoline and rations supplied to French forces in Germany, the links between the French and American Armies were severed. In mid-July, SHAEF was dissolved and the First French Army officially restored to the control of Paris. The great coalition that had liberated Western Europe was ended.[22]

Notwithstanding his withdrawal, de Gaulle achieved his objectives in northwest Italy. If his designs were as limited as he claimed, he exceeded even his triumphs of Syria, Madagascar, North Africa and Saint-Pierre and Miquelon, where he did no more than take over what France already possessed. In postwar negotiations France obtained new territory from Italy, though it amounted only to a few small frontier towns whose populations were ethnically French. In each town, the transfer was confirmed in plebiscites by substantial majorities. Italy barely noticed the loss. But it symbolized France's retribution for the Fascist "stab in the back" of 1940.[23]

More significant to France's quest for status was the outcome of the great conference of San Francisco. De Gaulle had declined the proposal made at Yalta that France be a sponsor. He explained that he preferred to be free to work for changes in the charter that had been drafted, without France, the previous year at Dumbarton Oaks. At San Francisco, Bidault, the chief of the delegation, was firm in pressing France's demands and was strongly supported, especially by the smaller nations. At San Francisco he found that France was, after all, still regarded as a great power. France emerged from the conference as one of the Big Five of the United Nations, with permanent membership in the Security Council and the power of veto. French, in deference to its tradition as the language of diplomacy, was adopted as an official language of the United Nations. Most of France's procedural amendments—which were, on the whole, constructive—were adopted. At San Francisco, France's restoration was confirmed by an overwhelming consensus of sovereign nations.[24]

In July, American, British, Russian and French representatives, meeting in London, finally resolved the question of the enemy occupation zones. The boundaries were drawn on the basis of the territory already held by the troops of the four powers. De Gaulle's determination to plant the French Army on the soil of Germany thus was vindicated. France was made responsible roughly for the territory held by the First French Army in southern Germany and for a strip on the Rhine to the north. Stuttgart remained the principal city of the French zone. France also participated as an equal in the Control Commission for Germany and the administration of Berlin. In Austria, the French retained control over the Tyrol region and shared in the rule of Vienna. Though France reigned over less of the enemy homeland than the other three victors, even de Gaulle acknowledged that he was satisfied with the arrangement.[25]

The United States, Britain and Russia met for the last time without France at Potsdam on July 17th. Their efforts to reach agreement on the questions that divided them came to failure. The Potsdam conference revealed brutally the fallacy of Roosevelt's conviction that Russia and the Western powers could serve harmoniously as arbiters for the postwar world. After Potsdam, France as the most important nation of Western Europe, took its seat at the major international conferences.

On September 2, 1945, General Leclerc stood on the deck of the battleship *Missouri* in Tokyo harbor. No French troops had reached the Pacific before the Japanese capitulation. France partook in the Pacific war with a few islands, a handful of ships and a few detachments of soldiers. Yet de Gaulle pressed the claim that France be represented among the victors. It was his country's ultimate act of rehabilitation. In behalf of France, Leclerc signed the document of surrender of Japan.[26]

The miracle was now consummated, the impossible achieved, the incredible realized. France, defeated and humbled in 1940, the only country that had surrendered to Hitler, had somehow emerged triumphant. The nation that had withered before Nazi might and laid down its arms had put a half-million men into the field to drive the enemy from its soil. The people who had cringed before the occupant had risen up to envelop him in terror. A man who had been condemned to death by his government now sat with presidents, prime ministers, and kings. France, disgraced in the eyes of the world, had returned to reclaim its greatness and its self-respect.

Without de Gaulle, the miracle would not have happened. Without him, there might have been a few French divisions fighting with the Allies. There would probably have been a Resistance; there would certainly have been a liberation; but there would not have been a France victorious, determining its own destiny, once again a major power. De Gaulle achieved that, almost alone. While the world sneered at a dishonored country, he asserted the premise that France was not beaten, and brought it to reality.

A man less sustained by a faith in the French nation could not have achieved his triumph. In 1938, de Gaulle wrote of his compatriots:

Poor people who from century to century carry with resignation the heaviest burden of sorrows. Ancient people, whom experience has never freed from its vices but who inevitably are redeemed by the sap of new hopes. Strong people who, if they deceive themselves by embracing shadows, are invincible from the moment they make up their minds to banish them. Oh great people, made for example, for enterprise, for combat, always the vanguard of history, whether they are tyrant, victim or champion.[27]

De Gaulle did not delude himself about the weaknesses of France. But he was certain, from the day he declared his rebellion against the *capitulards*, that beneath the stratum which crumbled before the Nazi Panzers was a reservoir of vitality and strength.

To de Gaulle, the collapse of 1940 was a vicissitude of history. He understood France not in terms of a few weeks or a decade of dishonor but in the perspective of two millennia of greatness. When Anthony Eden, his great advocate, once chided him for causing Britain more trouble than any of its allies, he had no apologies. "I don't doubt it," he said. "France is a great power." If France was temporarily enfeebled by a resurgence of its vices, he regarded it as inevitable that France would soon become itself again. As he understood his nation, France could never resign itself to inferiority and retire as a protagonist from the stage of history. "To me," he wrote, "France cannot be France without greatness." [28]

It was understandable that Franklin Roosevelt, in contrast to Charles de Gaulle, should have lost his confidence in France and its future after the debacle of 1940. It was justifiable that he was suspicious of a Frenchman whose relentless will he acknowledged but of whose motivation he was uncertain. Without initial reservations about de Gaulle, Roosevelt would have been remiss—to the United States and to France. But, for poor reasons, Roosevelt retained his reservations long after other responsible men had shed them. It was inexcusable that Roosevelt did not understand that France, under de Gaulle, was rising up to break its chains. It was indefensible that he should have honored a host of baser Frenchmen whom he could dominate to reject the one whom he could not.

Roosevelt, by his constant opposition, made de Gaulle's achievement more prodigious. Unintentionally, he assisted in giving France what it desperately needed, a hero who could overcome obstacles and triumph in crisis. Involuntarily, he helped de Gaulle emerge from the war enveloped in glory.

The unhappy conflict between these two men infected the ancient friendship between their countries. Both the United States and France paid for it heavily. Better for both, nonetheless, that France found within herself the resources to recover. In de Gaulle's victory, each has many times been repaid.

Epilogue

Two DECADES have gone by since de Gaulle consummated his miracle of French restoration and Roosevelt, on the threshold of triumph over the Axis, passed into history. The two decades offer perspective, not only on important events of another day but on a man who is again a dominant force in world affairs. De Gaulle has returned to lead the French nation. Discord once more characterizes his relations with the United States. In the bitter duel between Roosevelt and de Gaulle are the roots of the differences that separate the United States and France today.

Having won this duel in 1944, de Gaulle did not, as Roosevelt predicted, establish an authoritarian government with himself as its head. Instead, he tried to build a state that would be both democratic and strong. Having failed, he retired from politics. Without him, France embarked on a long period of drift, painfully reminiscent of the final years of the Third Republic.

But despite de Gaulle's failure to erect a strong governmental structure, democratic France survived. Under de Gaulle's leadership, the French state overcame the Communist challenges of 1944 and 1945. The governments that followed his, however frail, were sufficiently resolute to turn back the Communist threat in the succeeding years. The France restored by de Gaulle was thus able to meet its responsibilities, both foreign and internal. Almost certainly the France envisaged by Roosevelt at the time of the Liberation would have

243

collapsed. The impotent administrative organization that the President favored lacked the resources, both material and moral, to rally the French nation. With American aid, but without American arms, postwar France preserved its democratic system. The state de Gaulle brought to Paris in 1944 established the conditions which insured the perpetuation of democratic values in France and, quite certainly, in Western Europe. It is clear now that de Gaulle, offering decisive leadership at a critical juncture, was pursuing an objective that was in the national interest of the United States. It is also clear that he understood this better than Roosevelt.

De Gaulle's achievement does not mean, however, that he is in any conventional sense "pro-American." De Gaulle is only pro-French. Still, as a Western man, he is deeply committed to the values of a civilization which France and America share. In an era when this civilization is under attack, de Gaulle proclaims that the United States and France have a common purpose. "For us, the fundamental assumption of French-American relations," he said on July 23, 1963, "is friendship and alliance. For almost two hundred years that friendship has existed as an eminent psychological reality, basic to the nature of the two countries." But de Gaulle maintains that this common purpose does not obligate France to accept American leadership of the Atlantic community. "It is true that there are differences between the two countries over certain international problems," he also said. "Yet, for France and, I believe, for the United States the friendship which unites them and the alliance which binds them are unassailable." In pursuing policies that are independently French, de Gaulle does not pretend that he is motivated by a national interest other than that of France. But he rejects the contention that a divergent policy is necessarily hostile. In acting to preserve the civilization of which France and the United States are a part, he is convinced he can serve the goals of both countries.

But whatever the two countries possess in common, the quarrel between Roosevelt and de Gaulle was not a mere coincidence, proceeding from a chance incompatibility of two willful men. France and the United States, as the result of such factors as geography and economics, understandably have interests that conflict. Persisting differences of outlook, which Roosevelt and de Gaulle personally epitomized, add to the difficulty of resolving these conflicts. Roosevelt's generosity and idealism far exceeded de Gaulle's. De Gaulle had a more disciplined mind and, thanks to a superior sense of history, more perspective on events. Roosevelt was pragmatic, de Gaulle guided by principles and rules of conduct. Roosevelt, as a result, was more flexible but, unlike de Gaulle, frequently rudderless when confronted with a dilemma. Roosevelt, willing to defy convention, was free of stuffiness and indifferent to protocol, virtues which normally endeared him to those with whom he dealt. For de Gaulle, protocol and formality were proved instruments of diplomacy and human relations, which minimized the risk of misunderstanding and permitted attention to matters of substance. These divergent characteristics, these habits and conditions of mind, so much the product of a national culture, bred a constant distrust between the two men. As national characteristics they remain a constant source of vexation between the two countries.

But the quality in Roosevelt that most alienated de Gaulle was the Messianism the President brought to his dealings with France. De Gaulle, who had his own sense of mission toward his country, could not tolerate Roosevelt's claim that he knew what was best for France as well as for the rest of the world. It is worthy of note that de Gaulle has not hesitated, from time to time, to interfere in the affairs of lesser states. He has justified such interference on the grounds that these states, though sovereign, were not great. This, he contends, distinguishes them from France. He maintains that an intrinsic quality of greatness, earned over the centuries, has given France the right to influence the affairs of weaker countries but forbids France to mortgage its own future to a country that is stronger. De Gaulle found it offensive that France, during the years of postwar reconstruction, depended so heavily on the United States. He is committed to the proposition that France, restored to full strength, must now assume its full responsibilities. This is a view that Frenchmen, by and large, share with him, whatever their opinions of de Gaulle as political leader. It was this view that clashed most spectacularly with Roosevelt's sense of sacred mission toward the world as a whole. It conflicts today with the Messianic premises the American government brings to its determination of Western policy.

Shortly after de Gaulle returned to power in 1958, he proposed to President Eisenhower that France be accepted as an equal with the United States and Britain, the West's nuclear powers, in providing direction for the Atlantic Alliance. The proposal was rejected. Three years later, de Gaulle received a negative response to a bid for a greater voice in Western affairs from President Kennedy, who was under a pledge to increase, rather than diminish, American leadership abroad. Kennedy subsequently recognized that Europe, no longer in need of American assistance, was growing less and less tolerant of Washington's domination of Atlantic affairs. He began to speak out in terms of a Grand Design that would make Europe and the United States coequals in an Atlantic union. But at the same time his Defense Secretary, Robert McNamara, talked of plans to revise American strategy in a fashion that raised doubts about the willingness of the United States to risk nuclear war to defend Europe. De Gaulle, who looked on the Grand Design as a device for adapting American predominance to new European conditions, saw confirmed in McNamara's proposals his lingering belief that Europe could not allow its fate to be determined in Washington. In the fall of 1962, President Kennedy's threat to wage nuclear war to force Soviet missiles out of Cuba dramatically reinforced his apprehension about American leadership. Though he was not consulted in the decision, de Gaulle stood faithfully by Kennedy until the Cuban crisis was over. Then he pointed out that if Europe put its destiny in American hands it risked its existence for American interests. But as long as Washington made its decisions alone, Europe was without the certainty that its own interests were safe.

De Gaulle might have discarded the costly program to acquire his own nuclear weapons if the United States of the Eisenhower-Kennedy eras had not mirrored the posture of the Roosevelt Administration toward France. During World War II, Roosevelt, while declining responsibility for defending France's interests, put obstacles in the way of having France defend them herself. De Gaulle has found nothing since that time to persuade him that the United States looks differently on its relations with France. De Gaulle contends that the United States, which he regards as untrustworthy to make decisions for France, remains unwilling to admit France as a responsible partner in providing the leadership for the Western world. He sees no alternative to his conviction that France must therefore be the guardian of France's interests.

The profound disagreement that today separates France from the United States is an extension of the great battle for independence that de Gaulle waged against Roosevelt two decades ago. To accuse de

Gaulle, as have some, of dealing with Washington on the basis of a grudge is absurd. De Gaulle acknowledges the bitter memories of his wartime experiences, but the policies he has selected for the 1960's have sources that are far deeper. De Gaulle is currently engaged in a struggle to wrest the leadership of Europe away from the United States, which has possessed it since World War II. Europe, unlike France alone, contains the human, material and moral resources to act as an independent force in international affairs. If de Gaulle, with a nuclear deterrent, succeeds in replacing the United States as Europe's leader, he will be free to adopt his own course in foreign policy. He will also be strong enough to provide for the needs of France, which in matters of security he now regards as inseparable from those of Europe. De Gaulle is thus demonstrating, as he did two decades ago, his resolve that France, free of the United States, be able to determine its own destiny.

Comment on Sources and Notes

Hostile Allies would have been impossible without the memoirs of Charles de Gaulle and Winston Churchill, both magnificent works of art as well as of history. Fortunately for the historian, these two great men are generous in providing their documentary sources, which help fill the gap left by the absence of the memoirs of the third great figure in this study, Franklin Roosevelt.

The historian of the Second World War is also fortunate that so many of the principal participants, with varying degrees of reliability and candor, wrote of their experiences. Among those particularly helpful to me were Catroux, Clark, Eisenhower, Giraud, Hull, Juin, Larminat, de Lattre, Murphy, Passy, Stimson, Truman, Welles and Weygand. In fairness, I would like to acknowledge the usefulness of secondary works written by Aron, Benoist-Méchin, Blumenson, Funk, Hostache, Harrison, Howe, Langer, Michel, Pogue, Russell, Sherwood, Vigneras and Wright. The Department of the Army merits special credit for the superb studies produced under its sponsorship in the series *The United States Army in World War II*. The State Department has earned the appreciation of historians for its publications in the Foreign Relations series.

I am fortunate in having been granted access to a vast amount of unpublished material produced by the United States Army and stored in the World War II Records Division of the National Archives in Alexandria, Virginia. I have also consulted unpublished records in the

Franklin D. Roosevelt Library in Hyde Park and have read the diaries of Admiral William L. Leahy, stored at the Library of Congress. An unpublished compilation of documents prepared by Lieutenant Commander Tracy Kittridge for Admiral Harold Stark, who served as the liaison to de Gaulle in London, was made available at the Office of the Chief of Military History. The French Embassy graciously put at my disposal the press cables dispatched during the war by de Gaulle's mission in Washington.

To avoid the conventional but unwieldy Latin designations, the notes repeat wherever possible the name of the author of the cited work. If an author has written more than one work, his name is followed by a distinguishing word from the appropriate title. In the case of multivolume works, the number of the volume follows the author's name, except for Hull's *Memoirs*, which are paged consecutively. Publications without authors are cited by title. The Foreign Relations series is cited as "FR," followed by the year or name. All 1942 citations are from Volume II. The Stark documents have been listed under the name of Kittridge. Leahy's diaries are so marked, to distinguish them from his memoirs, and are followed by the volume number. Material from Hyde Park is prefaced by "FDR Library." All file numbers and letters—such as OPD and OCS—refer to the records stored in Alexandria, where the original Army filing system has been retained.

Bibliography

ANNET, ARMAND. *Aux Heures troublées de l'Afrique française, 1939–1943.* Paris: Editions du Conquistador, 1952.

ARON, ROBERT. *Histoire de la libération de la France.* Paris: Librairie Arthème Fayard, 1958.

———. *Histoire de Vichy.* Paris: Librairie Arthème Fayard, 1954.

D'ASTIER DE LA VIGERIE, EMMANUEL. *Sept Fois sept jours.* Paris: Les éditions de minuit, 1947.

———. *Les Dieux et les hommes.* Paris: Julliard, 1952.

AUPHAN, PAUL, and MORDAL, JACQUES. *The French Navy in World War II.* Annapolis: United States Naval Institute, 1959.

BARJOT, PIERRE. *Le Débarquement du 8 novembre 1942 en Afrique du Nord.* Paris: J. de Gigord, 1946.

BARLONE, D. *A French Officer's Diary.* New York: Macmillan, 1943.

BARNETT, CORRELLI. *The Desert Generals.* New York: Viking, 1961.

BARRE, GEORGES. *Tunisie 1942–1943.* Paris: Editions Berger-Levrault, 1950.

BAUDOUIN, PAUL. *Neuf Mois au gouvernement.* Paris: Editions de la Table Ronde, 1948.

BENDINER, ROBERT. *The Riddle of the State Department.* New York: Farrar and Rinehart, 1942.

BENOIST-MECHIN, JACQUES. *Soixante Jours qui ébranlèrent l'occident.* 3 vols. Paris: Editions Albin Michel, 1956.

BLUMENSON, MARTIN. *Breakout and Pursuit.* Washington: Office of the Chief of Military History, Department of the Army, 1961.

BONHEUR, GASTON. *Charles de Gaulle.* Paris: Gallimard, 1958.

BORDEN, MARY. *Journey Down a Blind Alley.* New York: Harper, 1946.

BRADLEY, OMAR N. *A Soldier's Story.* New York: Holt, 1957.

BRYANT, ARTHUR. *The Turn of the Tide 1939–1943.* New York: Doubleday, 1957.

———. *Triumph in the West 1943–1946.* New York: Doubleday, 1959.

251

BURMAN, BEN LUCIEN. *Miracle on the Congo*. New York: The John Day Co., 1942.

BUTCHER, HARRY C. *My Three Years with Eisenhower*. New York: Simon and Schuster, 1946.

BYRNES, JAMES F. *Speaking Frankly*. New York: Harper, 1947.

——. *All in One Lifetime*. New York: Harper, 1958.

CATROUX, GEORGES. *Dans la Bataille de la Méditerranée*. Paris: Julliard, 1949.

CATTAUI, GEORGES. *Charles de Gaulle*. Paris: Témoins du XXe Siècle, 1956.

CHAMINE. *La Querelle des généraux*. Paris: Editions Albin Michel, 1952.

CHARLES-ROUX, FRANÇOIS. *Cinq Mois tragiques aux affaires étrangères*. Paris: Plon, 1949.

CHURCHILL, WINSTON. *The Second World War*. 6 vols. Boston: Houghton Mifflin, 1948–1953.

CIANO, GALEAZZO. *The Ciano Diaries 1939–1943*. New York: Doubleday, 1946.

CLARK, MARK. *Calculated Risk*. New York: Harper, 1950.

COOPER, DUFF. *Old Men Forget*. New York: Dutton, 1954.

CRUSOE (JACQUES LEMAIGRE-DUBREUIL). *Vicissitudes d'une victoire*. Paris: Les Editions de l'Ame Française, 1946.

DECOUX, JEAN. *A la Barre de l'Indochine, 1940–1945*. Paris: Plon, 1949.

Documents on American Foreign Relations. Vol. I through Vol. VII, by various publishers under auspices of the World Peace Foundation, Boston. Published contemporaneously.

DUROSELLE, JEAN BAPTISTE. *De Wilson à Roosevelt, politique extérieure des Etats-Unis*. Paris: Librairie Armand Colin, 1960.

EISENHOWER, DWIGHT D. *Crusade in Europe*. New York: Doubleday, 1948.

FARMER, PAUL. *Vichy, Political Dilemma*. New York: Columbia University Press, 1955.

FEIS, HERBERT. *Roosevelt, Churchill, Stalin*. Princeton: Princeton University Press, 1957.

Foreign Relations of the United States. Volumes for 1941 and 1942 plus special study, "The Conferences at Malta and Yalta 1945." Washington, D.C.: Government Printing Office, 1955–1962.

FORRESTAL, JAMES. *The Forrestal Diaries*. Edited by Walter Millis. New York: Viking, 1951.

FUNK, ARTHUR L. *Charles de Gaulle: The Crucial Years 1943–1944*. Norton: University of Oklahoma, 1959.

GALIMAND, LUCIEN. *Origines et déviations du Gaullisme*. Paris: Editions de la couronne, 1950.

GANTENBEIN, JAMES W. (ed.). *Documentary Background of World War II*. New York: Columbia University Press, 1948.

DE GAULLE, CHARLES. *La Discorde chez l'ennemi*. Paris: Berger-Levrault, 1924 and 1944.

———. *Le Fil de l'épée*. Paris: Berger-Levrault, 1932 and 1944.

———. *La France et son armée*. Paris: Plon, 1938.

———. *Mémoires de guerre*. Vol. I, L'appel, 1954; Vol. II, L'Unité, 1956; Vol. III, Le Salut, Paris: Plon, 1959.

———. *Vers une Armée de métier*. Paris: Berger-Levrault, 1934.

———. *Discours et messages*. (In three volumes.) Paris: Egloff, 1944–1945.

GIRAUD, HENRI. *Un seul But: la victoire*. Paris: Julliard, 1949.

GOEBBELS, JOSEPH. *The Goebbels Diaries, 1942–1943*. Edited by Louis P. Lochner. New York: Doubleday, 1948.

GOSSET, RENEE. *Le Coup d'Alger*. Montreal: La Revue moderne, 1944.

GREW, JOSEPH C. *Ten Years in Japan*. New York: Simon and Schuster, 1944.

———. *The Turbulent Era*. Boston: Houghton Mifflin, 1952.

GRINNELL-MILNE, DUNCAN. *The Triumph of Integrity*. New York: Macmillan, 1962.

HALIFAX, LORD. *Fullness of Days*. New York: Dodd, Mead, 1957.

HARRIS, CHARLES R. S. *Allied Military Administration in Italy, 1943–5*. London: H. M. Stationery Office, 1957.

HARRISON, GORDON A. *Cross-Channel Attack*. Washington, D.C.: Office of the Chief of Military History, Department of the Army, 1951.

HASSETT, WILLIAM D. *Off the Record with F.D.R.* New Brunswick, N.J.: Rutgers University Press, 1958.

HATCH, ALDEN. *The De Gaulle Nobody Knows*. New York: Hawthorn Books, 1960.

HIGGINS, TRUMBULL. *Winston Churchill and the Second Front*. New York: Oxford University Press, 1957.

HOARE, SAMUEL J. G. *Complacent Dictator*. New York: Knopf, 1957.

———. *Nine Troubled Years*. London: Collins, 1954.

HOSTACHE, RENE. *Le Conseil National de la Résistance*. Paris: Presses Universitaires de France, 1958.

HOWE, GEORGE F. *Northwest Africa: Seizing the Initiative in the West*. Washington, D.C.: Office of the Chief of Military History, Department of the Army, 1957.

HULL, CORDELL. *Memoirs*. 2 vols. New York: Macmillan, 1957–1958.

HYTIER, ADRIENNE D. *Two Years of French Foreign Policy*. Paris: Librairie Minard, 1958.

ICKES, HAROLD L. *The Secret Diary of Harold L. Ickes*. 3 vols. New York: Simon and Schuster, 1954.

JUIN, ALPHONSE. *Mémoires*. 2 vols. Paris: Librairie Arthème Fayard, 1959–1960.

KAMMERER, ALBERT. *Du Débarquement africain au meurtre de Darlan*. Paris: Flammarion, 1949.

LANGER, WILLIAM L. *Our Vichy Gamble*. New York: Knopf, 1947.

———, and GLEASON, S. EVERETT. *The Undeclared War*. New York: Harper, 1953.

LARMINAT, EDGAR DE. *Chroniques irrévérencieuses*. Paris: Plon, 1962.

DE LATTRE DE TASSIGNY, JEAN. *Histoire de la Première Armée Française*. Paris: Plon, 1949.

LEAHY, WILLIAM D. *I Was There*. New York: McGraw-Hill, 1950.

MARCHAL, LEON. *Vichy, Two Years of Deception*. New York: Macmillan, 1943.

MICHEL, HENRI. *Histoire de la Résistance*. Paris: Presses Universitaires de France, 1950.

MOFFAT, JAY PIERREPONT. *The Moffat Papers*. Edited by Nancy H. Hooker. Cambridge: Harvard University Press, 1956.

MONTGOMERY, BERNARD L. *The Memoirs of Field Marshal Montgomery*. New American Library of World Literature, New York: 1958.

———. *The Path to Leadership*. New York: Putnam, 1961.

MORGAN, FREDERICK. *Overture to Overlord*. Garden City: Doubleday, 1950.

MORISON, SAMUEL ELIOT. *The Invasion of France and Germany*. Boston: Little Brown, 1957.

MURPHY, ROBERT. *Diplomat Among Warriors*. Garden City: Doubleday, 1964.

MUSELIER, EMILE. *De Gaulle contre le gaullisme*. Paris: Editions du Chêne, 1946.

———. *Marine et résistance*. Paris: Flammarion, 1945.

D'ORNANO, HENRY. *L'Action gaulliste aux Etats-Unis*. Paris: Central Press, 1948.

PASSY, COLONEL (ANDRE DEWAVRIN). *Souvenirs*. 3 vols. Monte Carlo: Raoul Solar, 1947.

PATTON, GEORGE S. *War As I Knew It*. Boston: Houghton Mifflin, 1947.

PENDAR, KENNETH. *Adventure in Diplomacy*. New York: Dodd Mead, 1945.

PERTINAX (ANDRE GERAUD). *The Gravediggers of France*. Garden City: Doubleday, 1944.

PEYROUTON, MARCEL. *Du Service public à la prison commune*. Paris: Plon, 1950.

PHILLIPS, WILLIAM. *Ventures in Diplomacy*. Portland, Me.: privately printed, 1952.

PICKERSGILL, J. W. *The MacKenzie King Record*. Toronto: University of Chicago, 1960.

POGUE, FORREST C. *The Supreme Command*. Washington, D.C.: Office of the Chief of Military History, Department of the Army, 1954.

REYNAUD, PAUL. *La France a sauvé l'Europe*. in 2 vols. Paris: Flammarion, 1947.

RICHARD, RENE, and DE SERIGNY, ALAIN. *L'Enigme d'Alger*. Paris: Librairie Arthème Fayard, 1947.

RIEBER, ALFRED J. *Stalin and the French Communist Party, 1941–1947*. New York: Columbia University Press, 1962.

ROBERT, GEORGES. *La France aux Antilles de 1939 à 1943*. Paris: Plon, 1950.

ROMMEL, ERWIN. *The Rommel Papers.* Edited by B. H. Liddell Hart. New York: Harcourt Brace, 1953.

ROOSEVELT, ELLIOTT. *As He Saw It.* New York: Duell, Sloan and Pearce, 1946.

ROOSEVELT, FRANKLIN D. *F.D.R., His Personal Papers.* Edited by Elliott Roosevelt. New York: Duell, Sloan and Pearce, 1950.

RUSSELL, RUTH B. *A History of the United Nations Charter.* Washington, D.C.: The Brookings Institution, 1958.

SCHMITT, GENERAL G. *Les Accords secrets Franco-Britanniques de novembre-décembre 1940.* Paris: Presses Universitaires de France, 1957.

SERANO SUNER, RAMON. *Entre les Pyrénées et Gibraltar.* Geneva: Constant Bouquin, 1948.

SERRIGNY, BERNARD. *Trente Ans avec Pétain.* Paris: Plon, 1959.

The Seventh United States Army in France and Germany 1944-1945. Heidelberg: Aloys Graf, 1946.

SHERWOOD, ROBERT E. *Roosevelt and Hopkins.* New York: Harper, 1948.

SHIRER, WILLIAM L. *The Rise and Fall of the Third Reich.* New York: Simon and Schuster, 1960.

SOUSTELLE, JACQUES. *Envers et contre tout.* 2 vols. Paris: Robert Laffont, 1950.

SPEARS, EDWARD. *Assignment to Catastrophe.* 2 vols. New York: A. A. Wyn Inc., 1945.

SPELLMAN, FRANCIS J. *Action This Day.* New York: Scribner's, 1943.

Stalin's Correspondence with Churchill, Attlee, Roosevelt and Truman, 1941-1945. New York: Dutton, 1958.

STETTINIUS, EDWARD R., JR. *Lend-Lease, Weapon for Victory.* New York: Macmillan, 1944.

——. *Roosevelt and the Russians.* London: Jonathan Cape, 1950.

STIMSON, HENRY L., and BUNDY, MCGEORGE. *On Active Service in Peace and War.* New York: Harper, 1947.

THOMSON, DAVID. *Two Frenchmen.* London: The Cresset Press, 1951.

TRUCHET, ANDRE. *L'Armistice de 1940 et l'Afrique du Nord.* Paris: Presses Universitaires de France, 1955.

TRUMAN, HARRY S. *Memoirs.* 2 vols. New York: Doubleday, 1955.

VIGNERAS, MARCEL. *Rearming the French.* Washington, D.C.: Office of the Chief of Military History, Department of the Army, 1957.

WELLES, SUMNER. *Seven Decisions that Shaped History.* New York: Harper, 1950.

——. *The Time for Decision.* New York: Harper, 1944.

WERTH, ALEXANDER. *Lost Statesman.* New York: Abelard-Schuman, 1958.

WEYGAND, MAXIME. *Recalled to Service.* New York: Doubleday, 1952.

WHITCOMB, PHILIP W. (ed.) *France During the German Occupation.* Stanford: The Hoover Institution, 1957.

WHITE, DOROTHY S. *Seeds of Discord.* Syracuse: Syracuse University Press, 1964.

WILLIAMS, MARY H. *Chronology 1941–1945.* Washington, D.C.: Office of the Chief of Military History, Department of the Army, 1960.

WILSON, HENRY MAITLAND. *Eight Years Overseas 1939–1947.* London: Hutchinson, 1951.

WRIGHT, GORDON. "Ambassador Bullitt and the Fall of France," *World Politics*, October, 1957.

Sources and Notes

CHAPTER ONE

1. Churchill II 178
2. Churchill II 182
3. A first-class biography of de Gaulle has yet to be written. The general facts of his life, however, are not in dispute. Those presented here have been compiled from Cattaui, Hatch, Grinnell-Milne and Bonheur.
4. De Gaulle *Fil* 51–52
5. De Gaulle *Métier* 202–203
6. Churchill II 42
7. Hull 767–68, Wright 82
8. Shirer 643
9. Churchill II 113
10. Spears II 174–77
11. Weygand 155–71
12. Reynaud II 298
13. Spears II 174
14. Benoist-Méchin I 353–54
15. Benoist-Méchin I 355
16. Spears II 139
17. De Gaulle I 50
18. De Gaulle I 44–45
19. Benoist-Méchin II 142–45, 163
20. Sherwood 134
21. FDR Library Secretary's Files
22. Wright 84
23. Churchill II 183–87
24. Weygand 163–65
25. Churchill II 207–11, de Gaulle I 62–66, Spears II 290–95
26. Burman 27
27. Quoted in Cattaui 51
28. De Gaulle *Fil* 48–49
29. Spears II 319–22, de Gaulle I 64–67, Churchill II 214–15
30. Churchill II 218

CHAPTER TWO

1. De Gaulle I 63, Stettinius *Lend-Lease* 29–32
2. De Gaulle I 67–71, 267
3. De Gaulle *Fil* 54
4. De Gaulle I 69, 268–69
5. De Gaulle *Fil* 78
6. Churchill II 230, Benoist-Méchin II 463–64
7. Benoist-Méchin II 464
8. Benoist-Méchin II 360–61, 376
9. Churchill II 219–221, Cooper, 283–84
10. Churchill II 645
11. De Gaulle I 269–70, 275
12. De Gaulle *Discours* 23–24
13. Benoist-Méchin II 303
14. Churchill II 230
15. Truchet 75
16. Reynaud II 379, Truchet 76, Weygand 182–83
17. Churchill IV 640
18. Marchal 20
19. Robert 44–45
20. Baudouin 207, de Gaulle I 118
21. De Gaulle I 270–71
22. De Gaulle I 272–75
23. Larminat 84
24. De Gaulle I 74–79
25. Hull 805

26. De Gaulle I 276
27. FDR Library Official File 203A Box 1, Ickes III 347
28. Hull 804–805
29. Churchill II 507–508, Hull 803, Hoare 70–75, Baudouin 368–69
30. The translation of de Gaulle's memoirs, published as *The Call to Honour* (Collins, London, 1955), contains these documents in the original English, 23–27
31. De Gaulle I 239, Bonheur 158–59
32. Churchill II 509
33. De Gaulle I 209
34. Borden 137
35. Passy I 33–34

CHAPTER THREE

1. Leahy *There* 1, 443
2. Churchill III 735
3. Churchill II 526, 622–24
4. Churchill II 526–27, Hassett 154
5. FDR Library Secretary's File Box 4
6. Leahy *There* 446–48, Welles *Seven* 34–35, *N.Y. Times* July 20, 1940
7. FR 41 108–109
8. Leahy diary 7, Leahy *There* 43, FR 41 129–30
9. Churchill III 736.
10. Leahy *There* 447
11. Leahy diary 7
12. FR 41 119–20
13. FR 41 134
14. Hull 955, FR 41 151
15. FR 41 110, 121
16. Weygand 261–62
17. Catroux 710–19, de Gaulle I 568–72, Churchill II 516, Churchill III 733
18. FR 41 207–11, Pendar 18–19, Weygand 281–83
19. FR 41 262–80
20. Weygand 253–54, 348
21. Weygand 347–50, Passy I 73–74, Passy II 333–44
22. Weygand 361–64, FR 41 211, 358–59
23. Aron *Vichy* 395, Leahy diary 7, Weygand 322
24. FR 41 186

CHAPTER FOUR

1. De Gaulle *La France et son armée* 1
2. Aron *Libération* 333, Soustelle I 270, 333
3. De Gaulle I 82–83, 219–23, Hull 1042, *Documents on American Foreign Relations* IV 632–34

36. Larminat 222
37. Passy I 122–23
38. De Gaulle *Fil* 50–51
39. De Gaulle *Fil* 69–70
40. De Gaulle *Fil* 79–80
41. De Gaulle I 89–120, Larminat 124–33, Charles-Roux 302
42. Passy I 94
43. De Gaulle I 97–109, Passy I 40–41, Larminat 171, Grinnell-Milne 123–38, Charles-Roux 340, Soustelle I 162–63
44. Churchill II 473–94, Catroux 20–22, Borden 300
45. Michel 8
46. Aron *Vichy* 282
47. De Gaulle I 303

25. Gantenbein 174, 192
26. Hull 962
27. Weygand 320–21, FR 41 176, 180, 355–59, 573–74, de Gaulle I 416–21
28. Aron *Vichy* 311–24, Weygand 320–28, Langer & Gleason 508, Langer 156
29. Churchill II 625, 709, Churchill III 86–88, Catroux 96–101, de Gaulle I 145–48
30. Churchill II 321–32, FR 41 707, 711, 748, 763, Hytier 278–82, de Gaulle I 149–60
31. De Gaulle I 149–80, 432–69, Catroux 160–64, 200–203, Passy I 215, FR 41 728–29, 771–79
32. Leahy *There* 460–62
33. Aron *Vichy* 373
34. Hull 961–62
35. De Gaulle I 181–93, 471–87, FR 41 573–78
36. FR 41 452–53, 578–82
37. Leahy *There* 59–60, Weygand 379–87, FR 41 407, 428, 456–58, 465–69, 479–80
38. Leahy diary 6, FR 41 197–202, 534–35
39. OPD 37/8–9
40. De Gaulle I 503
41. FR 41 205

4. FR 42 503
5. De Gaulle I 545, Soustelle I 363, *Documents on American Foreign Relations* IV 633–34
6. Hull 1160–64
7. FR 41 540–69, FR 42 654–71, de

Gaulle I 184–87, 486–523, Moffat 358–78, Muselier *De Gaulle* 260–65, Pickersgill 320–24, FDR Letters IV 1268, Churchill III 666–68, Welles *Seven* 61–64, de Gaulle I in translation 251 for Churchill letter

8. Sherwood 447–53, de Gaulle I 184
9. FR 42 564–96
10. De Gaulle I 188–92, 497–540, Kittridge 1–3, 7, OPD reports
11. Sherwood 548–50, Leahy *There* 86–92, Aron *Vichy* 359–67, Hull 1159
12. De Gaulle I 204–209, 581–605,

CHAPTER FIVE

1. Churchill III 645–51, 664–65
2. *FDR Letters* IV 1275
3. Churchill IV 533–35
4. Eisenhower 88
5. Churchill IV 482, 604–605, Sherwood 629, Bryant I 414, Pendar 10–20, Butcher 97–98, FR 41 416–17
6. FR 41 502
7. Weygand 386–93
8. Leahy *There* 75–76, 474–76
9. Langer 165, Passy II 97–99, 119, Hostache 25, Aron *Vichy* 38
10. Leahy diary 7
11. Leahy diary 7, Leahy *There* 92, Juin 67–69, Langer 238, OPD & OCS reports
12. Churchill IV 606
13. Giraud 15–17, 335, Crusoé 117–22, Langer 230, Butcher 115–16, Juin 72–73, Kammerer 77–78
14. Churchill IV 530
15. Churchill IV 527–43, Eisenhower 91–93, Butcher 72, 84, Clark 26–58, 134–35
16. Giraud 20, 348–52, Butcher 105–10, Howe 55–57
17. FR 42 392–94

CHAPTER SIX

1. Eisenhower 109
2. Howe 188–89
3. Howe 92–96
4. Howe 189, 239–49, Juin I 74–86
5. Howe 249–52
6. Juin I 96–103, Barré 80–86, Giraud 33–35
7. Clark 103–13, Juin I 91–96
8. Clark 114–16
9. FR 42 453–57
10. Eisenhower 109–10, Sherwood 652 and Langer 357–59 each give slightly

Churchill IV 222–37, Sherwood 550, FR 42 698–99
13. Rommel 213–20, Churchill IV 357
14. Soustelle I 343, de Gaulle I 604–607
15. De Gaulle I 529–33
16. De Gaulle I 232–37, 286–87, Passy II 143–57, 224–28, 275, Michel 91–97
17. De Gaulle I 533–34, II 330–38, Hull 1159–62, Catroux 277–78, Passy II 83–86, Leahy *There* 85
18. FR 42 512
19. De Gaulle II 340–41, OPD reports
20. De Gaulle II 343–45, Clark 36–37

18. FR 42 144–47, 392–96
19. Clark 68–91, Howe 80–82, Butcher 153–56
20. FR 42 408
21. De Gaulle II 360, OPD reports, Eisenhower 83–84, Churchill IV 604–606, Kittridge I 40–41
22. De Gaulle II 381–85
23. Letter from Herman Kahn, director at the time of the FDR Library, to author
24. FR 42 544
25. Churchill IV 605–606
26. Bryant I 421, FR 42 425
27. FR 42 423, Giraud 17–22, Lemaigre letter quoted in Kammerer 183–84
28. Clark 96, Eisenhower 100
29. Giraud 23–27, Clark 96–100, Eisenhower 100–101
30. FR 42 425, Gosset 312–315, Eisenhower 104–105, Churchill IV 611
31. De Gaulle II 393
32. Sherwood 645–647, Churchill IV 608
33. FR 42 430–31
34. Butcher 175–77, Western Task Force reports, Sherwood 629–30, Bryant I 421

different versions of this message, which is explained by a wartime requirement to paraphrase all coded communications.
11. Sherwood 648, *Documents of American Foreign Relations* V 540–1
12. OCS African report
13. De Gaulle II 41–45, 395–99, Kittridge II 9–25, Passy II 359–61, Soustelle I 461–62, II 8–23, OCS Africa
14. De Gaulle II 412–14
15. Sherwood 654

16. Sherwood 653-54
17. Howe 176-79, Patton 10-23, Butcher 193-95, Eisenhower 126-27, OPD 336 Africa, Kammerer 517, 555-57
18. Leahy *There* 135-36, OPD 336 France
19. Churchill II 239-41, IV 636-37, another translation in Butcher 206-207
20. Aron *Vichy* 532-38 contains probably the best account of this episode, figures cited are from Auphan 255-71
21. Howe 271-72, OCS 336.6
22. Churchill IV 641
23. Eisenhower 127-30
24. Vigneras 11-18, 23-29, Eisenhower 123-27, 140, Clark 126, 139-41, Howe 272-327, Butcher 224-29

25. Leahy *There* 137-38, Leahy diary 8, FR 42, 461-62, 481-82, Eisenhower 130-31, Hull 1198-1201, Butcher 208, OPD 336 Africa
26. Churchill IV 630-31
27. OPD 336 France, OCS 381 Africa
28. FR 42 546-47, de Gaulle II 388-428, Hull 1197-98, Passy II 361-62, Soustelle I 368-73, II 32-34, 61
29. Butcher 225-26, de Gaulle II 64-67, 394, Catroux 315-17, Soustelle II 30, 67-75, FDR Library Secretary's File Box 5
30. Churchill II 230
31. Clark 128-31, de Gaulle II 67, Gosset 217-22, Giraud 74-81, Butcher 229-35, Passy II 370, Hull 1205, Churchill IV 643-44, Eisenhower 129-30, Murphy 143, Kammerer 607
32. De Gaulle II 74, OCS 381 Africa

CHAPTER SEVEN

1. Eisenhower 130, OCS 336.4 France
2. Eisenhower 129-31, Giraud 79-80, Butcher 229-30, Clark 127-30, Howe 355-58
3. OCS 091 Africa, FR 42 492-5, Eisenhower 130
4. Butcher 232, FR 42 399, Murphy 145, OPD 336 France
5. OCS file
6. Churchill IV 630-31, 644-45
7. De Gaulle II 429-33, Kittredge II 84-87
8. De Gaulle II 74, Hull 1205-07
9. De Gaulle II 436
10. Murphy 165, de Gaulle II 437, Hull 1207, Churchill IV 671, Sherwood 678-79
11. De Gaulle II 437-40
12. Sherwood 678-83
13. Hull 1207-08, Sherwood 678-79

14. Sherwood 675-79, Eisenhower 130-31, Peyrouton 186-98
15. Churchill IV 680-81
16. De Gaulle's account of the Casablanca Conference II 75-86, Giraud 101, Catroux 318
17. Churchill IV 681-82
18. Churchill IV 682, Sherwood 685-86, 956
19. Giraud 101-108
20. Funk 70-71, Giraud 353-54, text in Crusoé 143
21. Vigneras 39-40, Stimson 558-59, Sherwood 691-93, Giraud 108-12, Crusoé 143-47, OCS 191 Africa, Churchill IV 693
22. De Gaulle II 440
23. Sherwood 685, 691, 956, *FDR Letters* IV 1400, Hull 1208, Hassett 152-53
24. De Gaulle II 441

CHAPTER EIGHT

1. De Gaulle II 54-58, Hull 1204, OCS 336
2. De Gaulle II 60-63, 440; Montgomery *Memoirs* 140, 331-32
3. De Gaulle II 445-46, Hostache 112-16, Passy III 188
4. Giraud 122-23, Pendar 129, 161-70, 220, Gosset 261-73, Kittridge III 23
5. Hull 1208-10, Crusoé 101-104, 148-51, Churchill IV 721-23, Vigneras 38
6. Vigneras 38-48

7. Vigneras 44, Murphy 179, Sherwood 678-79, Stettinius *Lend-Lease* 18-21, Pendar 163-64, Giraud 118-21
8. Giraud 117-24, Funk 106-107, *N.Y. Times* March 15, 1943
9. De Gaulle II 96-97, 454-60, Catroux 347
10. De Gaulle II 98-99, 457, Funk 408-10, Churchill IV 738, Sherwood 721, Hull 1214-16
11. Sherwood 702, 715, Churchill IV

212–13, de Gaulle II 410, FDR Press Conference V.21 140–141 [FDR Library]
12. De Gaulle II 80
13. De Gaulle *Discorde* 76, 213
14. OPD 336 CDC, de Gaulle II 129, 455–57, 467, Leahy diary 8
15. De Gaulle II, 128–29, 443–44, Robert 158–94, 206–10, OPD 336 CDC
16. De Gaulle II 87–88, Leahy diary 8, Auphan 282, Soustelle II 219, Kittridge III 26, 43, Hull 1219, OPD 336.3
17. Larminat 320–21, de Gaulle II 97–100, Giraud 184–88, Kittridge III 63
18. Giraud 67, Howe 668–70, Vigneras 58–59, Larminat 320–21, Churchill IV 778
19. Vigneras 221, Churchill V 625, Catroux 330–31, 354, Auphan 285–86, Giraud 173
20. Eisenhower 331, *N.Y. Times* May 11, 1943

21. De Gaulle II 487
22. De Gaulle II 473
23. De Gaulle II 100, 473–75
24. De Gaulle II 478–89, Catroux 354–55
25. Churchill IV 801, Kittridge III 65
26. De Gaulle II 103–105, 109–10, 488, Churchill IV 816, Butcher 318–19 *N.Y. Times* May 31, 1943
27. De Gaulle II 105–106, 484, Giraud 162–69, Catroux 365
28. De Gaulle II 106–107, 488, Larminat 324–25, Catroux 366–67, Butcher 320, Kittridge III 79, Juin 203
29. Catroux 367–70, de Gaulle II 106, 485, Peyrouton 231–36
30. De Gaulle II 107, 487–89
31. Murphy 180
32. De Gaulle II 490
33. De Gaulle II 110, Churchill V 174
34. Churchill V 174
35. Hull 1220–21
36. Churchill V 173–74

CHAPTER NINE

1. De Gaulle II 112–4, 493–98, Leahy diary 8, Giraud's memoirs are curiously silent on this entire period.
2. Churchill V 175, Leahy diary 8, Murphy 181–82
3. Churchill V 175–79
4. De Gaulle II 114–20, 500–501, Butcher 333–38, Vigneras 79–80, Kittridge VI 82–83
5. Leahy *There* 167–69, Leahy diary 9, de Gaulle 112
6. Giraud 188–242, Leahy *There* 170, Leahy diary 9, Vigneras 82–86, de Gaulle II 120–1, FDR Library Secretary's File 203A Box 2
7. De Gaulle II 112–13, *N.Y. Times* June 17, 1943
8. Robert 164–94, de Gaulle II 128–31, Leahy *There* 170, diary 9, Hull 1223, Roosevelt Press Conference July 16, 1943 [FDR Library]
9. De Gaulle II 125–26, 510
10. FDR Library Secretary's File 203A Box 2
11. Kittridge III 72, Butcher 338
12. De Gaulle II 133–36, Vigneras 86–87, OPD 336 France
13. De Gaulle II 133–36, Vigneras 80–89, Juin 204–207, Giraud 366–77
14. Churchill V 174–83, FDR Library

Secretary's File, Hull 1125–26, Butcher 365–70
15. Russell 114–16
16. Funk 159–62 contains a thorough discussion of the differences, de Gaulle II 137
17. Churchill V 182–83
18. De Gaulle II 137, Butcher 399
19. Passy III 44–47, 145–46, 209–12, 238–40, 258–61, 389–421, Michel 32, 38–39, 48–51, Aron 123–39, Harrison 200, Hostache 69–71, 157–59
20. Stalin 135, 139, Rieber 9–10
21. De Gaulle II 135–40, 520, 590–91, Stalin 152
22. Russell 140–41, Stalin 154–59, Murphy 209–10, de Gaulle II 191–92, Hull 1243–44, Feis 178–85
23. Russell 139–40
24. Giraud 243–61, Soustelle II 277–84, Williams 114, 133, 139, Vigneras 101, de Gaulle II 141–45
25. De Gaulle II 147–49, Washington *Post* Nov. 7, 1943
26. De Gaulle II 112–48, 532–37, Giraud 260–64
27. De Gaulle II 149–53, 542
28. *FDR Letters* IV 1453, OPD 400 France

CHAPTER TEN

1. Pogue 139–40, Hull 1239–42
2. Hull 1244–45
3. Stimson 559–60
4. Pogue 142, Hull 1244–45, SHAEF 091.112–64
5. Pogue 143–5, de Gaulle II 135, 211–12
6. De Gaulle II 134–35, 209–10, OPD 336 France, OPD 336.4 France
7. Churchill V 453–54, Peyrouton 244–45, 271, de Gaulle II 134, 616, Cooper 318–21, Leahy diary 9, d'Astier *Dieux* 54–55, Passy III 58–59, OPD 336 Security
8. De Gaulle II 260–62, 662–76, Vigneras 111–21, Sherwood 745–47, Butcher 473, SHAEF 475 France
9. SHAEF 092 France, SHAEF G–3 091.112–5
10. SHAEF 092 France
11. FDR Library Secretary's File Box 5
12. Stimson 545–52, 559–60, Leahy *There* 235–36, Leahy diary 10, Butcher 473
13. Leahy *There* 225, *N.Y. Times* February 13, 1944
14. Hull 1245–46, Harrison 116–17
15. Harrison 202–206, Kittridge IV 22, Vigneras 259–303, d'Astier *Dieux* 83, SHAEF 322–7 SO/SOE, Pogue 152–57, SHAEF G–3
16. Hull 1427, Stimson 547–48, OPD 311.23 CAD
17. SHAEF 092 France
18. SHAEF 092 France
19. De Gaulle II 167–69, Giraud 281–312, Soustelle II 284–96, 340–41, Vigneras 106, 151, Wilson 199–200, 210–11, Leahy diary 10, OPD 400 France, SHAEF 092 France
20. Hull 1428–9, SHAEF 092 France
21. De Gaulle II 631
22. De Gaulle II 176–77, 185–86, 212, 553, 559, 571–75, Aron 62, Hostache 269–70, Butcher 540–41, SHAEF 092 France
23. Vigneras 178–80, Clark 358, SHAEF 092, Juin 318–19, Eisenhower 281–84
24. Wilson 199–200, *Seventh* 1–26, Morrison 232, SHAEF 381 France
25. Churchill V 616–18, 699, Butcher 526, SHAEF 381 France
26. Harrison 202–7, OCS 091 France
27. Pogue 146–47, SHAEF G–3, SHAEF 092 France, SHAEF 091 111.2–5
28. Hull 1431, SHAEF 092 France
29. De Gaulle II 636–37
30. Churchill V 712, SHAEF 092 France, de Gaulle II 636–37
31. Hull 1432, Leahy diary 10, Cooper 326–9, Phillips 404–408
32. Pogue 231–35, de Gaulle II 606–607, Leahy diary 9
33. Pogue 236–7
34. De Gaulle II 215–27, 640, Churchill V 627–30, Cooper 330–32, Pogue 232, Aron *Libération* 62–93, Butcher 562–63, d'Astier *Dieux* 145–47

CHAPTER ELEVEN

1. De Gaulle II 641–48, OPD 311.23 CAD
2. Aron *Libération* 52–88, 21 AG Operations & Policy #302
3. SHAEF G–3 091.112–5, SHAEF 014.1 France
4. De Gaulle II 229–31, 644–45, Aron *Libération* 76–97, Montgomery *Path* 99
5. Aron *Libération* 87
6. 21 AG Field Report #304
7. 21 AG Field Report #302, SHAEF OCS 322.01/21, de Gaulle II 553, 9
8. Pogue 233
9. Stimson 550–51
10. Hostache 371–72, SHAEF 522–25 Resistance, OPD 336 TS, Pogue 234
11. SHAEF G–3 091.711–12, SHAEF 014.1 France VI
12. SHAEF 014.1 France, SHAEF OCS 332.01/21, OPD 311.23 CAD
13. De Gaulle II 231–35, 642, 651–52, OCS 091
14. De Gaulle II 235–43, 653–55, Hull 1433, Leahy diary 10, Hassett 261, Washington *Post*, July 6–10, 1944
15. Leahy *There* 244, diary 10, de Gaulle II 655, 659, OPD 336 France, SHAEF 014.1 France VI, SHAEF 092 France, 311.23 CAD TS, Civil Affairs Handbooks for Denmark and Norway
16. De Gaulle II 658
17. Bradley 379, SHAEF Resistance, Aron *Libération* 325–30, Hostache 275

18. Pogue 241, Cooper 336, SHAEF 014.1 France VI, OPD 336 TS
19. De Gaulle II 319–21, SHAEF G–5 115.4, SHAEF 092 France, OPD 336 France, Soustelle II 436–40, Whitcomb 561, Aron *Libération* 381–91, Thomson 106
20. De Gaulle II 702–703
21. SHAEF 092 France, Blumenson 601–608
22. Blumenson 608–10
23. De Gaulle II 292–319, Hostache 402–404, Aron *Libération* 437–47, Rieber 154–55
24. De Gaulle II 710, Pogue 241–43, Blumenson 607, 618–25
25. Eisenhower 297–98, Bradley 395–96, Pogue 242–43

CHAPTER TWELVE

1. Hull 1642–43
2. Churchill VI 248, Feis 471, de Gaulle III 350–59
3. FR *Yalta Conference* 286–87
4. Churchill IV 208–14, Halifax 261, Stettinius *Roosevelt* 211–14, de Gaulle III 258, Hull 1596–97, Forrestal 33, 57, *Documents on American Foreign Relations* V 205
5. De Gaulle II 285–86, 680–83, III 332–33, 353, 469–70, Leahy *There* 286, Leahy diary 9–11, Decoux 305–10, Hull 1597–1601, Vigneras 390–99, various OPD and SHAEF files
6. Churchill VI 253–58, Stalin 272
7. Pogue 397–402, Churchill VI 281, de Gaulle III 475–82, Eisenhower 362–63, de Lattre 346–58, 382, *Seventh* 561–82
8. SHAEF 092 France, SHAEF 091. 112–5, SHAEF OCS 332.01/21
9. Vigneras 335–8, Pogue 391–92
10. FR *Yalta Conference* 293–94
11. De Gaulle III 387–88, FR *Yalta Conference* 296–97
12. De Gaulle 389–92, Sherwood 847–48
13. FR *Yalta Conference* 572
14. Feis 555–56, Sherwood 851, 858–59, Rieber 192–95, Churchill VI 353, 510, Pogue 348–52, FR *Yalta Conference* general account

26. De Gaulle II 243, 306–307, Pogue 319–20, Hull 1433–35, 6AG 091.1–1 (France), SHAEF 014.1 France VI, OPD 014.1 ETO
27. SHAEF 092 France
28. De Gaulle III 8–39, Aron *Libération* 548–76 6AG 370–72
29. De Lattre 176–204, 6AG 670–72, SHAEF OCS 381 France, Aron *Libération* 666–67
30. De Gaulle III 8–21, 57–80, 100–101, 297–333, Aron 548–52, 633–37
31. SHAEF 092 France, 6AG 091.1, SHAEF 371 France
32. Churchill VI 242–9, Russell 178, Hull 1434–35, 1567, Pogue 325–26
33. De Gaulle III 44
34. Leahy *There* 273

15. De Gaulle III 87, Sherwood 847–48, 859–61
16. De Gaulle III 489
17. FDR Library Press Conference V 25
18. De Gaulle III 402
19. De Gaulle III 153–55, 490, de Lattre 470–77
20. De Gaulle III 320, 334, 493–96, de Lattre 567–71, Pogue 425–32, 456–61, Vigneras 356, 360–66, Truman 237–39, SHAEF 475 France, G–3 322.011 France, *Seventh* 803–804
21. De Lattre 582–83, 602–10, Pogue 487–92, *Seventh* 848–61
22. De Gaulle III 515, 533–39, Truman 239–42, Vigneras 367–72, Allied Control Commission files on Northwest Italy incident
23. Letter from director of the *Archives Départementales* of the Prefecture of the Alpes-Maritimes to author, September 8, 1961
24. Russell 625–26, 633–34, 649, de Gaulle III 201, Churchill VI 209, 354, Feis 430–31
25. De Gaulle III 205, 503, 540, Pogue 348–52, Truman 16, OPD 336 France
26. De Gaulle III 227–28
27. De Gaulle *La France et son armée* 237
28. De Gaulle I 1, II 102

Index

Administration transition from occupation to liberation, 183. *See also* France, administration of, at liberation

Alamein, rout of Rommel's *Afrika Korps* at, 109

Alexander, General Harold, praises French Army in Italy, 195; in French-Italian frontier dispute, 237

Algiers, confusion and fighting at, in North African invasion, 116-17

Allied Advisory Council for Italian occupation, 179

Allied Control Commission for Germany, France granted seat on, 232, 239

Allied Control Commission for Italian occupation, 179; French Committee given seat on, 191-92

Allied indifference to rights claimed by Free French in behalf of France, 86

American diplomacy, French press reflects deep resentment against, 221

American Division parades through Paris and passes in review before de Gaulle, 216

American plans for chain of landing fields in Pacific for ferrying heavy bombers, 70

Anderson, General Kenneth, leads British contingents toward Tunis, 120

Anfa agreement, *see* Casablanca agreement

Anglo-American Conference in Quebec, August 1943, 175

Anti-Semitic measures remain in force under Darlan's administration in North Africa, 125; under Giraud's administration, 150, 152

Appel aux Français by de Gaulle over B.B.C., 27; reaction to, 34, 35

D'Argenlieu, Admiral Thierry, Free French commander of New Caledonia, 84-85; to Casablanca with de Gaulle, 142; in liberation parade, 215

Armée de métier, de Gaulle's campaign for, 5-6

Armistice Day, 1944, Churchill and de Gaulle march together down Champs Elysées, 223

d'Astier, Emmanuel de la Vigerie, of Resistance, received in Washington, 91

d'Astier, General François de la Vigerie, on mission to Algiers, 130-31

Atherton, Ray, of State Department, 107-8

Atlantic Alliance, de Gaulle's demand for equality in, 245-46

Barré, General Georges, Army chief in North African French Army, 120

Battle of Britain, 30

Battle of the Bulge, 227, 229

Battle of France, 7-25 *passim*

Baubé, Jean, de Gaulle's press representative in Washington, 123

Bayeux, first town liberated by Allies, 202-4

Montgomery, General Bernard, Leclerc makes contact with, on coast at Tripoli after dash from Chad, 149; administration of Normandy beachhead under direction of, 202; acquiesces in de Gaulle's assumption of administration, 203

Montoire, meeting of Pétain and Hitler at, to agree on collaboration, 50

Morgenthau, Henry, U.S. Secretary of the Treasury, Pleven's visit with, 69; presents new proposal for accord with French, 208-9

Moulin, Jean, on mission in France to effect a union of French Resistance under direction of de Gaulle, 89-90, 149-50; succeeds in uniting Resistance, 159; tightens grip on direction of Resistance, 177; killed by Nazis, 177; dominated Communists, 178

Munich, effect on Roosevelt, 17

Murphy, Robert, favorable reports to Hull on Weygand in North Africa, 60; continues endorsement of shipments to North Africa after Weygand's dismissal, 71; activities of, in planning North African invasion, 99-112 passim, 115; makes sweeping predictions of French cooperation in Torch, 101; at battle of Algiers, 116-17; continues to identify himself with Vichyites, 125; recommends Peyrouton, former Pétain cabinet member, for post in Algiers administration, 128; collaborates with Giraud on memorandum on promises made to Giraud in Casablanca, 143-44; cooperates with those in Algiers of Vichy stamp, 150; acts as guide for Giraud in power struggle with de Gaulle, 167; transferred from Algiers, 185-86

Muselier, Vice Admiral Emile, commander in chief of Free French Navy, takes control of Saint-Pierre and Miquelon, 78-79; in Algiers at meeting between Giraud and de Gaulle, 162

Mussolini, Benito, declaration of war on France, 18

National Resistance Council, beginnings in Unoccupied Zone, 90; extension to Occupied Zone, 150, 159, 178; accepts truce with von Choltitz in Paris, 212; greets de Gaulle in Paris on day of liberation, 214; de Gaulle informs, that his regime alone governs France,

214; de Gaulle disbands, after liberation of Paris, 215

"National Revolution," Pétain's plan, 37

Nazi defeats in northern France, 210

Nazi pressure on Vichy causes Pierre Laval appointment as head of government, 86

New Caledonia joins Free French, 50; use of, by U.S. as landing field for heavy bombers, 70; difficulties between Free French and U.S. over bases in Pacific, 84-85

New Hebrides joins Free French, 50; use of, by U.S., as landing field for ferrying heavy bombers, 70

New York Times, on efficiency of French Committee, 171-72

Noguès, General Auguste Paul, opposed to Breton redoubt, 16; de Gaulle's wire to, offering services, 27; arrest of Mandel and dissident French in Casablanca, 30; after protest at armistice, remains with Pétain Government, 33; commander of French North African Army, 33; named by Pétain as Vichy commander in North Africa, 118; relinquishes his mandate in North Africa to Darlan, 121; unacceptable to U.S. as successor to Darlan, 135; retains identification with Vichy, 150; de Gaulle's demand for dismissal of, 161; Giraud abandons, 163

Normandie and other French ships in American ports seized by U.S. Navy after Pearl Harbor, 72

Normandy beachhead, administration of, 202-7; breakout from, 210

North Africa facet of Hull's Vichy policy, 59; French resistance nullified by Weygand's dismissal, 71; 1942 invasion of, planned by U.S. and Britain, excluding Fighting French, 93-94; invasion plans based on premise that the French would not resist, 95; invasion, Roosevelt's objective to give it appearance of act of liberation, not of aggression, 97; relative strength of Allies and French defending force, 100; invasion, development of strategy for, 100-11 passim; date of landings withheld from French conspirators, 102, 109-10, 111; landings begin in face of vigorous French defense, 114; question of government of, after invasion, 120-22; fiction of Pétain's authority mesmerizes administration, 127; Roose-

N

W E

S

IRELAND

ENGLAND

NORTH
SEA

London

NETHERLANDS

BELGIUM

GERMANY

ATLANTIC

OCEAN

Abbeville

Cherbourg
St.Lô Isigny
Bayeux

Laon

Karlsruhe

Stuttgart

Rennes

Paris

Strasbourg
Colmar

Ulm

Tours

FRANCE

Bern

TYROL

Limoges

Vichy

SWITZERLAND

Bordeaux

Lyon

ITALY

Toulouse

Montpellier

Marseilles
Toulon

PORTUGAL

Barcelona

CORSICA
Ajaccio

Rom

Lisbon

Madrid

SPAIN

SARDINIA

Gibraltar

MEDITERRANEAN

SP. MOROCCO

Cherchel Algiers

Bône Bizerte
Tunis

Oran

Philippeville

Rabat

Casablanca

Marrakech

FRENCH
MOROCCO

ALGERIA

TUNISIA

LI

0   100   200   300   400   500

MILES